David E. Ruth

Inventing the Public Enemy

The Gangster in American Culture, 1918–1934

The University of Chicago Press
Chicago & London

David E. Ruth is assistant professor of history and
American studies at Pennsylvania State University.

The University of Chicago Press, Chicago 60637
The University of Chicago Press, Ltd., London
© 1996 by The University of Chicago
All rights reserved. Published 1996
Printed in the United States of America
05 04 03 02 01 00 99 98 97 96   1 2 3 4 5

ISBN: 0–226–73217–7 (cloth)
0–226–73218–5 (paper)

Library of Congress Cataloging-in-Publication Data

Ruth, David E.
  Inventing the public enemy : the gangster in American culture,
  1918–1934 / David E. Ruth.
      p.   cm.
  Includes bibliographical references and index.
      1. Gangsters—United States—History—20th century.   2. Gangsters
  in popular culture—United States.   3. Gangsters—United States—
  Public opinion.   4. Public opinion—United States.   I. Title.
  HV6446.R87   1996
  364.1′06′6097309041—dc20   95-22480

Inventing the Public Enemy

Contents

Acknowledgments

While researching and writing this book, I have accumulated many debts. The staffs of the Wisconsin Center for Film and Theater Research, the Library of Congress Film Archive, and the Museum of Modern Art Film Stills Archive helped with publicity stills and access to prints. Librarians at Northwestern University and the Chicago Historical Society guided me to other hard-to-find materials. The Chicago Crime Commission granted access to its files.

It would be difficult to overstate my indebtedness to Robert Wiebe, who provided encouragement, timely advice, and penetrating critiques. Michael Sherry contributed thoughtful readings and good advice on matters large and small. I am also grateful to other teachers and colleagues who stimulated my thinking about crime and American culture: Henry Binford, Paul Boyer, Lane Fenrich, Karen Halttunen, Naoko Shibusawa, and David Zimand. Lewis Erenberg, Mark Haller, and Lary May graciously read the manuscript and made many useful suggestions. My editors at the University of Chicago Press, Doug Mitchell and John McCudden, have been helpful at every turn.

Early in my research Philip Hauser shared his memories of studying the underworld—as an assistant for the landmark 1929 analysis *Organized Crime in Chicago*. His experiences included being pressed into service as a pallbearer at the funeral of a victim of the St. Valentine's Day Massacre. I have striven to achieve a somewhat different familiarity with our mutual subjects.

My parents, Jean and John Ruth, have been unwaveringly supportive. Daniel Johnson Ruth, born as this book was nearing completion, has provided welcome distractions and delightful reminders of the joys of discovery. My greatest debt is to Karen Johnson Ruth, whose companionship, support, and understanding have enriched this book—and every other aspect of my life.

Introduction:
The Gangster and
Urban America

Inventing the Public Enemy is an attempt to understand mass media images and the culture that produced them. As such it is a study of values. Shortly after the First World War many Americans came to believe that rampant crime was a defining element of their society. Attention soon centered on the gangster, the paragon of modern criminality and eventually the subject of innumerable newspaper and magazine articles, scores of novels and plays, and more than a hundred Hollywood movies. The media gangster was an invention, much less an accurate reflection of reality than a projection created from various Americans' beliefs, concerns, and ideas about what would sell. This study, concerned with the meanings rather than the facts of crime, addresses questions whose answers provide a fuller understanding of American culture in the interwar years. Why was the invented gangster such a compelling figure? What messages did he convey? What values did he promote?

The rhetoric of crime gained a resonant new term in April 1930 when the Chicago Crime Commission released a list of the city's twenty-eight most dangerous "public enemies." Journalists across the country published the list, adopted the term, and dubbed the notorious Al Capone "Public Enemy Number One." The next year Warner Brothers and James Cagney assured *The Public Enemy*'s cultural longevity with an electrifying portrayal.[1] Though the label was still new, Cagney's Tom Powers, like Capone, embodied a collection of attributes that had coalesced in media portrayals of criminals since the end of the First World War. The public enemy, energetic and confident, was successful in a competitive, highly organized business. A model of stylish consumption, he wore fine clothes, rode in a gleaming new automobile, and reveled in expensive nightlife. He rebelled not only against the law, but against established behavioral codes, especially involving gender, and his lovers flouted the conventions of female propriety. In all these characteristics he was resolutely urban, a product of the city and an enthusiastic participant in its culture.

So too was the gangster markedly urban in his most notorious activity: flaunting national prohibition. As saloon and cabaret scenes in *The Public Enemy* suggest, Americans generally associated drinking with two distinct urban groups: the ethnic working class and free-spending pleasure seekers. Among the strongest supporters of prohibition were conservatives who cast the reform as a bolstering of sober, small-town values against the encroachments of foreign, big-city decadence.[2] In the vanguard of modern society's perceived assault on traditional restraint, Tom Powers, Al Capone, and their underworld peers were men of the city.

This constellation of attributes made the gangster an emblem of changes affecting the lives of millions of Americans. Indeed, he was a "public" enemy in two senses: a predator on the public, he was also part of it. The underworld dramatized the development of an impersonal, highly organized, consumption-oriented urban society. More and more Americans, like the gangster, worked out their daily lives in large cities or their suburbs. Even for those remote from the major centers, the consolidation of mass commercial culture in the 1920s meant that urban images proliferated in daily news and entertainment. Urbanization and modernization reoriented the individual's relationship to society. Especially in their work, millions of Americans, the gangster among them, faced the challenges and opportunities of pursuing individual goals within and alongside the large organizations of a modern society. At the same time, twentieth-century commercial society, selling consumption and display, promised new opportunities for individual fulfillment. This array of changes in turn transformed older ethnic, gender, and class systems. The behavior of urban Americans, like that of the gangster and his associates, conformed less than ever before to the norms of inherited social typologies.

Inventing the Public Enemy argues that the gangster was a central cultural figure because he helped Americans master this changing social world. The study draws on the anthropological notion that people develop cultures—shared systems of thinking, belief, and values—in order to make sense of and control the social facts they encounter in their daily lives. The primary stuff of which cultures are made is stories, repeated tales that carry moral truths, prescriptions for behavior, lessons about success and failure. Among the stories that play the most constructive cultural roles are those that fit into genres, whose evolving conventions of setting, character, iconography, and plot offer highly compressed but accessible symbolic vocabularies deeply relevant to the concerns of audience members. Story genres are not, of course, organic creations of "the culture." Instead they owe their promulgation to individuals and groups in positions of power, and, to some degree, they inevitably reflect the interests and biases of those groups. In early twentieth-century America it was the creators of nationally standardized news and entertainment, and the social groups they represented, who gained an unprecedented role in the production of cultural texts. With increasing success the common stories of the new commercial culture of mass-circulation magazines, movies, and radio vied for the allegiance of Americans also tied to cultures localized around such groupings as gender, ethnicity, class, and neighborhood. Nevertheless, even as audience participation in the production of cultural texts became more remote, consumers collectively retained the power of veto, for the economic viability of this national storytelling depended on its resonance with millions of Americans. Image producers did their best to respond to public desires and, often, to infuse their products with such a variety of messages that they might appeal to the widest possible audience. Participants in a commercial culture, they registered success or failure every day in the marketplace.[3]

In the 1920s and early 1930s the gangster genre's countless offerings established the invented criminal as one of the new mass culture's preeminently powerful, easily recognizable symbols. The task to which his creators put the gangster was to confront the urban society he epitomized. The genre's symbolic vocabulary was a rich cultural resource that journalists, filmmakers, and others used in efforts to explain and change the behavior of urban Americans. The various composites of flashy clothes, gats, fast cars, and bad attitudes represented a compelling personalization of sweeping social change and carried a multitude of messages, some contradictory, for a public still adjusting to the city. Readers and moviegoers who examined the gangster saw complex social issues played out in simplified, manageable form. Like any other successful invention, the gangster performed a useful function. While it is impossible to gauge popular acceptance of specific messages, the essential fact is that millions of Americans literally bought what was being sold.

The criminal subject of the gangster genre made it a particularly capacious vessel for this kind of communication. Beginning with functionalist sociologists who suggested that groups foster and publicize deviant activity to mark boundaries of acceptable behavior,[4] scholars have often noted the unique cultural utility of criminals. A growing body of historical research shows how men and women have constructed new understandings of the criminal to shape values about race, gender, class, responsibility, and sexual morality.[5] Contemporary fascination with criminals confirms their special cultural utility. In his recent study of "what makes crime 'news,'" sociologist Jack Katz shows that news consumers recognize the considerable shortcomings of journalistic accounts as credible guides to a threatening criminal world. Nevertheless, skeptical readers value this apparently flawed genre because each story speaks to problems encountered in daily life. Crime reports grapple with such issues as the limits of individual competence, the legitimacy of social and political claims of various groups, and the security of revered institutions. "The reading of crime news," Katz concludes, "is an eminently practical, future-oriented activity. In reading crime news, people recognize and use the moral tale within the story to orient themselves towards existential dilemmas they cannot help but confront." Katz suggests, in other words, that the criminal is a rich cultural resource men and women use to understand and shape their social worlds.[6] In his instructive nonconformity, the invented gangster played a familiar and powerful cultural role.

To understand this role, I have examined gangster images in films, fiction, popular nonfiction books and pulps, and newspaper and magazine reporting. As Katz's work suggests, to concentrate on whether a particular depiction is or is not factually accurate is to miss the point: that a large audience found it compelling. In a publicity piece for the 1933 film *Blondie Johnson,* Warner Brothers studio provides further justification for discounting the conventional differentiation between "factual" and "fictional":

> When serious historians begin to piece together the picture of our modern times they will give particular thanks to four people, James Cagney, Edward G. Robinson, Paul Muni and Joan Blondell. These young players, more than any other, are supplying future generations with the true picture of our own hectic current problems by their work on the talking screen. Those future writers may call this the age of rackets, the years when the youth of the world went wild, revolted against law and discipline, or they may refer to it as the gangster era when law enforcement went under an eclipse. Whatever they name it, however they explain it, the truest pictures of all this strange international phenomena will be provided by the then ancient rolls of film known now by such names as "The Public Enemy," "Little Caesar," "Scarface" and "Blondie Johnson." The value of these films now is entertainment. Their priceless ingredients for future historians is their truth.[7]

The publicity boilerplate—written by a studio employee about a purportedly "true" fictional account and intended for inclusion in local newspapers as a legitimate feature article—suggests the irrelevance of conventional literary categories. "Factual" journalistic accounts relied on imaginative conjecture and regularly included material, from the dialogue at ultra-secret meetings to the unuttered thoughts of dying men, beyond the range of even the most capable reporter. "Fictional" accounts, among them *Blondie Johnson* and the successful films to which studio executives hoped to link it, invariably claimed authenticity, asserting the author's intimate knowledge of gangland, highlighting the use of shady underworld consultants, or incorporating well-known real settings and events. Warner Brothers, Hollywood's most prolific exploiter of the underworld, declared its films "Snatched from Today's Headlines!"[8] Neither fact nor fiction, these accounts are most reasonably aggregated as invention or even myth, forms in which other categories are irrelevant.

Whether packaged as news or storytelling, the central project of gang imagery was the exploration of a fascinating, troubling urban world. Many of those who invented the gangster brought special skills and a long interest to the task of explaining the city. This was especially true for those in the most important participating occupational group, writers for large metropolitan newspapers. As Gunther Barth has suggested, the big dailies thrived by feeding a steady stream of information about the mystifying realm of the city to virtually insatiable audiences.[9] And it was not only through their newspaper writing that crime reporters explained the city, for many applied their journalistic skills of storytelling and interpretation to successful ventures elsewhere in the new mass culture. Atypical only for his prominence was *Scarface* screenwriter Ben Hecht, who came of age in Chicago newsrooms and gained national renown as a *Daily News* columnist. A large portion of gang imagery, probably most of it, shared *Scarface*'s provenance in the stories of reporters who moved easily from medium to medium, capitalizing on their ability to present the city.[10]

The imagined gangster, of course, fit into a long series of attempts to come to grips with urban society. American distrust of the city dated at least from independence, and since the late nineteenth century the difficult transition of a rural society into one predominantly urban had captured the attention of millions of Americans. The native-born middle class, reared to be suspicious of the city, drawn to it because of economic change, and enjoying relatively easy access to political and cultural power, was the group most vocally preoccupied with the transition. Especially in the first two decades of the new century, middle-class men and women combined professional organization with political and social activism to impose their vision of order on the apparent chaos of the new urban, industrial society. These progressives marshaled bureaucratic organization, expert management, and the creed of efficiency to construct social institutions that would regulate otherwise dangerous urban phenomena: huge corporations, impersonal markets, and unprecedented concentrations of workers and immigrants. Issues that commanded middle-class attention—from public health, to the assimilation of immigrants, to housing, labor, and civil-service reform—were pieces of the era's most challenging puzzle: How to live with the city?

Many efforts to cope with urban society were, like the gangster image, cultural rather than explicitly political in nature. Some sought to provide the temporary, therapeutic respite believed necessary to those immersed in the jangling, competitive life of the modern city.[11] Other responses, rejecting even that brief escapism, confronted the city more directly and attempted to take cultural possession of it. William Taylor has argued that many middle-class men and women became preoccupied with urban photography from the 1890s into the 1920s because visual representation helped them construct a reassuring understanding. Portraits by Lewis Hine and others showed that human dignity was not incompatible with the giant new cities. Skyline views metamorphosed office towers—each built to project corporate power and ambition—into quasi-mystical expressions of civic greatness.[12] Equipped with the mental images inspired by these photographic ones, some Americans could now celebrate their new urban environments.

This acceptance of some elements of modern urbanism informed even the most aggressive middle-class and elite attempts to take cultural control of the city. Social Gospel ministers, Richard Wightman Fox has shown, embraced urban commercial amusements by the early twentieth century. Discarding the conventional Protestant mistrust of theater and other commercial entertainment, they believed that urban amusements provided essential regeneration and could be a strong force for moral uplift.[13] A similar confidence spurred city planners and others who sought to establish cultural authority by reconstructing the physical environment of the city. The creators of the grandiose neoclassical settings of the 1893 Chicago World's Fair did hope to reorder unruly urban society along the edifying lines of their architectural models. But, as James Gilbert demonstrates, a major goal of that reordering was to make the modern city, with its diversity and exciting new pleasures, accessible to respectable folk.[14] These men and women, and the generation of planners and reformers they inspired, strove not to repress the modern city but to make it their own.

That the long project of coming to grips with urban society was generally successful is suggested by the waning of some of these efforts after the First World War. Progressive reform faded from public discussion and political significance, as did the city-planning movement. Unlike his counterparts of an earlier decade, George Babbitt, the perceptive Sinclair Lewis's middle-class composite, could ignore the blighted patches of his beloved hometown.[15] When reform returned, it was the New Deal blunderbuss aimed at the ills of an entire society in which cities seemed no sicker than small towns or the countryside. By the 1920s the city had become the accepted, normal setting in which all kinds of Americans might work out their lives.

Nevertheless, the acceptance of urbanism as a norm did not constitute resolution of all the problems it entailed, and the gangster images of the twenties and early thirties belong to the long effort to devise solutions. The gangster represented a reformulation of long-standing concerns for a new cultural context. As staged in the underworld, the city was a disorderly place of dangerous strangers, of rapacious capitalists, of unmanly men and unwomanly women, of seekers of pleasure and shirkers of responsibility. In every scene, however, the drama played out by this familiar cast had been rewritten to meet the needs of a new audience. Gender, strangers, pleasure, and business were still problematic, but in new ways. At the same time, the inventors of the gangster, like others who grappled with the meaning of urban society, found much to admire in their new surroundings. However troublesome, the underworld's city was a place of exciting possibilities.

The gangster genre's discussions of city life clustered around problems of social categorization. This common concern reflects the powerful cultural role of systems of classification in ordering the social world and the inadequacies of existing systems to structure urban experience. Boundaries between law-abiding and criminal, respectable and disreputable, male and female, moral and licentious, individual and group: all seemed at the same time blurry and crucially important. The inventors of the gangster walked these boundaries, reported what they saw, and blazed new lines where the old ones had been trampled away or headed in dangerous directions. The commercial success of the genre indicates that millions of Americans valued this guidance and joined in the expedition.

The following chapters of *Inventing the Public Enemy* examine this cultural mapping of new social territory. The first chapter analyzes crime writers' efforts to survey the most fundamental cultural boundary and the one that had become most perplexing in the developing urban society: the line that defined the individual. In the early and mid 1920s a contentious media debate about an apparently explosive growth in lawlessness centered on the issue of the criminal's responsibility. Some writers publicized "scientific," determinist views that seemed appropriate to an impersonal, interdependent urban society. Distant, external forces overwhelmed the inconsequential human will. By the middle of the 1920s, a counterargument prevailed, contending that criminals were responsible for their actions and thus that individual agency remained undiminished even in the face of modernization's assaults. The inventors of the gangster would build on this reinforced foundation of traditional moral values.

The second and third chapters study the gangster genre's exploration of the crucial boundary of respectability, and of several lesser territorial lines as well. Chapter 2 examines the portrayal of the gangster as that paragon of middle-class occupational respectability, the businessman. Using the underworld to scrutinize the developing corporate society, the inventors of the gangster at once celebrated the values of efficiency and warned of their potential dangers. The third chapter studies the ways Americans used the underworld to examine the developing urban mass-consumption society. The stylish gangster verified that consumption brought recognition and fulfillment, but, for some, he also served notice that the standards of style blurred supposedly more reliable categories of social classification, especially ethnicity and class. Others, more comfortable with the new ethos of consumerism, smugly saw in the overdressed gangster buffoon reassurance that even in the modern city filled with strangers outward display broadcast inner character.

The fourth chapter examines the ways Americans used the underworld to explore the shifting terrain of gender relations in urban society. The gangster and his female associates experimented with a range of roles men and women might now play. On gender, as on business and consumption, the genre offered an alternately enthusiastic and critical evaluation of urban social change.

The final chapter studies accounts of the individual gangster Americans found most compelling, Al Capone of Chicago. Capone came to prominence in 1926, and from the St. Valentine's Day Massacre of 1929 through his conviction on income tax violations in 1931, his career generated extraordinary attention. Countless newspaper articles, magazine features, books, and pulps constructed an elaborate fable of his rise to wealth, fame, and power. At once a responsible individual, an organized businessman, a hedonistic consumer, and a champion of traditional morality, Capone illuminated urban society's problematic boundaries by his flagrant transgressions or ironic observance. His tale of success, as hortatory as it was cautionary, helped explain the possibilities and the dangers of the new urban society.

The epilogue considers the persistence of gangster imagery after a fading of media attention in 1933 and 1934. In particular it examines an invention of the mid and late 1930s: the gangster as a rural desperado. John Dillinger, Pretty Boy Floyd, and their celluloid counterparts suggested that the long accommodation to the city no longer ranked as the nation's preeminent cultural challenge. Americans put the gangster, this rich resource, to other tasks.

The Individual, Society, and the Uses of Crime

In the apparent explosion of crime of the early 1920s many saw the key to understanding a society in turmoil. That Americans murdered, stole, and assaulted with unmatched regularity was the starting point for endless searching of the national soul. "The United States is the most lawless nation on the globe, barring only Russia under Bolshevist rule," one typically grim observer concluded; "No subject has attracted more attention and caused more serious discussion."[1] This discussion, aired in the mass media and capturing the attention of its huge audience, concerned much more than the causes of lawbreaking, for participants used the issue of criminality to grapple with some of the most troubling cultural dilemmas of their time. Most fundamentally, the criminal served as an important cultural resource for men and women working to understand—and shape—the structure of their society and the place of the individual within it. Through him, Americans considered difficult problems, tested controversial ideas, and promoted basic values.

The criminal was a rich symbol, and Americans in the early 1920s struggled over who would use him. Observers divided most significantly, and most contentiously, over whether the typical criminal was responsible for his actions and whether he resembled "ordinary" (native-born, middle-class) Americans. Answers had cultural significance far beyond the issue immediately at hand. Placing lawbreakers apart as a peculiar, distinctive class suggested that indelible lines of difference separated unequal groups in an inevitably heterogeneous society. But if the criminal and the noncriminal could be lumped into a coherent whole, then the lines of difference faded, and it was a largely homogeneous populace that faced the challenges and promises of modernity. In pronouncing the criminal's irresponsibility, many determinists voiced broader concerns about the diminution of individual competence in a mass society. Moralists for their part evoked the culpable criminal to shore up eroding standards of individual responsibility. It was their vision of the typical criminal, fraught with implications for other ordinary, responsible Americans, that prevailed in the early 1920s and spawned the gangster imagery soon to follow.

Many Americans argued that crime was the result of powerful forces external to the individual will. Popular accounts drew on recent scientific ideas to trace criminality to defective breeding, racial proclivities, diseased teeth, over- and under-active glands, mental illness, low intelligence, and pernicious childhood environments, often in terrible combinations.[2] "Modern scientific investigation," they typically explained, "has shaken to its foundations" the assumption "that crime is the voluntary choice of a free agent."[3] These determinist explanations diverged over whether the lawbreaker's lack of individual agency was unique or whether it was merely an extreme example of a general powerlessness.

The brand of determinism that most often pronounced the criminal's essential differentness attributed crime to innate hereditary factors. Since the turn of the century the notion that behavioral traits passed from generation to generation had regularly captured public attention. Well publicized eugenicists argued that a host of social problems, from violent crime to pauperism and sexual promiscuity,

were the inevitable consequences of the "breeding" of "defectives."
Though the eugenics vogue had peaked in the decade after 1910, it
continued to receive favorable press coverage in the 1920s, especially
early in the decade.[4] As crime became an ever-greater matter of public
concern, it regularly drew the attention of the eugenics popularizers.
The eugenicists assured that lawbreakers had little in common with
ordinary folk. In his contention that "nature fashioned [the criminal]
beyond the reach of his own will," *Collier's* contributor Wesley O.
Howard typically offered an implicit contrast with law-abiding citizens presumably well within the reach of their wills.[5] "The criminal,"
another eugenicist explained, "is a unique and highly differentiated
individual, deviating sharply from the normal."[6] Criminals were a different breed. A terrible national problem was best understood by di-
viding society into types, rigid natural categories of ability, behavior,
and worth.

The eugenicists' message of difference was amplified by its incorporation of the markers of important social divisions. The born criminal validated existing ethnic and racial categories. The pickpocket
described by Howard's *Collier's* account—a "little, lithe, slender,
peak-faced . . . cunning" man with "keen, quick, narrow, shifty
eyes"—conformed neatly to stereotypes about Jews, who were believed to have an affinity for that crime. Nature imprinted a typical
"thug" with troglodytic characteristics routinely ascribed to southern
and eastern European immigrants: "His face was unchangeable—the
heavy, brutal jaw; the surly lowering brow; the dull, cruel eyes; the
defiant, dishonest glance; the vulgar gluttonous mouth; the pimpled,
pitted skin; the thick, bull-like neck; the guttural, unmannerly
speech."[7] Appearance distinguished the criminal from respectable
folk and linked him to dangerous ethnic groups.

Occasionally the ethnic connection was more explicit. Most eugenicists fretted about Nordic "race suicide" and pointed to crime as
another reason to close the gates to immigrants. *Scribner's* contributor Edwin Grant Conklin was one of many to match "alien races"
with their "peculiar forms of lawlessness and crime": Irish were
drawn to crime by alcoholism resulting from an inherited "unstable
nervous organization"; Italians, with their "highly excitable and
emotional disposition," excelled at kidnapping, blackmailing, and
crimes of violence; Russians and Poles, at "gainful crimes such as
robbery, larceny, and receiving stolen goods"; Jews, at white slavery

and prostitution.[8] In an odd manifestation of nativist chauvinism, a *Woman Citizen* contributor warned that as Poles, Jews, Slavs, Italians, and others made "the American type ... smaller and darker [and] more mercurial," unsavory immigrant offenses would displace the old "Anglo-American crimes of burglary, drunkenness and vagrancy."[9]

The message of difference also invoked economic divisions, as some observers employed the rhetoric of class to understand the criminal. Though some writers, reflecting the scientific origins of determinist thought, referred to a criminal "type," "class" offered richer associations. "The 'criminal class,'" one writer concluded, "is practically a caste," drawn from the same families "generation after generation."[10] The rhetoric of class was often coupled with nativism and buttressed by science. "We are now admitting large numbers of persons of low intelligence," Conklin wrote, "and it is this class which constitutes the greatest biological danger. . . . Any measure which would prevent the growth of this class of persons of low intelligence would to a large extent reduce the immense amount of crime and lawlessness in this country."[11] Warnings about the rapid growth of this deviant class reflected the fears of many native-born Americans that respectable society would be overrun by the rapidly multiplying immigrant laboring class. "This class of defectives . . . from which nearly all our criminals come," as one eugenicist warned, "is giving American society five children for every one contributed by the class of highest intelligence."[12] Decent society was under siege from a dangerous lower class, and the criminal exemplified the threat.

Setting the problem of crime in the big-city slum cemented the association of criminals with the lower class. Many writers placed criminals in the teeming, decayed urban areas inhabited by immigrant and other laboring "hordes," and they imagined that the criminal class behaved much like other stereotypical slum dwellers. Repackaging standard conservative dogma about the lower class in general, eugenicists explained that even though criminals came from the slums, their behavior could not be attributed to that environment. Instead, members of the defective (lower) class would make a slum of any decent neighborhood into which misguided reformers placed them.[13] Some eugenicists' choices of offenses to highlight owed more to notions about slum behavior than to concerns about crimes that were particularly violent or resulted in large property losses. "Exploring the Criminal Mind," a *Literary Digest* report on the work of psychologist and eugenicist William J. Hickson, featured a Chicago mother of seven children, two of whom had died. Her transgressions consisted of repeatedly deserting her husband and children by "running away with drunken 'bums' for four or five days at a time and consorting with the lowest class of men and women" and keeping her home "in frightful condition; disorder everywhere, children and house neglected and filthy." Fecundity, promiscuity, drunkenness, uncleanliness, sickness, chaos: this criminal's life was a catalog of middle-class stereotypes about the slum and those who lived in it.[14]

The portrayal of the criminal as an exotic, biologically driven alien reflected some Americans' basic values and promoted powerful cultural and political messages. Its conflation of crime and ethnicity argued for the restriction of immigration and for the vigilant oversight of "foreigners" already here. The assertion that a lower deviant class inevitably produced its own environment cast any attempt at social amelioration as a misguided effort in futility: the lower orders lived as they were born to live. It was this division of society into higher and lower orders that was the most insistent message. Society did not conform to the classical liberal conception of an aggregation of rational, autonomous individuals. Instead, its lower reaches were filled with people whose actions were to a greater or lesser extent determined not by individual choice but by the awesome workings of nature. Categories of defect and criminality blurred into categories of economic class, race, and ethnicity. The eugenics popularizers assured that respectable Americans, their presumed readers, were different: they possessed complete self-control. These good citizens were imperiled by the members of dangerous foreign classes so inferior that they could not control themselves. Respectable Americans need neither deny nor take responsibility for the disorder around them: it emanated from others.

Another group of observers used deterministic explanations to put forth a very different set of cultural messages. Many psychiatrists, academic social scientists, and their popularizers shared the belief of eugenicists that irresistible forces impelled the criminal, but they insisted that ordinary, noncriminal individuals were subject to the same influences. In their view criminals were not exotic aliens governed by unique biological or psychological rules. Instead they believed that scientific study of criminals, as one endocrinologist explained in *Collier's,* "promises to revolutionize our whole understanding of human behavior."[15] The task for scientists was not to explain deviant oddities but to uncover "the forces that determine the conduct, social or ethical, of men and women."[16] Criminologists could understand the lawbreaker, a *Current History* contributor reported, because science "is able today to explain human conduct . . . with an accuracy and helpfulness that far exceed anything of which it was formerly capable."[17] Professor Fred E. Haynes, responding to the eugenicists' message of difference, wrote in the *Independent* that new research "emphasizes the fact that the study of the criminal is the study of human behavior, and not that of a special biological variety of the human race, nor of a separate social class."[18]

Such study led many to believe that powerful forces external to an individual's will controlled criminals and law-abiding citizens alike. They assumed, the *Literary Digest* summarized, "that the actions of men are predetermined and that personal responsibility is a myth."[19] The prominent sociologist Harry Elmer Barnes was a leading popularizer. "We have given up the notion of man as a free moral agent," he wrote, "and have come to the conclusion that human conduct is the resultant of a vast number of influences, alike hereditary and cultural, which make our action at any time as thoroughly determined as any other natural phenomenon. . . . There is not the slightest iota of freedom of choice allowed to either the criminal or the normal citizen in his daily conduct."[20] "Science has brought the matter of human conduct or misconduct down to a physiological and even to a chemical basis," an endocrinologist explained in *Collier's;* "Men do not err because they are evil, but because of chemical disturbances in that marvelously intricate machine, the human body."[21] French Strother, writing in *World's Work,* used the same mechanical metaphor: the criminal's "physical machine that registers emotions is . . . a defective machine."[22] The focus shifted easily from the criminal to the ordinary citizen. "Any reader," Edward H. Smith wrote in the *New York Times,* "can test the chemical theory for himself" by observing his or her own involuntary reactions to certain stimuli.[23] Barnes explained that "the act of a criminal is as inevitable as that of a clergyman or a missionary."[24] Strother graciously assured his readers that "your own son couldn't commit a deliberate crime if he tried."[25] Clergymen, well-reared boys, and felons were united in the slight credit or blame they merited for their behavior.

For some writers, the putative goal of explaining criminality seems to have been far less important than highlighting the absence of free will. As they pointed to myriad explanations, the message of the inexorability of powerful forces took precedence over causal consistency. "We have discovered that a large part of crime is inevitable," Francis Bowes Sayre explained in the *Atlantic*, "the result partly of inherent physiological abnormalities and mental defects, and partly of social environment and economic conditions."[26] According to Barnes, it was "heredity, past experience, and present environment" that excluded "the slightest iota of freedom of choice."[27] In his *Times* article, Smith adduced the research of behaviorists, Freudian psychologists, and two physicians who believed "that human behavior is controlled by chemical action"—one of whom blamed defective glands and the other "focal infections in the teeth, the tonsils, the lower colon and other parts of the body." Conceding the inconsistencies of these explanations, Smith acknowledged that his real theme was the lack of free will: "If the reader feels a great schism between the Freudians and the physicists here he is asked to reflect that both these schools agree that man behaves in certain ways not because he wills to do so but because he must, because he has no control over his actions in the last analysis."[28]

The determinists realized they advocated controversial and troubling ideas. The enlightened understandings of "the philosophic and scientific order," Smith contended, had come into conflict with "the ancient attitude toward guilt and personal responsibility."[29] Barnes provocatively promised "the entire repudiation and elimination, once and for all, of the theological and metaphysical interpretations of criminal conduct and responsibility."[30] A few writers struggled with their own discomfort with the broader implications of their ideas about crime. French Strother acknowledged that "this explanation somewhat shocks us at first, because it seems to destroy at once the proudest conception of himself that man has built up through the ages—the conception of man as a free moral agent." If "our acts are controlled by a machine," could a person still proclaim himself "master of my fate . . . captain of my soul"? Criminal irresponsibility challenged "the whole structure of theology." Strother attempted unconvincingly to reconcile this individual-as-machine with conventional notions of responsibility. How can we continue to maintain that people have free will, he asked. "The answer," he assured, "is a little complicated, but quite intelligible." The free will that leads to the desire to obey the law, he concluded, exists for those who have "the machinery with which to feel that way."[31] Strother's contortions did convey one clear message: some Americans used the criminal to air difficult ideas with which they themselves were not entirely comfortable. Starting with the message that deviants did not control their actions, Strother and others could experiment with the riskier, more explosive notion that moral responsibility was a sham.

As the determinists and their readers pondered responsibility, they took part in a larger cultural consideration of the status of the individual within the new mass society. Since the late nineteenth century many Americans had come to believe that social change had rendered individuals increasingly inconsequential. Walter Lippmann offered his assessment in a 1931 essay on crime. "Our civilization," he wrote, "has become so extensive and complex that we are for the most part mere spectators of events in which by a hidden chain of causes we are implicated."[32] Others matched Lippmann's sentiment, if not his ability to express it. Ordinary people seemed to lose power as nationwide markets and huge corporations displaced the face-to-face economy of earlier decades. Success seemed to depend less on character and hard work than on the ability to situate oneself within a promising professional or corporate bureaucracy. For many workers technology made obsolete the skills on which personal identity had been founded. Changes in the factory were mirrored on the battlefield. Critics of the First World War contended that even the best soldiers were not courageous heroes but standardized accessories to the modern machinery that could so easily obliterate them. Even one of the mainstreams of Protestantism, under the banner of the Social Gospel, discounted individual agency by preaching that society bore much of the burden for salvation. With the explosive growth of mass leisure and consumption, critics in the 1920s began to see excessive conformity as a national problem. At the same time, many advertisers detected widespread fears that individuals had become insignificant parts of an undifferentiated crowd. Buy our product, they promised, and stand out.[33] The unfortunate criminal, bounced along by powerful forces he could not control, confirmed the individual's loss of agency in an impersonal world.

It was the connection of criminal irresponsibility to individual insignificance that, for some determinists, made the Great War an important precipitating factor in contemporary lawlessness. Understandings of the war inevitably reflected understandings of society; for some determinists the battlefields of Europe provided stark evidence of the inconsequentiality of the rational will. "The crime wave now afflicting the entire world," a *Nation* contributor contended, was "a logical aftermath of the war," with its "loosening of men's animal passions."[34] "Weaker men were broken in moral fiber under the experiences of war," another *Nation* contributor believed.[35] The excitement and upheaval of war, Strother wrote, "threw off their balance thousands of boys and men whose emotional centers were unstable."[36] An editorialist excerpted in the *Literary Digest,* noting "that terrible conflict's disturbance of all normal conditions," ascribed criminality to "the unsettled frame of mind in which it left the young men who lived in a feverish state of excitement in the army."[37] In linking the war and the criminal, determinists exploited two of the most powerful symbols available to Americans in the 1920s to show the individual's loss of agency in a complex world.

If overwhelming excitement and upheaval had their temporal center in wartime they had a specific geographic location in daily life: the metropolis. Many determinists placed the criminal in the big city and suggested that there modern society's assaults on individual potency were most intense. In his *Collier's* account of the criminal career of "a young New Yorker of the sensitive type," Edward Smith linked individual powerlessness to the stresses and clamor of urban life. After serving in the army, the young man became an employee in a Wall Street brokerage, that symbolic locus of urban pressure. "Suspense and anxiety" combined with an overactive thyroid to drive the "harried" young man to embezzlement and armed robbery. "There are countless human beings," Smith concluded ominously, "who are ill adapted to their environment and the stresses and struggles of life."[38] French Strother, citing economic uncertainty, a lack of fixed social relationships, and an overabundance of excitement, concurred that the urban environment strained the weak emotions of potential criminals.[39] Max Schlapp, a neurologist featured in the *New*

York Times, saw crime as "a pathological matter" attributable to "a basic disturbance in the nation's emotional stability." The instability was most dangerous to immigrants who "have left a peaceful, orderly life without any particular emotional shock and have been plunged into a nervous maelstrom." Somewhere in the journey from European village to American city, Schlapp's verbs suggested, immigrants lost control over their lives. Others faced "the enormous increase in the nervous stimulation and shock of American life" with only somewhat deeper emotional reserves. Tracing the overpowering disturbance to "immigration, automobiles, jazz and the movies," Schlapp located it squarely within the boundaries of the modern city.[40]

The links between crime, individual powerlessness, and urban complexity were most explicitly delineated by Harry Elmer Barnes. The disruptive consequences of modernity had come about so abruptly, he suggested, that Americans of the early nineteenth century bore more similarity to their prehistoric ancestors than to their modern descendants. "If crime is actually on the increase in this country," he wrote,

> it is only what we should expect as a result of the changes in society and culture that have occurred since the scientific and industrial revolutions. Man originated and has spent more than 95 per cent. of his existence in a highly simple environment with relatively few stimuli operating upon him. Today society and civilization have become extremely complex, so that the average citizen is subjected to a greater variety of stimulation (with the resulting increase of strains and stresses) in one week than his great-grandfather had to encounter in a decade. It is inevitable that these increased strains and stresses should have their effect in producing a breakdown of the less tough and hardy human types. Some increase of crime and degeneracy is bound to result from the growing complexity of contemporary civilization. . . . Therefore, if there is such a thing as a growing crime wave in the country, it is something which we should naturally expect as the outcome of the greater difficulties which an animal that arrived at his present nature in the cave age encounters in attempting to live in modern metropolitan areas in the era of machines and movies.[41]

Understanding the criminal meant understanding human beings in their alien contemporary environment. In the transition from the cave to the modern city, with its technology, mass entertainment, and constant bombardment of stimuli, men and women had lost control of their lives.

Writers who attributed crime to individual powerlessness in the face of irresistible external forces conveyed an insistent message about the proper location of social authority. If actions resulted from individual choice, then any reasonable person could understand and potentially influence the behavior of others. But the determinists argued that in modern society causation was so remote that ordinary people could not hope to understand, let alone mold, the actions of those around them without the guidance of highly educated experts. If, as physician Edgar A. Doll wrote, "crime is caused by an intricate complex of related influences," then only the "intelligent cooperative effort" of specially trained professionals could lead to the understanding or prevention of it.[42] Not surprisingly, appropriately qualified experts most ardently publicized this view. "The human personality," sociologist Barnes wrote, "has been revealed as a proper subject for the cooperative study of biologists, physiologists, psychologists, psychiatrists and sociologists, and it is to these men that we must in the future refer the problem of determining the nature of moral conduct and the degree of personal responsibility therefor."[43]

Some publicists used their accounts of the experts' competence in dealing with accused criminals to propose a much broader role for the scientific elite. For criminals highlighted the possibilities of scientists as social managers. Thus among the suggestions in a *Literary Digest* forum on "Murderous Maniacs at Large" was that "trained psychiatrists examine children in all the schools."[44] After advocating a central role for scientists in the criminal justice system, Barnes called for "a general inquisition and investigation of the whole population in order to put in segregation or bring under treatment the feeble-minded, psycho-neurotic and other types likely to be guilty of criminal conduct."[45] Watson Davis, a *Current History* contributor, agreed that "eventually it will not be necessary for the community to wait until crimes of certain sorts are committed before detecting the potential criminal. Experience and tests will allow the person with criminal tendencies to be spotted in early life at a time when his destructive tendencies can be corrected or curbed." Moreover, Davis confidently extended the expert's purview beyond the problem of lawbreaking, actual or potential. "The new psychiatry," he wrote, "reaches far beyond the asylum, jail or courtroom. The experience and technique of the mental expert can be applied with success to the irascible employe, the retarded school child . . . the compulsive drinker and the multitude of other unhappy individuals who do not find themselves in step with society."[46]

In their exaltation of expertise, these determinists replaced the eugenicists' vision of a society divided along lines of ethnicity and class with one divided along the single line between scientific experts and nearly everyone else. Ordinary people created social problems; scientists knew how to solve them. The distinction was apparent in experts' assessments of nonscientists involved in the criminal justice system. While many critics attacked judges and jurors for laxity, sentimentality, or overzealous attention to defendants' rights, these determinists accused them of ignorance and stupidity. One physician contended that "the judge unaided can no more be expected with any degree of accuracy to differentiate between the human material before him than he could be expected to differentiate between pure water and water containing typhoid bacilli by looking at it or tasting it." Juries fared worse. A psychiatrist complained that "complicated medical questions" were often left to jurors "of very low mental calibre."[47] Barnes dismissed juries as "twelve men who are for the most part unconscious of what is being divulged to them, and who would be incapable of an intelligent assimilation and interpretation of such information if they actually heard it."[48] Such limitations, these determinists explained, reflected the huge chasm between the gifted few and the unlucky many. "A considerable majority" of the population, Strother reported, "grades no higher than high grade moron in intelligence."[49] No wonder society needed the wise guidance of men with graduate degrees.

The determinists who portrayed the criminal as essentially ordinary in his lack of free will presented their audience with two consistent messages about the structure of their society and the place of the individual within it. First, their explanation of criminality buttressed the perception that individuals had little control over their own lives. Especially in the big cities, individuals were helpless in the face of irresistible external forces. Second, this common powerlessness united ordinary people, even across the lines of class and ethnicity that the eugenicists insisted were so important. Nevertheless, the social vision of this brand of determinism, like that of the eugenicists', which denied equality to entire class and ethnic groups, was deeply undemocratic, for the general homogeneity ended at the sharp line of expertise, beyond which was a small group distinguished by the ability to use science to understand and control their world.

In many ways the determinist explanations of crime resonated with compelling strains of progressive-era social thought. The determinists' faith in scientific experts was at the heart of countless reform movements. So was the belief that in an interdependent, complex society causation was frequently remote or esoteric. Just as important, native-born, middle- and upper-class whites were driven to social activism by an acute awareness of working-class Americans' rejection of bourgeois culture. Reform often had as its goal the social control of groups that seemed dangerously distant from middle-class values.[50] When characterizing the lawbreaker as a threatening other external to respectable society, eugenicists echoed the reformers' warnings about the dangerous classes. The determinists' explanations of crime fit comfortably in the rambling, capacious structure of progressive social thought.

Despite the apparent congeniality of the determinists' ideas, they never enjoyed preeminence in 1920s media discussions. Instead, these theories of criminal causation seemed to be holdovers from an earlier era of progressive scientific certainty. Like other strains of prewar reform thought, they persisted in the twenties but only in the shadow of the prevailing conservative sentiment. Their proponents argued most regularly in elite magazines like *Current History* that presented a diversity of often controversial viewpoints. In more popular magazines sympathetic discussions of determinist theories became increasingly infrequent, brief, and full of qualifiers. For example, after the mid-1920s they virtually disappeared from *Collier's* and became much less prominent in *Literary Digest*. The nation's most widely read magazine, the *Saturday Evening Post*, provides the clearest case. Editor George Horace Lorimer, staunchly moralistic and hostile to intellectuals, had never permitted his pages to be used as a platform for deterministic ideas. Nevertheless, writers in the early 1920s occasionally suggested that criminality might be at least partially attributable to a pernicious environment or mental and physical deficiencies.[51] By the end of the decade, Lorimer not only took an active role in banishing such heresies from the *Post* but also made refuting them one of the magazine's many ideological missions.[52]

Most mass media accounts instead contended that criminals possessed free choice and the responsibility that accompanied it. However complicated society seemed to have become, and regardless of the experts' slick arguments, criminal behavior was easily understandable using long-established legal and moral principles. This conventional legalistic and moralistic understanding of crime, like the determinist explanations, carried strong messages about the social order and the place of the individual within it. Society was imperiled not by dangerous outside groups but by individuals hiding behind the flimsy excuse of irresponsibility.

The cultural significance that moralists attached to the criminal was evident in their vehement denunciations of the determinists. Despite the somewhat one-sided nature of the media debate, the opponents of deterministic theories gave them extraordinary attention. The influence of determinists in universities, elite periodicals, and a few institutions in the criminal justice system accounted for much of the moralists' concern. More important, however, the vitriol of the moralists' attacks suggests that they were engaged in a defense of sacred ideological ground. The determinists had to be thoroughly discredited lest they further undermine the individual accountability that was the foundation of true morality. In countless incantations the moralists accused the "flabby," "so-called experts" of engaging in an "orgy of sentimentality" that made them utterly incapable of understanding the world around them. Richard Washburn Child, former United States ambassador to Italy, admiring ghostwriter of Mussolini's autobiography, and founding member of the new National Crime Commission, included most of the standard harangue in his long, singularly influential *Saturday Evening Post* series on crime in 1925. Determinists—the criminal's sympathizers—were "bearded gentlemen" reminiscent of hairy radicals, "blithering sentimentalists," "floppy-minded persons," and "a lot of professors, social workers, amateur philosophers, ladies' sympathy circles and rescue leagues."[53] Flabby, muddle-headed, or feminine, the proponents of irresponsibility deserved only scorn.[54]

As they attacked the determinists, the moralists dismissed the modern notion that only science could explain the supposed complexities of society and human behavior. *Saturday Evening Post* writer Charles Francis Coe, promising an explanation of the current crime wave, boasted that he was "not a quoter of statistics" and had no special training.[55] The experts, a *Scribner's* contributor asserted, were "an intensely artificial lot" blinded by "their unnatural way of regarding things."[56] The rejection of science often took the form of intense hostility to abstract theories and arcane terminology. Criminal psychology, according to Child, was "nonsense . . . the introduction of phraseology which calls old, recognized human traits by new names." "A sensible citizen," Child explained, "wants facts and not theories." Another founder of the National Crime Commission insisted that "the true study of crime in America must be based on a matter-of-fact knowledge of existing conditions, and not on a theory that will complicate the situation and end only in confounding us. We have got to stop theorizing."[57] Several magazines, refuting the scientific approach, appropriately turned to convicts as the persons with the greatest matter-of-fact knowledge. "All the pretty theories of parole and pardon boards, all the sophistries contrived by sentimental reformers must give way before the smashing evidence of a thousand police blotters," was the obliging conclusion of Prisoner No. 4000X in *Scribner's*. Combined with common sense, such simple evidence would obliterate the dangerous notion that the criminal was "drawn by powers beyond his control."[58] This hostility to theoretical understandings was at the ideological center of the attack on the determinists. Understanding human behavior required little more than common sense and observation of readily apparent facts, for mysterious, distant forces played no significant role. People chose to act the ways they did, and others were more or less equally capable of understanding those choices. Experts could claim no special competence.

In addition to his responsibility, the criminal's salient characteristic, according to the moralists, was his normality. Criminals thought, looked, and, for the most part, even acted like respectable Americans. The *Saturday Evening Post* suggested the ordinariness of one criminal in the pseudonym it assigned him: John Doe.[59] A typical young criminal, *Collier's* writer William G. Shepherd reported, was "to all intents and purposes . . . as normal a boy as you would care to meet."[60] Many writers, responding to the notion that lawbreakers were monstrously different, echoed the apparent revelation of George S. Dougherty's *Saturday Evening Post* expose "The Criminal as a Human

Being."[61] "To any one who has observed and studied the criminal over many years," Judge Charles C. Nott concurred in *Scribner's,* "he seems intensely human—much more human and normal than do the neurasthenic philosophers who proclaim his abnormality."[62] Basil Thomson wrote that criminals "are men and women of like passions with ourselves and our neighbors . . . if we know how we would act in a crisis we should make very passable detectives."[63] Understand the criminal, the moralists said, and understand yourself.

For many writers, the basis of the criminal's normality was his rationality and intelligence. Here the contrast was with the scientists' tales of bad brain chemistry and defective thinking machines. As Shepherd characteristically reported about one criminal, "his mind was all right. You couldn't call him wrong in the head."[64] Writers routinely compared the thoughts and motivations of lawbreakers with those of their presumably ordinary readers. "Actual as well as potential criminals go through the same mental processes as the average citizen," a *Scientific Monthly* writer explained.[65] That criminals were rational, calculating, and intelligent was a staple of crime writing in the twenties and thirties. The dangerous criminal, according to Louis E. Bisch, was "the normal crook, the man who is able to think as you and I do, who can plan, who can reason, who is clever, who is daring."[66] Such abilities were essential, according to countless writers, for criminals had to overcome enormous obstacles in the planning and execution of crimes. Crimes of passion were rare.[67] Like other skilled workers, most dangerous criminals broke the law for financial gain. Crime was a lucrative field, pursued by professionals who carefully evaluated the risks and rewards of possible "jobs."[68]

Nor was the criminal set apart by appearance. After the mid-1920s Hollywood rarely characterized him as the physical monster previously popular in the films of Lon Chaney and his imitators.[69] Now the criminal was indistinguishable from the respectable, law-abiding citizen—"far from being a stage Bill Sikes," as one writer put it.[70] The criminal's unremarkable appearance was especially significant because it contradicted Cesare Lombroso's widely popularized writings about physical stigmata. As Child explained, for example, gang leaders were "young men whose appearance, expression and contour of features would perplex any of those scientific old gentlemen who talk about a 'criminal type.'"[71] "For centuries a certain school of illustrators and cartoonists, egged on by an army of

well-meaning criminologists," another *Saturday Evening Post* writer complained with more passion than precision, "has done its very best to portray burglars and stick-up men as an unsightly breed of plug-ugly individuals. Their facial lines have been distorted and devolutionized to such an inferior complex that today they are pictured in the minds of most people as direct descendants from Darwin's pet image."[72] "With his straight, good features, his bright eyes, his slender hands and his appearance of physical well-being and cleanliness," a convict described by William Shepherd was a neat, ironic contrast to the stereotypical flabby, cloudy-eyed determinist who declared the lawbreaker's abnormality.[73]

Some writers contended that the criminal's normality extended to his very soul. They stressed that lawbreakers possessed good moral traits along with the bad. Like the respectable, otherwise decent citizen who cheated on a tax return, the criminal was a morally ambiguous figure. Ed X., a "typical" young criminal featured by Child, loved animals and was scrupulously honest. His desperate desire to hide his occupation from his sister and wife revealed conventional domestic values that could come only from some deep well of decency.[74] Morally attractive traits confirmed the criminal's humanity. One criminal, featured in *Collier's*, "proved himself a human being" through his distraught reaction to his wife's planned suicide.[75] "Everybody is human," the *Christian Science Monitor* explained, "and we have found in the underworld that the guerrilla is a man of courage and heart and that he has well-defined virtues."[76] "You can appeal to their better natures the same as to any other human being's," Louis Bisch explained; "They are capable of sentiment, love, loyalty, truthfulness, patriotism—any and all of the highest and best emotions—even self-sacrifice in behalf of a principle or of an individual."[77]

By presenting criminals who so resembled ordinary men and women, the moralists showed their middle-class readers that serious threats to social order originated within the boundaries of supposed respectability. Men and women who looked and thought and loved *like you* were to blame for the crime wave and the greater disorder it symbolized. What made this message even more alarming was the suggestion that this internal threat was new, a challenge never faced before. According to many of the moralists, criminals in the past, and even contemporary old-timers, in fact had belonged to a different human type. Numerous writers noted the disappearance of "the

seasoned criminal of the olden days, who had outlaw written all over his face."[78] William Shepherd contrasted the appearance of recent convicts with the obviously "stolid, stupid" look of longtime inmates.[79] Child compared the attractive Ed X. with a sixty-year-old "weasel-faced department store thief" in a nearby cell. The older man, according to Child, "continually patted a swatch of long red hair plastered across a bald spot on his absurdly small skull. Here was disease indeed; here was the stunted, twisted character."[80]

So too, the changing geography of the underworld announced a troubling new universality of disorder. "Criminals of nowadays do not haunt particular sections of New York," *Atlantic* writer Morris Markey noted; "In the old days there were the 'honky-tonks,' those fantastic embellishments of city life which were recognized haunts for all types of blackguards. . . . They were the ganglia, as it were, of Manhattan's criminal life. . . . The underworld no longer has a habitat—it is everywhere."[81] Hollywood confirmed the change in 1928 and 1929, replacing the seedy, dark hangouts of earlier films with glittering, spectacular cabarets and penthouse apartments.[82] "In the old days there was a definite geography of crime," *Outlook* contributor Jack Grey remembered; "All big cities had their underworld zones and underworld joints, where crooks gathered in rooming houses and saloons." "The new underworld," he concluded, "is here, there, everywhere."[83]

One category of difference that persisted in some of the moralists' accounts was ethnicity. For as much as the moralists located social peril in the new behavior of native-born, "nonethnic" Americans, they were not entirely reconciled to urban diversity. Richard Washburn Child expressed this undercurrent. In accordance with his major objective of critiquing new standards of middle-class behavior, most of the lawbreakers he depicted, including typical criminal Ed X., had no discernible ethnic background. Yet one of the articles in his "The Great American Scandal" series included a lengthy digression on the dangers of "imported trouble makers," the "stream of criminal material from nations where the climate, the racial background or centuries of oppression has provided explosive, passionate or sneaky natures."[84] Here Child undermined his usual emphasis on the criminal's lack of distinctiveness and uncharacteristically echoed many of his determinist opponents. Subtler hints of racial determinism would persist in moralistic accounts of Italian and Jewish gangsters in the

late twenties and early thirties. Casting lawbreakers as members of minority ethnic groups remained a powerful cultural tool for exposing the perils of urban diversity. This use of the criminal is unsurprising among a native-born population only beginning to shed its xenophobia about ethnically different whites. Indeed, what is remarkable is that the vast majority of the inventors of the gangster, Child included, usually submerged these fears in pursuit of a new cultural agenda.

The criminal's normality set him up as the ostensible subject in a wide-ranging critique of other ordinary, responsible Americans, especially members of the urban middle class he so closely resembled. For the insistence on individual responsibility did not preclude sweeping social commentary. While explaining the upsurge in criminality, the moralists offered a vigorous conservative critique of modern urban society. Their vision of society and the challenges it faced differed fundamentally from that of the determinists. The social order was imperiled by an aggregation of individual choices, not by dangerous forces external to the individual will. Moreover, their critique of the social developments encouraging criminality contradicted the common middle-class, nativist notion, picked up by the eugenicists, that groups external to respectable society constituted the threat to order. It was social change among middle-class, native-born Americans that seemed to spawn the great postwar crime wave.

Some observers attributed modern criminality to the erosion of the work ethic and the new middle-class celebration of leisure.[85] "The morale of our industrial civilization has been shattered," United States Solicitor General James M. Beck warned in a widely reported 1921 anti-crime speech. "Work for work's sake, as the most glorious privilege of human faculties, has gone, both as an ideal and as a potent spirit. The conception of work as a degrading servitude to be done with reluctance and grudging inefficiency, seems to be the ideal of millions of men of all classes and in all countries."[86] Richard Washburn Child, perhaps nostalgic for the discipline of fascist Italy, linked crime to prosperity, laziness, and the moral weakness they bred. Society was "getting soft," he warned, because "America has yielded too much resource too suddenly. The hardening processes of struggle to succeed, of work for daily bread, no longer are sufficient to give enough moral sinew." Like Beck, Child adopted a historical perspec-

tive: modern lawlessness was a story of moral declension caused by social change. Drawing on a powerful symbol of the bootstraps mythology, Child argued that "the kind of quiet wrestling with life which produced President Coolidge's father and the President himself produced a fiber that mere advantages and luxuries will not beget." Would that everyone knew the hardship of a poor Vermont farm. The social locus of the change in values made it especially threatening. Even the nation's business "leadership at the top" succumbed to the new softness. Young executives, unlike their heroic predecessors, were more likely to be found vacationing than in the office.[87] The man who took up crime because of an aversion to hard work seemed to be modeled after the most respectable and modern of his contemporaries.

Many traced the postwar crime wave to Americans' loss of their religious bearings. Fewer than one in six juvenile delinquents, one minister reported, had heard of the Ten Commandments.[88] Crime flourished because "unbelief and luxury and vanity and loose manners have weakened our moral nature," a Methodist journalist wrote. The explanation echoed the regular lamentations of religious conservatives that the urban middle class had abandoned orthodoxy for secularism and permissive liberal religion. "Carelessness and willfulness and greed and fun have warped our higher sensibilities. . . . The churches have been laughed at, Puritanism has been scorned, and too lively a conscience has become a joke."[89] This specter of jaunty, fashionable irreligion redirected Christian concern away from the unbeliever who had been its customary object, the laborer unreached by the preaching of middle-class churches. Now the threat of godlessness seemed to originate within the boundaries of respectability.

Concerns about godlessness, materialism, and the disintegration of the work ethic came together in the attribution of criminality to the failure of the American home. From many, rampant criminality among youths called forth, as the *Literary Digest* put it, "an indictment of the domestic hearth." That the failure was not isolated but general was apparent in the sweeping terms of condemnation: "Parents have shirked their responsibilities. . . . The home as a source of spiritual culture, education and moral training is not functioning."[90] The failure of middle-class homes caused the greatest alarm. Richard Washburn Child noted that "the lads and girls of good families" were well represented among recent criminal recruits, and he blamed par-

ents caught up in spending. The "abandonment" of children "in favor of the touring car, the card table, the movies, trips, and a round of wet or dry social engagements" had become a national catastrophe. "The home—the old home, with the whole family in it at night, has flapped away," he lamented; "Everybody is excited, everybody is on the move, the move, the move! That's one cause of crime in America."[91]

Writers associated the dangerously frivolous, pleasure-oriented middle-class home with a threatening new urban society. Child's account of a typical young offender made the connection clear. Until he reached the age of fourteen, J.S. had lived with his modestly prosperous family in a small house on an acre of land. He was an intelligent boy, did well in school, attended church, and helped his father in the backyard vegetable garden. After his father, a building contractor, made "large profits," the family moved to an apartment, his father bought an expensive automobile, and both parents spent most of their spare time out on the town. "Life changed from the moment his parents got money and began going out." His fifty-year-old mother bobbed her hair and "read books or novels showing that too much restraint for boys and girls prevented self-development." The inevitable product of this "parental neglect" was the boy's sordid criminal career.[92] Parental movie-going, apartment living, easy spending, permissive child-rearing, and a short-haired mother added up to a life in crime.[93]

The attribution of crime to the failure of middle-class homes represented a critique of some of the fundamental cultural developments of the early twentieth century. Economic, social, and cultural forces had transformed middle-class families since the last decades of the nineteenth century, but the changes received greatest recognition in the 1920s. The new family reflected the erosion of nineteenth-century values about discipline, ascetic morality, and age- and gender-based hierarchy. New notions of the ideal family endorsed democratic, expressively affectionate relations between family members. In the increasingly impersonal modern society the family was no longer geared to affirming its members' social status by insuring their sober propriety. Instead, one of the new ways men and women conceived of the home was as a base for pleasurable consumption—the automobile jaunts and theater-going of Child's moral tale. As he recognized, the new experts on child-rearing replaced the inculcation of

discipline with a cultivation of psychological well-being as the family's primary goal. The image of the criminal youth was in large part an attack on the modern middle-class home.[94]

Many seized on crime to expose an even deeper source of corruption: a general disrespect for authority and a dangerous spirit of indiscipline. Illicit drinking, shady business deals, and fast driving indicated that disrespect for the law characterized not just the hardened criminal but the average citizen as well.[95] Lawless indiscipline was not a problem of an exotic "they" but of a newly irresponsible "we." "We are apparently drifting toward chaos in matters of convictions on fundamental questions, which in former years were looked upon as settled and operative on conduct," Frederick Hoffman explained in *Current History.* "We are failing grievously in teaching the duty of discipline and restraint."[96] Attributing the problem partly to geographic mobility, Child lamented that "we have lost much of the responsibility which comes from being settled for life in one place."[97] The fundamental source of the crime wave, according to Child, was the nationwide infatuation with "self-expression": "We are all out to get ourselves expressed. So in music, we have strange novelties and grotesques; in poetry, free verse; in morals, do as you please."[98] Disrespect for the laws of society seemed the natural companion of disrespect for the laws of conventional literature and classical composition. At every turn, traditional forms of discipline seemed to have been cast aside. Crime was merely the most alarming symptom of an endemic condition.

Some moralists traced this explosion of indiscipline to the most catastrophic event in recent memory, the Great War. Disappointed in their early hopes that the crisis of war would bring a fortifying infusion of martial discipline, moralists now saw wartime upheaval as the consequence of Americans' willful severing of ties of authority, discipline, and order.[99] While determinists stressed the role of war in making criminals, the moralists emphasized individual agency. A *Current History* contributor believed that the war brought a lessening of "regard for the sacredness of human life and the inviolability of property."[100] It sapped respect for life and law, a *Saturday Evening Post* writer agreed.[101] Editorialists surveyed by the *Literary Digest* concurred that lawlessness stemmed in part from "a general loosening of old standards by the war-spirit."[102] Far from driving helpless individuals to lawlessness, war corroded the values of culpable free agents.

The moralists, associating discipline with the acceptance of responsibility, contended that modern indiscipline—and criminality, its extreme manifestation—sprang from a pervasive current denial of responsibility. Pleasure, self-expression, acquisitiveness: the key pursuits within mass society seemed antithetical to the dutiful acceptance of responsibility. Criminologist George W. Kirchwey told the *New York Times* that American lawlessness was among "the results of our lack of moral fibre, of an absence of public and social responsibility among us."[103] Charles Francis Coe, like many other writers, believed that professional criminals took their cue from businessmen who followed the letter of the law but ignored "morals and moral responsibility."[104] Richard Washburn Child saw the terrible consequences of "a new sense of irresponsibility" in the apparent disorder everywhere around him. "We are living in an age of irresponsibility," he thundered; "the whole philosophy of freedom at any price and irresponsibility at any cost has been turned loose on the world." The remedy for crime, he contended, was "to substitute sane and able authority for the sense of irresponsibility that has taken hold of the youth of today."[105] As they traced crime to the shirking of responsibility, the moralists shared the determinists' preoccupation with the status of the individual in modern society. But the moralists insisted that "the sense of irresponsibility" was a sham, that the "absence of . . . [acknowledged] responsibility" was a catastrophe. Their pronouncements on crime exposed the fraudulence of the modern notion of individual irresponsibility.[106]

Thus the moralists responded to the same apparent deterioration of individual competence that preoccupied the determinists. While most moralists left implicit the relationship between the vogue of irresponsibility and the development of mass society, United States Solicitor General James Beck addressed the connection in his widely discussed speech on the moral roots of American criminality. Beck recognized that the tension between mass society and the status of the individual was the real subject of the debate about criminal responsibility. Lawlessness reigned because "a mass morality has been substituted for individual morality." "The individual," he continued, "has been submerged in group formations, and the effect upon the character of man has not been beneficial." Yet Beck insisted that social and technological change had not rendered individuals morally irresponsible. He acknowledged the potential threat to "the human soul" posed by "our complex mechanical civilization." But he confronted directly the determinists who suggested that the war was the prime example of individual inconsequentiality. Instead, he contended that in combat "all the horrible resources of mechanics and chemistry were utilized to coerce the human soul, and all proved ineffectual." Hold individuals to the standards of responsibility that mass society had shrouded—but that machine guns and nerve gas could not displace—and social order would return.[107]

The competing visions of the criminal fueled a contentious 1920s media debate about how best to confront the problem of crime. In this debate the moralists' and determinists' messages about the individual and the social order were especially clear. As in the discussion about the causes of crime, the determinists' positions were as notable for provoking the moralist response as for their own popularity. Conventional notions of punishment, the determinists reasoned, made sense only if criminals were rational and chose to commit crimes and therefore could be held responsible. Punishment might then serve justifiably important retributive and deterrent functions. But criminals were impelled to their actions by irresistible forces of heredity, disease, or environment, the determinists believed. Given this absence of individual agency, punishment was a barbarous carryover from unenlightened times.[108]

The new scientific understandings, the determinists contended, called for the replacement of punishment with treatment or segregation. The eugenicists advocated permanent segregation: the menaces to good society were inexorably, biologically different. They had to be excluded. Nevertheless, incarceration would not attempt its traditional goals of retribution, now exposed as illogical, or deterrence, now seen as impossible. Publicists of a generalized determinism advocated permanent segregation only when the preferred option, treatment, was ineffective. Otherwise, the criminal should be placed in the highly capable hands of the experts on whom society should depend. This extension of scientific authority represented a step from a barbaric past to a progressive future. "Just as the medicine man, the witch doctor and shaman of savage cultures have been replaced by the physician, surgeon and psychiatrist of modern civilization," a *Current History* contributor explained, "so the 'eye for an eye and tooth for a tooth' doctrine of medieval justice is being superseded in modern courts and prisons by sane and scientific remedial procedure."[109] For all the determinists, the cause of the criminal's condition, not the particular symptomatic act he had committed, needed to be the focus of society's actions. In the determinists' constant refrain, society needed to "stop making the punishment fit the crime and begin making the treatment fit the criminal."[110] Attention to irresistible external forces rather than individual moral choices reiterated the determinists' message about the insignificance of the individual will. As Fred E. Haynes wrote in the *Independent*, "Modern science recognizes that crime, like disease, has natural causes and that penal or remedial treatment cannot be indiscriminate, but must be adapted both to the causes and to the individual resulting from the causes."[111]

The moralists countered with a legalistic response to crime that carried a very different set of cultural messages. George Dougherty succinctly stated their premise in his observation that "all people are reachable somewhere, and criminals are only people."[112] Such was the rationale behind a widely publicized New York City poster campaign to convince criminals "YOU CANT WIN." "The 'CANT' strikes sharply," an enthusiastic journalist explained; "It is printed in large, bold-faced capital italics and is heavily underlined in black. Even the apostrophe has been omitted to give it greater force and sharper appeal."[113] Criminals are essentially ordinary, and ordinary people are controlled by a rational will that others could hope to persuade. Since would-be lawbreakers carefully calculate their deeds, the crime wave could be stemmed by improving the efficiency of law enforcement agencies and curbing the "abuses" of constitutional protection of the rights of the accused.[114] Additionally, many moralists contended that lawlessness resulted from the "coddling" of convicts by probation officers, parole boards, and prison administrators. Ignoring the wretched conditions in most penitentiaries, writers focused on the reforms enacted in a few. Well-intentioned but foolish reformers, they charged, had made imprisonment such a pleasant experience that few potential lawbreakers actually feared it. The experts' errors betrayed their lack of a common-sense understanding of human nature. As the *Philadelphia Inquirer* editorialized, "if the average thug knew that his punishment was going to be the rock pile, we would have fewer thugs."[115] Civilian clothing, baseball games, and theater—"to see which," one critic noted, "the unconvicted citizen has to pay five or six dollars a seat"—had robbed prisons of their terror. Restoring it would clean up the streets.[116]

Underlaying these calls for discipline was a moralistic notion of punishment aimed not at a select group of others but at the population generally. While the determinists urged the treatment of pathological victims or the segregation of alien others, moralists advocated punishment as a deterrent aimed at every person in society. The prospect of unpleasant consequences of particular acts stood as a powerful incentive to acceptable behavior. "We are all potential criminals," restrained only by fallible consciences and social sanctions, the *Outlook* explained.[117] Certain punishment would be effective, Thomson wrote, because "there is something of the schoolboy in all of us."[118] Child concurred that punishment was understood by "almost every human being, eugenically bred or not, psychoanalyzed or not, educated or not, rehabilitated or not."[119] Another writer asked rhetorically if his readers would violate the Volstead Act if they knew that inevitable punishment would follow.[120] The criminal is one of us. In the face of appropriately unpleasant potential consequences, men and women would act with proper discipline. Individuals are responsible for their actions, they consider the consequences of their behavior, and they must be held accountable.

The passion brought by the participants to the debates about crime suggests that they recognized the criminal's broad cultural significance. The debates constituted a struggle over who would exploit this rich cultural resource, and to what ends. By the mid-1920s the moralists emerged the clear victors. Their portrayals of the criminal promoted a coherent set of values about the social order and the position of individuals within it. Individuals, they said, had not become insignificant or powerless. Human behavior is a result of individual choices, not irresistible external forces. People control their own lives. They are responsible for what they do. "Respectable" society faced serious threats, but not from the outsiders demonized by the eugenicists. An urban middle class, rebelling against authority and apparently seeking pleasure at any cost, now constituted the gravest danger. The examination of the new urban culture intensified in the mid-twenties and after, in a more vividly imagined version of the ordinary criminal: the gangster.

Our crime wave coincides with an economic golden age which manifests itself otherwise in industrial expansion, crowding inventions, huge building programs, and intense interest in material achievements. I argue that we have more crime *per capita* than the British for the same reason that we have more automobiles, more telephones, more ton-miles of freight moving, and more horse power of electrical energy *per capita*. In other words, a good deal of our crime . . . flows from our "go-getting" spirit.[1]

Criminal

Businessmen

Americans' "go-getting spirit" was the true subject of much of their discussion of the criminal. For it was as a businessman that the stereotypical lawbreaker most uncannily reflected an ordinary, middle-class American. From the crime waves of the early 1920s through the gangster imagery of the mid-1920s and after, crime was presented as an industry and its perpetrators as businessmen after the main chance. As Richard Washburn Child put it, "The ignorant and vicious are becoming capitalists."[2] Through these criminal capitalists, Americans examined the businessman, that most powerful and problematic of modern urban types.

The prevalence of these images in the mass media, graphic evidence of how compelling Americans found them, suggests that the media's predominantly middle-class audience and producers in the twenties did not adjust as easily to their business society as historians have conventionally assumed. For the inventors of the gangster offered ambiguous and often disturbing revelations about the businessmen they exposed. At once marvelously capable and frighteningly dangerous, the gangster businessman cast a harsh light on his legitimate counterpart. Perhaps because this light of exposure was a reflection, a powerful but indirect illumination, it could convey critical messages normally absent from the generally conservative media of the twenties. Through the gangster genre, Hollywood, the *New York Times, Collier's,* and even the *Saturday Evening Post* became the unlikely vehicles of subversion.

The incorporation of crime exemplified the vast expansion of the social and economic role of big business since the late nineteenth century. In that period business thrived on the enormous jumps in productivity made possible by new manufacturing techniques, economies of scale, and innovations in management and distribution. In the thirty years ending in 1929 manufacturing output increased 264 percent; in the twenties alone it nearly doubled. The corporations' newly abundant consumer products profoundly affected daily life. The most visible product of the revolution of goods, the automobile, proliferated during the period when Americans began to envision the criminal as a businessman: from 1910 to 1928 the ratio of automobiles to people in the United States grew from 1 in 265 to 1 in 6. So too, a myriad of other products focused attention on their corporate creators. By the end of the twenties chain stores provided a physical reminder of the new ascendancy of the corporation, even in small towns and ethnic enclaves that had long resisted the large retailers' enticements.[3] The large corporation had assumed an ever greater role in Americans' daily lives since the closing decades of the nineteenth century; by the 1920s its influence had reached recognizably modern levels.

The gangster's apparent consolidation of the business of crime was, of course, paralleled in the larger consolidation of economic control. In 1880 few firms other than the large railroads had assets of five million dollars or more. "By 1929," Louis Galambos writes, "a list of the five hundred or so largest industrial corporations—even if one left out the railroads—would include companies with assets ranging from around thirty-five million to almost two and a half billion dollars."[4] That year two hundred companies possessed almost half the nation's corporate wealth. Mergers with existing firms were the most important source of this growth. Though the greatest number of mergers occurred from 1898 to 1902, more significant to the twenties portrayal of the gang as an expanding corporation were the sizeable lesser peaks in merger activity during the Great War and again in the late twenties.[5]

The organizational revolution had profound consequences for Americans not only as consumers but also as members of these large groups. For millions of middle-class men, the corporation became the setting for career achievement and fostered new bureaucratic values. After the turn of the century middle-class women encountered corporate values as employees in the mushrooming clerical workforce. Similarly, professionals enthusiastically grasped the benefits of business-like organization, joining with their peers to advance their economic position and social influence. For countless Americans individual identity had become intimately associated with membership in large organizations.[6]

The trend toward organization transformed not only the private economy but public life as well. Problems arising from industrial growth were, of course, the impetus behind many of the movements for progressive reform. But while many reformers hoped to rein in the "trusts," an ultimately more influential group envisioned reform as a means to enable businesses to operate smoothly and profitably. More generally, the reform movements gained their strongest support from middle-class professionals at the forefront of the organizational revolution. New regulatory and ameliorative agencies took the bureaucratic organization and efficiency methods of the corporation as their guiding light. Government became suffused with the techniques of hierarchical organization, specialization, and scientific expertise developed by private corporations.[7]

The movement toward increasing organization extended beyond the progressive years. During the war, business and organizational values in the public sphere assumed new importance as government and industrial leaders attempted to meet the extraordinary demands for conservation, better information, and increased production. Public groups like the War Industries Board furthered the expansion of business influence. Even the military borrowed from the model of the well-run corporation.[8] The trend continued into the 1920s, as the conservative Republican administrations were uncharacteristically activist in their promotion of business cooperation and association-alism.[9]

The social and political prominence of big business in the twenties was matched in the broader realm of popular culture. Commentators have long remarked upon the cultural elevation of the businessman. According to the popular media, he was a visionary who would solve daunting social problems where reformers had failed. New corporate benefits programs would ameliorate the problems of poverty, and company unionism would dampen nagging class tensions. Universities aligned themselves with the heroes of harmonious prosperity by expanding offerings in management, advertising, and retailing. It was the equation of business and religion, however, that most loudly proclaimed the businessman's exalted status. Bruce Barton's *The Man Nobody Knows,* the best-selling nonfiction book of 1925 and 1926, cast Jesus as a go-getter young executive.[10] As Frederick Lewis Allen quipped in 1931, "So frequent was the use of the Bible to point the lessons of business and of business to point the lessons of the Bible that it was sometimes difficult to determine which was supposed to gain the most from the association."[11]

Through the gangster-businessman, writers, filmmakers, and others explored the meanings of this new corporate society. Audiences were subtly encouraged to examine the businessman, to understand what their urban society had produced, the organizational values it increasingly upheld, and what they themselves might be or soon become. The inventors of the gangster offered a simplified version of the businessman, a social phenomenon that was, because of its variety and profusion, otherwise inscrutably complex. Shorn of obscuring detail, the gangster stood as an invitation to see the businessman as he really was.

The similarity of the gangster and the businessman began with appearance. In 1925 Richard Washburn Child suggested that "the lean business man" who headed a burglary ring might easily be mistaken for a realtor.[12] A bootlegger in a 1926 *Collier's* account was a "well dressed young fellow" who looked like a life insurance agent or bond salesman.[13] Clothing and appearance no longer seemed reliable guides for differentiating between good and evil. "The bigger figures in the environs of the underworld," a 1929 *New York Times* feature on racketeers explained, "are not easily distinguishable from the broader business types."[14]

Editorial cartoons provide graphic evidence of the gangster's new resemblance to the businessman. In the early 1920s cartoons generally depicted criminals in one of two ways. Often they were creatures apart—undersized, grotesque, contorted, skulking figures in caps and jackets that signified working-class status and ethnic origins. Other cartoons depicted the innocent youth, newly arrived from the countryside, drawn in by the lure of easy money. By the middle of the decade criminals often wore the attire of middle-class urbanites. Moreover, cartoonists increasingly imagined that underworld leaders, like business movers and shakers, were not youths but middle-aged, fleshy men who strained the buttons of conservative vested suits. No longer topped by a scruffy cap, the new criminal seemed perfectly attired in a stylish hat more appropriate to the business district than to a taproom.[15]

Crime remained an urban problem, but Americans in the 1920s shifted its setting from ethnic ghettos to downtown business districts. Earlier notions of the urban criminal's geographic remoteness had been manifested by magazine exposes of the nefarious crimes within sharply defined immigrant neighborhoods, occasionally illustrated by a street map of the exotic, unfamiliar territory.[16] Now the pestilence had come to environs familiar to middle-class readers, as suggested by a 1925 cartoon of huge rats labeled "crime" overrunning a dense business district. Another cartoon, from 1931, featured a colossal racketeer surveying his realm from a throne of downtown buildings. The gangster inhabited a world of office buildings and skyscrapers, the new shrines to business achievement.[17] Within that world, his immediate environment looked much like that of his legitimate counterparts. Child's typical burglar planned his affairs from within "a fairly respectable office building," perhaps behind a door emblazoned with the name of a real estate company. He worked "behind [a] large golden-oak desk with a telephone and a stenographer."[18] Business offices with expensive furniture, office equipment, filing cabinets, and large staffs of typists, stenographers, and other clerical workers were the routine settings for the businessman-gangster's activities.[19]

Films of the late twenties and early thirties offered the most vivid portrayals of gangsters' businesslike appearance and settings. Through the mid-1920s dishevelled members of celluloid gangs were usually attired in caps and drab or garish cheap clothes. They gathered in rough subterranean rooms, drank in dirty, raucous saloons, and generally confined their prowling to such areas as dockyards and congested tenement districts.[20] Reflecting both the changed notions about criminals elsewhere in American culture and Hollywood's new commitment to "realism," movies in 1928 abruptly began to depict gangsters as nattily dressed, office-using businessmen. Pleasant-featured, they wore three-piece suits, ties, hats, and watch-chains—a stylish version of standard middle-class business attire. Their offices covered the conventional range of business taste, from heavy Victorian probity to sleek Art Deco modernism.

A 1931 film, *The Finger Points,* typified the use of physical appearance and settings to connect the businessman to the racketeer. The middle-level gangster boss operates out of an office with an executive's impressive desk and an oil painting on the wall. His young associate, played by Clark Gable in a tasteful vested suit with silk handkerchief, pocket watch, tie-bar, and bowler hat, has his own office suite with all the standard accoutrements: a waiting room, batteries of filing cabinets, and a busy typist. Floor-to-ceiling bookcases and carved paneling cover the walls of Gable's private office, where he works intently at a large desk with an in-basket. Like any executive he conducts much of his business over the telephone, has a receptionist place his calls, and talks convivially to his colleagues. His language is appropriate to this sanctum of business. After proposing a joint venture he asks, "Well, do we play ball?" "Yep, we play ball," is the reply. "All right," he concludes, "you'll hear from me later." Crime operated in business's conventional, mundane metaphorical realm of sport.[21]

The criminal's new businesslike exterior carried with it a number of unsettling messages. While depictions of the criminal had once confirmed for middle-class Americans the dangers of people who wore shabby clothes, spoke indecipherable languages, and dwelt in the wrong parts of town, by the middle of the twenties such reassuring cultural and physical distance had collapsed. No longer an abnormal outsider, the criminal had become the ultimate middle-class insider in the years when, as Calvin Coolidge intoned, the business of America was business. Like everything else, the doing of evil seemed to have been taken over by men in three-piece suits. For some Americans, the message must have been: Here is what really happens inside those skyscrapers. Theft, violence, and other lawlessness symbolize their true influence. For others closer to the center of the business society, the message took the form of a series of questions: How different are the things you do inside your busy office? What are the consequences of the way you play ball? In either case, businessmen merited the scrutiny once reserved for anarchists, immigrants, and beer-drinking unionists.

In telling the gangster's story, Americans followed—and commented on—the conventional script of business and success literature. The portrayers of the businessman gangster of the midtwenties and after devoted little attention to his motivation, so important to earlier observers, because they knew that the criminal, like any businessman, did what he did to make money and rise in the world. As something approaching a natural law, self-interest required no explanation. Of much greater concern were the gangster's avenues to wealth. Intricate descriptions of criminal enterprises attempted to answer the basic question asked about every successful man: How did he make his money? Portrayals of gangs and their leaders were thus, in large part, accounts of strategies, techniques, and guiding principles. In form and even substance, the accounts read very much like those of legitimate business. Unlike most popular success accounts, however, stories of the gangster suggested that lawless violence and defiance of broadly espoused moral principles were the legacies of the successful man.

The fundamental business strategies explored by the inventors of the gangster were growth, consolidation, and organization. Countless observers remarked that the scale of operations of the typical criminal enterprise had grown explosively. From its inception in 1919, the highly visible Chicago Crime Commission directed public attention to this growth. "The business of crime," its leaders preached at every opportunity, "is being more expertly conducted. Modern crime, like modern business, is tending towards centralization, organization and commercialization. Ours is a business nation. Our criminals apply business methods." "No longer have we to deal with the individual alone," commission director Henry Barrett Chamberlin warned. "The men and women of evil have formed trusts."[22] Criminals, concluded mystery writer and radio personality Arthur B. Reeve, exemplified the American "genius for organization on a vast scale."[23] As in legitimate business, growth was accompanied by successful efforts to limit competition. "The day of cutthroat competition between individual and irresponsible criminals is passing," noted Richard Washburn Child, an admirer of the Chicago group; "Just as in the development of American big business, the time comes when the investment is so large a stake that conference and cooperation are the watchwords."[24] Looking at a single field, one observer noted the consolidation of dealers in stolen goods and contended that their trade dwarfed the business of United States Steel, Ford, and General Motors.[25] "The once familiar notion that a 'fence' was a squalid person hidden in some cellar, bartering with desperadoes for a few dollars worth of loot," another feature revealed, "has given way to the latter-day realistic conception of an operator in stolen goods who is a big business man in crime."[26] The trend, fueled by the same internal growth and combination as the expansion of the legitimate corporation, prevailed across the lines of criminal enterprise. "Unlike the old gangs as are the modern 'mobs' of the underworld," a *New York Times* feature summarized, "modern gangdom simply has followed the trend of business, perfecting its organization, merging when necessary."[27] Unprecedented wealth rewarded those who grasped the opportunities of organization.

The reward for those who failed to organize, or who stepped outside the organization, was considerably more bleak. The critic Robert Warshow was among the first to note that for the gangster "it is dangerous to be alone." In *Scarface*, gang leader Big Louie is killed, Warshow explains, because "through some monstrous lack of caution, he permits himself to be alone for a few moments."[28] His eventual successor, Tony Camonte, is gunned down by police after he is isolated from his mob. The heroes of *Little Caesar* and *The Public Enemy*, the other most successful and acclaimed gangster movies of the early thirties, similarly separate from their companions before meeting equally violent ends.[29] If organization brought success, independence, the gangster taught, brought terrible failure.

It was bootlegging and racketeering that provided the clearest evidence of the expansion of criminal enterprise. In the latter half of the 1920s the kinds of lawbreaking in which profit-seeking criminals reportedly engaged shifted in accordance with the new ideas about the organization of crime. Until then most observers reported that the businesslike gang existed primarily to commit crimes of theft—the same types of burglaries and robberies undertaken by earlier, less organized criminals. For example, early in the decade the Chicago Crime Commission gave its attention to such crimes as warehouse burglaries and payroll robberies.[30] Popular writers included other armed robberies, residential burglaries, and even shoplifting among the gangs' regular enterprises. Contrary to the assumptions of later commentators, the modern gangster predated his bootlegger incarnation.

After 1926 media portrayals of the gangster devoted less and less attention to traditional crimes of theft. New crimes especially conducive to modern rationalization increasingly seemed to threaten the social order. The media first focused on gangsters' involvement in a relatively new field: violation of the Volstead Act. Two years later, in 1928, a second figure, the racketeer, joined the bootlegger in the cultural spotlight. The two fields seemed to offer unprecedented opportunities for the application of business methods. Their cultural prominence constituted an intensified effort to understand the new corporate society.

Bootlegging had received considerable attention in the popular media through the mid twenties. Yet few writers before 1926 included it in their surveys of the crimes that seemed to threaten decent society. Accounts of bootlegging typically featured nonviolent, gentlemen suppliers, swashbuckling high-seas adventurers, or exotic, isolated foreigners. When not remote, most of the offenders seemed more quaint than dangerous.[31] The prevailing attitude was summed up by the *Literary Digest*'s inclusion in 1925 of sellers of intoxicants, like drivers who ignored traffic signals, among the petty offenders who encouraged others to "go farther . . . in their disregard of law."[32]

Bootlegging emerged in the latter half of the 1920s as a serious crime and the perfect field for turning business's masterful coordination of capital to criminal ends.[33] More than ever before it became clear that the supposedly benevolent methods of modern business could serve lawlessness with equal efficiency. Americans devoted enormous attention to the concerted efforts of producers, distributors, and sellers that constituted the illegal alcohol industry. In a report on one city's bootleggers, *New York Times* writer R. L. Duffus betrayed the suspicion of concentrated economic power he shared with his former teacher and eventual biography subject, Thorstein Veblen. "The day of the independent retailer has passed," he explained. "Philadelphia's bootleg industry . . . was no back-room, down-cellar affair. It had capital. When it needed more funds it went into the money market and borrowed, or attracted investors, exactly as though it were making clothes or automobiles. It was well organized. It was centralized. Probably in these respects it was a picture in miniature of the bootleg industry of the United States."[34] The "kingdom of rum," another feature explained, "is scientifically organized. It uses the long-distance telephone, the telegraph system and even bootleg wireless plants to maintain communication. It has fleets of trucks, warehouses and arsenals representing a huge investment."[35]

Movies provided the most vivid portrayals of the extensive industrial and commercial resources behind each bottle. A scene in the 1930 film *Doorway to Hell* provided a sweeping view. James Cagney drives all over the city informing underworld associates of a meeting called by his superior, who has realized "we're a big business and it needs organizing and it needs a boss." Cagney's tour takes him from headquarters to saloons to a cigar store to the Acmo Brewing Company, a bustling plant with dozens of workers, trucks to be loaded, and a huge pyramid of barrels, all presumably full. Beer, the film proclaimed, is a major industry.[36]

Racketeering similarly offered steady profits to the well-organized enterprise. Racketeering encompassed an enormous variety of activities linked by the use of coercion to influence the buying and selling of goods or services in legitimate businesses. Though small businessmen who resisted the racketeer's advances received considerable sympathetic attention, his primary victims, according to many writers, were the consumers who paid higher prices to businesses under his control. But because these consumers rarely faced significant levies on any single purchase, they tolerated the new crime. "The gang has oriented itself to contemporary conditions, and, while it touches the lives of ordinary citizens as closely as ever, it does so with more finesse and less violence," a feature explained. "It is less painful to pay a few extra cents for your artichokes . . . than it is to be thumped on the head with a lead pipe and have your valuables and cash removed. It comes to about the same thing economically."[37] And because the racketeer's net stretched so wide—from laundry to produce to taxis to pinball machines—big-city consumers contributed evenly, and thus relatively painlessly, to his haul. Like many other entrepreneurs, racketeers had discovered the virtues of making their fortunes in tiny increments.

Bootlegging and racketeering befitted the organization of crime because they seemed more open to the steady, highly rationalized operation rewarded in the modern economy than were traditional property crimes. Larceny had an inherent volatility that defied even the most advanced applications of the methods of modern business efficiency. Success depended on the occasional big score and the frustration of outraged victims. Perpetrators could count on few defenders in the legitimate world. "Outright robbery or burglary is at the best a precarious and unprofitable business," a *New York Times Magazine* feature explained; "the work of preparation is arduous, the risks of the operation are great, the disposition of the stolen property difficult, and the danger of subsequent penalties quite real and enduring."[38] Despite the gangster's managerial efficiency, larceny often seemed a risky, boom-or-bust proposition more suited to the nineteenth-century financier than to the twentieth-century middle manager. The robber baron, aptly named, had given way to the businessman.

As a result, according to many observers by the end of the twenties, gangsters had left the fields of house-prowling, safe-cracking, and armed robbery. "Mental-defectives or unfortunate chaps momentarily in need of a good meal and out of a legitimate job" had taken over the traditional fields. "The night burglar prowling about for petty hauls has become almost as obsolete as kerosene lamps. . . . All of these once prominent forms of crook exploits," continued *The Whole Truth About Racketeers*, "are condemned, by the men who once gloried in their criminal accomplishments, as awkward, small in profits, and too liable to incur detection."[39] In contrast, the new crimes such as racketeering were easy, safe, and "continuously profitable," according to future Brain Trust member Raymond Moley. "The human being," he explained in terms that portended early New Deal industrial policy, "is always anxious to have his sporadic and casual efforts brought into a regular system."[40]

While tracing the consolidation of crime, the inventors of the gangster simultaneously celebrated the productivity of corporate methods and gave new airing to old concerns about the concentration of economic power. Banding together replaced the uncertainty of the individual operator with the stability, resources, and economies of ever larger units of production. Corporate methods brought their adherents an enviable windfall. But the accounts revealed that the gigantic corporation was as adept at producing lawless disorder as at churning out closed touring cars. Thus crime reporting, films, and genre fiction carried forward the claims once raised by progressive politicians and muckraking journalists.

The internal workings of the modern gang also commented on the well-organized modern business. One way to highlight the sophisticated organization of crime was to attempt to disabuse readers of archaic notions about rudimentary mobs. "The average person . . . being innocent of true conditions," Child wrote, had little understanding of the operations of a modern gang. The typical person imagining a burglary ring "has in mind a picture of four or five tough-looking customers sitting in some cellar around the stub of a candle. They determine that they must go forth to get money in a burglary. Skulking in the shadows, they glance up at a store or warehouse. One says, 'That place looks as if it might yield something.' Another produces a jimmy and they go to work, with one of their number ready to blow a blast on a whistle if the patrolman comes along." Rough denizens of a shadowy, subterranean world, the criminals imagined by the public, according to popular writers, relied on spontaneity, luck, and no excess of wit. The image, Child and others concluded, was a myth.[41]

To redirect readers' attention to the new phenomenon of organization, writers explained in minute detail the ways lawbreakers exploited efficiency methods. Depictions of gangs emphasized hierarchical leadership, individual job specialization, and up-to-date technology. The structures and innovations of modern business culture pervaded gangdom. At every turn, the methods of the businessman seemed ominously well suited to the conduct of crime.

One of the business developments that the inventors of the gangster most closely examined was the institution of elaborate hierarchies of authority. The development of vast, efficient managerial structures had been one of the signal achievements of American business in recent decades, and criminals seemed to share the benefits.[42] Accounts of gangs stressed their multi-tiered leadership. Crime showed that any enterprise required a clear, smooth chain of command. At the top was often a mysterious individual far removed from daily operations. He engaged in long-term planning and exploited far-ranging political and economic contacts. Contacts with respectable bankers and other "capitalist[s]" were among the mastermind's essential assets.[43] "As a rule," a *New York Times* feature explained, "this man is not generally known as an underworld character. He has means, credit, a certain reputation."[44]

The descriptions of these men read like vague criticisms of industrial magnates who maintained a spurious distance from their organizations' unseemly affairs. "He keeps himself very much aloof" from his workers, according to a *Saturday Evening Post* article, "transmitting his orders . . . through a few trusted lieutenants."[45] His role was often that of a distant financier. According to the *Times,* the masterminds "do with their field men—the actual bandits and burglars and thieves—what amounts to grub-staking. They tide their criminal agents over periods of famine and stress; they furnish them with the 'nut money,' which means the funds needed to launch a big criminal enterprise." Like other chairmen equally distant from production, the mastermind profited handsomely—and safely—from the labors of others beneath him on the corporate ladder. "Rarely" was he "caught and put out of business."[46]

Of far greater concern was the "boss," gangland's middle-manager, who directed the daily operations of a relatively small group. Often the boss worked as a bureaucrat in the service of the mysterious higher-up. In this capacity bosses were "the middle men," according to the *New York Times,* implementing the higher-up's strategy and acting as a buffer between the "respectable" leader and his employees, who ranged from cultured men like himself to rough ex-convicts.[47] The boss's role was that of the successful, middle-level corporate executive. The emphasis on middle management reflected recent developments in commercial enterprises. As businesses grew increasingly complex and far-ranging, top managers came to rely on subordinates for an ever-expanding role in the conduct of day-to-day affairs. Mid-level John Doe criminal managers mirrored their legitimate contemporaries.[48] Child described one boss, Joe, "the manager for a group of men who are engaged in the lively business of wholesale-house, fur and silk robbery." Despite the tendency of some observers to label Joe a "mastermind," Child wrote, "he may only be a good criminal business man." His work encompassed the ordinary activities of any executive. "It is his job to superintend, to plan the work ahead, to get orders for goods and set forth the program on which the 'workers out' are to proceed." He analyzed information, monitored demand, covered the overhead, and oversaw the finances. "Joe," Child concluded, "is the general manager."[49]

The mundane quality of the criminal boss's activity opened the possibility that the routine duties of ordinary executives might have similarly disruptive consequences. A *Saturday Evening Post* report on one boss's correspondence captured the normality of wrongdoing. In the process of "filling an order" for stolen goods, he informed "his Eastern correspondent" of the ready market in his area. Not in any mysterious code, "it was a straightforward letter, written in plain English, just as one legitimate business house might write to another." The stationery was unremarkable. So closely did the letter conform to convention that initials in the bottom corner indicated the separate identities of the person who dictated it and the secretary who typed it.[50] An ordinary businessman, the criminal boss spent much of his day at recognizably ordinary tasks.

Nevertheless, success as a manager, according to the inventors of the gangster, required a combination of intelligence, leadership, and charisma. The 1930 film *Little Caesar* opens with a scene of small-time, small-town crook Rico Bandello, played by Edward G. Robinson, holding up a gas station. In the next scene Rico establishes an alibi by turning back the hands of a clock in a diner and asking the counter man for the time. "Gotta hand it to you, Rico," his partner comments, "little bean's workin' all the time." Rico, viewers learn, is destined for achievement. His managerial savvy emerges in the scene in which he begins to gain control of a big-city gang. Eight men are standing around an office desk examining the diagrammed plans for the New Year's Eve robbery of a nightclub. Rico watches coolly while the boss assigns each man a spot to cover, but he suddenly thrusts his finger on the overlooked position that would have brought the gang's downfall. His authority established, Rico soon becomes the decisive leader. His primary skill is the intelligent direction of men; he formulates plans and barks orders to carefully chosen underlings who follow him absolutely. This man of action is a model executive.[51]

The general managers of crime, like their legitimate models, reportedly relied on several tiers of subordinate managers to whom they delegated tasks and authority. Like the corporation, much of the gang organization consisted of workers who shared a common middling status. Many crime movies made through the mid 1920s soon would have looked out of date in their depictions of motley bands of social inferiors commanded by a single upper-class mastermind who provided the only brains the outfit possessed.[52] The modern bureaucracy was arranged according to more subtle distinctions best described in the vocabulary of business. According to the *Saturday Evening Post,* gangs were divided into territorial units, each with "an undisputed boss" and central control. "This boss has clustered about him an efficient staff composed of the most daring and energetic gangsters in his district." From "headquarters," these men "act as whips over intermediate or secondary gang leaders commanding minor groups of predatory gangsters."[53] The criminal had become another worker enmeshed in a new white-collar bureaucracy.

The gangster also showed the necessity—and danger—of specialization within an organization. The boss, himself a specialist in management, relied on the coordinated efforts of diverse experts within his corporation. "Crime, like industry, if it is to flourish on a large scale, must depend on the perfectly coordinated efforts of sundry groups of specialists, each group under central direction, knowing just when and where and how it is to function," a *Saturday Evening Post* editorial explained.[54] Specialists performed their jobs with efficiency unmatched by nonexperts. Like organization, specialization seemed rife with potential for social havoc. The criminal specialist highlighted the danger that experts, single-mindedly pursuing their professions and the wealth they offered, might ignore the social consequences of their actions.

In accounts of burglary and robbery gangs, expert finders—"research men"—received particular attention. Writers emphasized that the careful collection of information was essential. "The first requirement" of a successful gang, according to the *New York Times,* was "a competent information system."[55] The "spot man," explained another *Times* feature, "goes out and finds stores to be robbed, studying their defenses and getting all the advance information in the greatest detail, so that an absolutely mathematical plan, timed to the second, can be laid."[56] Sometimes these specialists constituted an entire gang division. "Up to the minute" "research departments," according to the *Saturday Evening Post,* "locate the prospects [and] separate the good ones from the poor." They then converted all this information "to maps and diagrams for the benefit of the gang master who does the planning."[57]

Accounts also placed salesmen among the most highly valued specialists, for the gangsters' products or services could bring a profit only if someone wanted to purchase them. Functioning much like their legitimate counterparts, criminal salesmen suggested the nefarious potential of one of the era's most widely discussed specialties. By the twenties sales had become regarded as a profession that required special techniques and expertise. Not only did selling gain legitimacy, but it also became more closely associated with the corporate society as increasing numbers of salespersons were corporate employees rather than independent agents.[58] The criminal salesman was equally an inhabitant of the corporate world. According to one account of a gang of bootleggers, a "crew of salesmen" work "certain districts allotted to them," check out any likely "prospect," "quote" prices, and relay orders to stenographers at headquarters. As much as the sales staff tries to strike excessively profitable deals, the "market price" prevails. Sales, their boss concludes mundanely, is hard work.[59] In *The Big Shakedown*, a 1934 Hollywood release, well-dressed salesmen meet, listen to their boss's harangue about declining sales, and attempt to blame their poor performance on a sagging market.[60] While slow sales provoked criticism, success brought wealth and recognition. One successful gangster, according to a 1928 *New York Times* feature, "was particularly good as a salesman, for he knew exactly how to persuade people to buy what he had to sell."[61] Coercion might have replaced psychological manipulation, but the criminal salesman's willingness to do almost anything to close a deal must have seemed disturbingly recognizable.

Another specialist reportedly essential to the success of any gang was the lawyer. When charged with a crime, the gangster depended on his lawyer to protect his life and freedom. But accounts devoted equal attention to the day-to-day relationship of the attorney and the gangster, who like any other businessman, routinely required competent legal counsel. He obtained it in the conventional manner: from an attorney on his staff or on retainer. The lawyer negotiated difficult financial transactions and provided the expert legal advice required by any enterprise. "Like the corporation lawyer," a *Saturday Evening Post* feature explained, "he is a specialist who endeavors to guide the policies of his clients with such wisdom that they will not find it necessary to engage in litigation."[62] The willingness of lawyers to provide these services perhaps constituted the harshest indictment of the cult of specialization. Practicing law required extensive education and certification in legitimate society. The gangster's lawyers showed the willingness of specialists to betray that legitimate society for financial gain.

Not all the gangsters were managers or specialists, of course. Like most employees of any business, the majority of workers were near the bottom of the hierarchy. Writers emphasized that leaders always found men willing to perform dangerous, semi-skilled work for relatively low pay. While bosses and masterminds were rarely caught, low-level bandits were expendable and constantly risked arrest. Weak, stupid, and often addicted to narcotics, these misfits filled the positions in the corporate hierarchy best suited to them. "The big master criminals constantly recruit new men," Smith explained. "They have aids who are always training street arabs and other strayed children in the criminal arts. . . . The crop of new fools to do the bidding of the big, safe crime barons never fails." [63]

In addition to organization and specialization, the other business tool commented on by the inventors of the gangster was technology. Technological innovation was important in many realms of the underworld, but nowhere more so than in the commission of violence. Fast cars, explosives, and the recently developed Thompson submachine gun became the iconographic instruments of underworld maiming and killing, and the gangster became a paragon of technological modernity. [64] "This extraordinary improvement in equipment for the commission of crimes of violence is an indication of a new adaptability which must be conceded to the criminals of the younger generation," a *Saturday Evening Post* editorial explained. "No invention is too modern for their purposes." Portrayals of gangland violence examined some of the implications of modern technology. Most important, new technology vastly increased productivity but, in the wrong hands, could serve terrible ends. "The attainment of higher efficiency in merchandising and industry during the past twenty-five years has not been more notable than the steadily increasing effectiveness of criminal methods," the *Post* editorialist contended. [65] "As in the case of our manufacturers," Franklin Roosevelt's political adviser Louis Howe explained in the *Saturday Evening Post,*

> the success of this new and evilly thriving national organization has been largely due to modern invention. Successful holdups, gang killings and profitable kidnappings have been made possible largely by the

automobile and the machine gun. . . . Revolver shootings were, at the best, an uncertain form of murder, and in the old days rival gangs would shoot for hours at each other without serious damage being done. But the victim of the modern gang is sprayed with a hundred bullets a minute and is certainly marked for death beyond hope.[66]

The gangster showed that the technological inventiveness that had multiplied the productivity of legitimate enterprises could be a powerful force for evil.

Accounts of criminal gangs provided a virtual blueprint for success in the new corporate culture. Their messages were profoundly ambiguous. On their surface they claimed to be matter-of-fact expositions of how real gangs had taken up the innovations of modern business. On another level they functioned as enthusiastic endorsements of corporate methods. Crime was once thought to have dismal prospects as an occupation: seedy haunts, high risk, low pay. Now that the gang had learned from the corporation, however, lavish rewards beckoned the potential criminal. Follow these simple steps, the accounts seemed to say, and the world will be yours. But despite this enthusiasm, the underlying message was ultimately foreboding. Well-dressed, office-using specialists, organized into elaborate hierarchies and armed with the latest technology, took property that did not belong to them, sold illegal, dangerous alcohol, and kidnapped infants.

In the use of violence criminals pursued the same goal of efficiency that lay behind the more general appropriation of business methods. Descriptions of smooth-running illegal enterprises were rife with assessments of the gangsters' marvelous efficiency. Specialization, expertise, technology, and hierarchy were important because they enabled criminals to pursue business's guiding light. The changed meaning of crime, and of violence, centered on efficiency, crime's new connotations of order, rationality, and subtlety. Gangsters showed that business culture's most cherished ideal, like its methods and structures, could function equally well in the service of evil. Efficiency brought not only prosperity and happiness but lawlessness and death. Its disciples, lawless or not, were dangerous men.

Ironically, it was discussion of the ways the gangster used violence, the activity that might seem to distance him furthest from law-abiding counterparts, that provided the most incisive commentary on the development of modern business. Violence was a business tool, and explorations of the motivations for it and the techniques used to accomplish it yielded disturbing insights into the legitimate models of its practitioners.

Writers often highlighted the businesslike nature of contemporary violence by contrasting it with the gang mayhem of a legendary past. Oddly warm, nostalgic accounts of old-time gangsters appeared frequently beginning around 1926. In New York City, according to a *Times* feature, gangs like "the Car Barn Gang of Harlem and the Gas House Gang of Yorkville had passed with the horse cars" to become the stuff of "city folklore."[67] As the archaic gangster provided a historical perspective on the development of criminal business he also illuminated the development of modern economic behavior. A mythic figure who embodied the values of a bygone era, his crude, irrational violence threw the modern mercenary spirit into sharp relief. Knives, clubs, paving stones, an occasional pistol, "and plain hard fists" were the old gangsters' weapons of choice, for technological advances had not yet revolutionized the instruments of violence.[68] Nor had specialization limited its practitioners. Gangs were enormous, disorganized mobs of men who worked other jobs and gathered to socialize, drink, and brawl. "In the old days the gangsters worked at honest jobs six days of the week and became fighters at night and on Sunday," John R. Chamberlain explained.[69] They were linked by ethnicity, neighborhood, and other bonds formed in childhood, not by occupational ties or training. None among them were the designated perpetrators of violence. Passion and brute strength, rather than expertise or discipline, led to success. Leaders earned their positions through demonstrations of courage and ferocity, and they fought alongside their followers. Men were joined in the fray by neighborhood women, who "developed proficiency in eye-gouging and ear-biting."[70]

Descriptions of this quaint old-time violence approvingly evoked an era when men and women supposedly pursued adventure unrelated to financial gain. Lacking "the cold acquisitiveness of their successors,"[71] old-time gangsters brawled to defend the reputation of their neighborhoods and to prove their individual honor, for the fierce fighter enjoyed heroic local status. Just as important, "they practiced violence for the fun of it," "for the pure love of scrapping."[72] These simple, chivalrous fighters brawled on the open streets and roundly condemned stealth of any sort. "The score was only half evened up," one reporter reminisced, "unless an enemy was warned in advance that trouble was headed his way."[73] Far from epitomizing atavistic brutality or callous disregard for life and limb, the gang battles of old, according to nostalgic writers, expressed the honorable, uncorrupted values of a dreamlike precapitalist past.

Though the legendary gangs—the Bowery B'hoys, the Hudson Dusters, the Dead Rabbits, and a host of equally colorfully named bands—had passed with the nineteenth century, many writers saw traces of their values and methods well into the new one. The sentiment of these accounts was less nostalgia for the old ways than astonishment at the change the old-timers represented as benchmarks of an earlier era. Men like Whitey Igow, featured in *Collier's* in 1927, represented a transitional phase in the shift from premodern to modern forms of organization. Walter Davenport recounted Whitey's career in terms that suggest deep concern about this transition. Now a "relic" picked up for purse-snatching, just twenty years earlier Whitey had been the leader of a fearsome mob renowned for having "the distinction of being the first to put rough stuff on an over-the-counter basis." Despite this accomplishment, Davenport presented Whitey as an instructive period piece. His operation had been confined to a small neighborhood out of which he rarely ventured. Its colorfully named dives, among them the Bucket of Blood, Suicide Hall, and the Flea Bag, suggested his isolation from the developing cosmopolitan world. Even his gang's schedule of fees and services seemed to be a reminder, more quaint than gruesome, of bygone days. Though murder cost at least a hundred dollars, Davenport reported, "for twenty-five you could have your neighbor's ear (right or left) shorn from his head or for thirty-five you got both ears." Whitey had been a businessman. Yet his story, preserved with antiquarian zeal, was that of countless other ambitious but shortsighted local entrepreneurs whom times had passed by.[74]

Writers lamented that the quaint violence of the old-time gangs disappeared like the earlier patterns of industrial organization on which they were modeled. Nevertheless they celebrated the cold, efficient violence that replaced it. Rudimentary technology, lack of specialization, participation by women as well as men, and the priority of honor over short-term profits gave way to the new patterns of twentieth-century industrial society. Importantly, the decision to commit violence became a matter of rational, businesslike deliberation. In fact, many accounts contended that the modern gangster first had refined the new techniques of violence while working for businessmen, breaking strikes or intimidating competitors.[75] As a business tool, violence retained its power only when carefully controlled. "As long as things run smoothly, his business of crime flourishes and profits pile within his coffers, the gangster will not murder," a *Saturday Evening Post* writer explained. When someone disrupted this smoothness, the gangster "murders promptly, ruthlessly and unrelentingly."[76] "The mercenary gangster," R. L. Duffus explained, "kills for business reasons. He kills in a struggle for money."[77] Murder is not "personal," a seasoned killer typically explained in a *Liberty* short story; "you gotta remember that business is business."[78] Shootings, bombings, and beatings, or threats of the same, were the quotidian techniques used to eliminate rivals, enforce agreements, and spur sales. Passion, honor, and pleasure played a much diminished role in the creation of violence. The gangster who killed for noneconomic reasons was either a small-timer or headed for trouble.[79]

Those who traced the development of mercenary violence confirmed that the delegation of tasks often brought the most profitable results. Gang leaders had ceased to carry out violence personally and instead directed it, like research or sales, from afar. Violence showed how any executive could distance himself from his actions. The makers of a 1931 film, *The Star Witness*, felt compelled to explain at length why the mob-leader antagonist himself gunned down a squealer instead of using hired killers.[80] "Almost never do modern gangsters stand up and shoot it out," F. Raymond Daniell explained. Direct involvement would be "foolhardy exhibitionism," because "things are not done that way today." Instead, violence had become the province of a relatively small group of specialized experts. "The super-businessmen at the top" had realized that the large, undifferentiated mobs of an earlier era had become obsolete.[81] Now gang leaders used "hirelings . . . carefully selected for their qualifications for the task," explained a feature on gunmen.[82] Expert machine-gunners and bombers reportedly took pride in their specialized skills. They were often independent professionals who sold their services to various gangs in an intercity market; like the activities of the increasingly nationally minded corporation, violence had ceased to be a local matter.[83]

Considerations of the changing nature of gangland violence carried the message that individual honor was of slight importance in the new corporate society. Unencumbered by the protocol of honor, the up-to-date gangster had no desire to offer his opponent a fair fight and so turned to cunning and stealth for whatever advantages they could provide. "In no case do they give their victim a chance if they can avoid it," Duffus explained. Killers preferred a safe shot in the back to a riskier one head on.[84] "Where the modern gangster . . . differs most from his old-time prototypes is in subtlety," Chamberlain explained. "He does not kill in the open, nor with ferocity; his attacks are planned so as to leave no tell-tale trail."[85] With honor disappeared a host of corollary traits, observers noted regretfully. "There used to be some adventure in crime," a gray-haired former bandit told the *New York Times;* "In the old days a criminal took a chance, and he gave the other fellow a chance. . . . Nowadays when a man goes out with a machine gun, there isn't any thrill."[86] R. L. Duffus linked the unseating of honor in crime to its deterioration elsewhere. "The modern gangster," Duffus explained, "is not . . . quite like the gangster of prewar vintage. Like many other features of present-day life he has lost some of his boldness and picturesqueness under the pressure of efficiency methods."[87]

As Duffus's remarks suggest, the gangster confirmed many Americans' sense that the war marked a crucial stage in the displacement of honor by efficiency. The gangster genre contained a highly critical commentary on modern warfare that elaborated on many of the themes of the critique of business culture. The parallel concern was perhaps inevitable, for, as Americans learned during mobilization and belligerency, success in war and success in business depended upon many of the same factors: technological advances, specialization, and organization. Films and news reports commented on criminals' appropriation of "war's most devastating weapons," machine guns and even gas bombs.[88] The weapons' most efficient operators received their training in the Army.[89] Not only had these weapons and their operators failed to make the world safe for democracy, they had brought unprecedented danger into American life. More significantly, however, the disappearance of honor and adventure in criminal violence closely paralleled their perceived irrelevance on the battlefield, the site of supposedly legitimate violence. Less eloquently but no less passionately, the inventors of the gangster echoed Ernest Hemingway's anguished discovery that glory, honor, and courage were meaningless in the face of modern technology and organization.[90]

The critique of corporate society, and especially its exaltation of efficiency and devaluation of honor, articulated the same concerns about the status of the individual expressed by the moralists and the determinists in their arguments about the causes of crime. Just as conservatives rejected theories that attributed the criminal's actions to distant forces beyond his control, they feared that the modern organizational imperative threatened to render the individual insignificant. A *Current History* writer observed that "the modern tendency to combination" had rendered nearly inconsequential the actions of "single individuals."[91] A *Saturday Evening Post* account of a holdout "free-lance crook" read like a regret-laden commentary on the depersonalizing consequences of modern organization. The "independent" free-lancer, according to the *Post,* "owes allegiance to no one." He pays for this independence when caught, however, for without organization he lacks political influence and funds for high-priced legal representation. "Still he remains obdurate. He simply cannot bring himself to work under orders, to loot by rules and regulations. He will not join a looting corporation to become just a cog in the wheel of the crime industry. The work is too grinding. He is temperamentally unsuited for cooperation. He is a thorough individualist." Less a villain than a hero, the independent crook was, lamentably, a dying breed.[92]

Charles Francis Coe's novel *Ransom,* serialized in the *Saturday Evening Post,* concurred that individuals must struggle heroically against the huge organizations that threatened to overwhelm them. Narrator Alec Davers, a "masterful lone wolf," kidnaps the infant daughter of a wealthy banker but is arrested for another crime before he can arrange to collect ransom. Sentenced to a long prison term, he looks forward to a huge payoff, for the girl remains in the care of the decent couple with whom he had left her. Upon his release nineteen years later, in 1933, Davers discovers that crime "had become a vast business" and that, as a result, independent operators faced perilous odds. Therefore he enlists the help of a major gang to collect the long-awaited ransom. He worries, however, about the consequences of submitting to the organization. "I grew afraid. Afraid of the bigness, the organization, the mighty scheming of modern crime. Would I be able to compete with new methods?" His fears prove well founded. The gang plans to cheat him out of his profit and kill the girl, now a fine young woman. A sympathetic character and at heart an honorable man, he plots to save her and even wins the admiration of her long bereaved father. But Coe is so pessimistic about the individual's capabilities that only a highly implausible deus ex machina can save the day. Coe concludes, as Davers had feared, that the individual is virtually powerless in the face of the corrupt huge organization.[93]

When the inventors of the gangster cast their critical gaze at the big businessman, they did not contrast him with an otherwise blameless public. Instead, accounts of bootleggers and racketeers insisted on broad public complicity with those most modern and dangerous of criminals. Involving much of the population, not merely a dangerous subgroup, crime suggested that only public consent permitted unethical business to flourish.

Broad popular complicity was, of course, most apparent with bootleggers, who quenched the thirst of countless enthusiastic patrons. No longer a disreputable crook, the criminal had become the efficient provider of highly desired merchandise. As an indignant gang leader exclaimed to an impudent police captain in *Doorway to Hell,* "I'm no thief—my racket is beer and you know it—I'm in a legitimate business."[94] One journalist suggested that some readers might be sipping the same hijacked Scotch whose path he had traced.[95] Prohibition, another writer argued, "created a fresh tolerance for lawbreaking. Who could look at his bootlegger as a serious offender when he supplied him with his drinks?"[96] Even bankers, executives, professionals, and socialites seemed not merely to tolerate these lawbreakers but to boast of their association with them.[97]

Racketeering provided more evidence that pernicious enterprise could exist only with significant public toleration. The racketeer also reportedly enjoyed widespread support, not from consumers but from producers whose industries he infiltrated. Accounts emphasized that small businessmen failed to combat the racketeer, and indeed often courted him, because he offered stability and greater profits in previously tumultuous, unrewarding fields. "A racket," Raymond Moley explained, "often sells something of very definite value and perhaps at no unreasonable price."[98] Numerous articles gave examples of gangster-operated associations that had used violence to enforce price agreements to the benefit of everyone involved except the consumer. According to Gordon Hostetter, the author of an exposé of racketeering in Chicago, rackets were "seized upon by business men and labor leaders as a quick solution of their problems of competitive conditions and labor-organization control."[99] Journalists trumpeted the economic benefits reaped by the owner of a large Chicago cleaning and dyeing firm who took Al Capone for a partner in 1928. The "business man's alliance with the vice king," as one explained the relationship, paved the way for the criminal's businesslike pursuit of his vocation.[100]

In the case of racketeering it often seemed nearly impossible to distinguish the crook from the businessman. The outright criminal, the unethical proprietor desperate to survive amidst fierce competition, and the upstanding businessman merged into a single suspect figure. The racket was "a manifestation of human activity deeply embedded in the normal processes of economic competition, labor relations, business practice and psychology . . . in short, of almost the sum total of what we call, for lack of a better name, civilization," Moley explained. "The reason the racket is so hard to stop is that it looks like normal life."[101] Racketeer-based combinations in restraint of trade seemed little different than baseball's organization under its commissioner, Judge Kenesaw Mountain Landis, or Hollywood's under movie "Czar" Will Hays.[102] The collaborator seemed no more—or less—sympathetic a character than his underworld associate. Gangster and industrialist merged in the new, ever-expanding sphere of "gangsterized industry."[103] Underworld and upperworld threatened to become one.

Explanations of the racket's semilegitimate functions became especially common during the great business disorder of the early years of the Depression. It is not surprising that intellectuals like Raymond Moley and Walter Lippmann projected their concerns about the destructive consequences of unregulated competition onto the image of the racketeer and the conditions that spawned him. The racketeer epitomized the profoundly ambiguous meanings of the gangster businessman. He endangered the standard of living of the consumer, that most unorganized of Americans, and after the Crash he increasingly came to symbolize the pervasive corruption of the business system. Yet he also represented an organizing force to Americans who believed that the modern economy demanded rationalization that transcended petty private interests. The racketeer, R. L. Duffus explained in the *New Republic*, "steps in because other agencies have failed. He meets a need for order that otherwise would not be met." [104] "The underworld through its very crude devices," Lippmann concurred, "serves that need for social organization which reputable society has not yet learned how to satisfy." [105] Dangerous and marvelously capable, the gangster again exposed the complex meanings of organization.

Various commentators, responding to the standout gangster films of the early thirties, have recognized the genre's critical assessments of modern business culture and the success ethic. Failing to note the close similarity of these films to earlier stage, print, and even celluloid portrayals, they have generally concluded that these criticisms resulted from disillusionment prompted by the stock market crash of October 1929 and the subsequent economic upheaval. [106] Yet even the racketeer, the gangster incarnation most obviously expressive of concerns about the business order, predated the Crash by more than a year. A more comprehensive examination reveals that continuity after the collapse was more important than change in depictions of gangsters as businessmen. Nevertheless, significant changes did occur.

Depictions shifted somewhat during the early 1930s precisely because gangsters had already been portrayed as businessmen. As a business, crime was subject to general economic forces. Gangster-businessmen had therefore risen on the swell of prosperity throughout the 1920s. In the early 1930s, however, according to many observers, they began to feel the effects of the Depression, which were exacerbated by the repeal of national prohibition. Prices for bootleg alcohol reportedly dropped, and rackets in struggling industries yielded shrinking profits. [107] Scrambling to replace lost income, gangsters jacked up their levies on legitimate businesses and turned to a new, highly organized enterprise, kidnapping. [108] Economic necessity had driven the gangster to dangerous, provocative actions he had avoided in more flush days. As a result, the criminal businessman seemed to hit closer to homes already vulnerable because of the economic collapse. [109] But as a businessman he acted in ways set long before October 1929.

3 Dressed to Kill:
Consumption, Style,
and the Gangster

A journalist in 1930 could credibly explain why Chicago area police had no difficulty labeling the headless, legless torso pulled from the bottom of a local canal: "Pin stripe tailoring, diamond stick pin and silk shirt proclaimed him a gangster and a gang victim."[1] For along with business organization and violent criminality, stylish consumption defined the public enemy. As Americans developed a new kind of consumer society, many deployed the gangster in efforts to understand its promises and control its course.

As they dressed the criminal in fine clothing, adorned him with jewelry,[2] and placed him in a luxurious nightclub, writers, filmmakers, and their audiences explored the abundance of goods that had transformed their society. Through the gangster image Americans previewed new paths to individual fulfillment apparently opened by a mass-consumption economy. At the same time they pondered how the new standards of consumerism affected older categories of social order, especially class and ethnicity. These were crucial cultural concerns, and the gangster offered not just illumination but guidance as well. The inventors of the public enemy used him to promote values about the urban consumer society he epitomized.

It was at the culmination of the development of a new consumer society that Americans became fascinated with the gangster. The new consumerism had its roots in the revolutionary innovations in production, management, and distribution that swept across the American economy in the decades around the turn of the century.[3] The scale of consumerism increased most dramatically in the 1920s, when a flood of goods transformed the daily lives of millions of Americans, particularly within the urban middle class. Easy credit brought more and more goods within the reach of the middle class. Automobiles were the most significant single item, with production jumping from four thousand annually in 1900 to 4.8 million in 1929, the majority of the increase coming in the 1920s. Telephones, radios, refrigerators, prepared foods, and a host of other goods saw comparable gains. Sales of the commodity of entertainment increased apace, with the major industry, movies, jumping from forty million admissions a week in 1922 to 100 million in 1930.[4]

To a remarkable extent the consumption patterns established in the prosperous 1920s persisted in the next decade. Aided by lower prices and credit purchasing, families struggled, often successfully, to maintain the standard of living they had enjoyed in the 1920s. Even as Americans scrambled to live on smaller, less reliable incomes, many of them continued to regard as necessities goods and services that ten or twenty years earlier had been luxuries. Automobiles, telephones, and commercial entertainment had become essential products.[5]

The new consumerism involved more than just quantitatively greater use of purchasable goods. Sellers sought to invest products with intangible value beyond any utilitarian function they served, a strategy that buyers seemed to validate with each purchase. Increasingly, mass-production goods were touted on the basis of mysterious qualities that had little to do with the product's actual use. To exploit the diverse associations that consumers might make with specific goods, manufacturers marked their products with racy brand names and graphically appealing logos. Sellers attempted to make their offerings exude gentility, sophistication, modernity, or any of a multitude of other desirable traits. In the 1920s, department stores staged spectacular pageants to impart new meanings to featured goods, and manufacturers introduced a spectrum of color to automobiles, telephones, kitchen appliances, and even furnaces to imbue them with distinctiveness. In sum, what the new economy promised in abundance was style, once limited to a small number of product groups and available to a relative few. More than ever before, products were important not only because of the immediate function they served, but because of the images they conveyed.[6]

Leading in the promotion of style was the burgeoning advertising industry, which achieved unprecedented cultural influence in the 1920s. National advertising volume, just 682 million dollars in 1914, jumped to 1,409 million dollars in 1919 and then to 2,987 million dollars in 1929. Magazines carried six times as much advertising in 1926 as they had ten years earlier. Moreover, the content of ads changed to emphasize stylistic appeals. By the early 1920s advertisers abandoned the sober text extolling tangible qualities that had been the staple of earlier ads. Instead, sensuous illustrations, often evoking scenes far removed from a product's putative function, sold the rewards of style. Soap ads promised business success, mouthwash promised love, automobiles promised a return to Arcadia.[7]

The promoters of style sought to capitalize on the erosion of old values and social arrangements, especially those that had provided middle-class Americans with a sense of place and identity. Employment in corporate hierarchies deprived many men of the sense of visible, invigorating accomplishment enjoyed by the owners and employees of smaller units of production. The new work-place emphasis on specialized skills, education, and professional identification undermined the culture of character, in which status had depended more largely on the quality of one's reputation. The new celebration of play toppled the older producer ethos, long tottering, that exalted hard work and condemned frivolous consumption and aimless leisure. Heightened perceptions of geographic mobility, ethnic divisions, and class-segregated neighborhoods weakened the notion of elite social stewardship and the obligations of social-uplift work that had provided a mission for respectable women's activities outside their homes. Elite women saw their traditional roles further eroded by professionals' usurpation of uplift and relief work. Women's role as moral uplifters within their own homes was weakened by the growth of commercial amusements that increasingly left parlors empty and lessons untaught. For some, even the certainties of religion seemed to succumb to modernity as liberal Protestantism moved ever further from the stern absolutes appropriate to a hierarchical society. Because of these changes wrought by modernization, T. J. Jackson Lears suggests, for many educated Americans the "sense of selfhood . . . had grown fragmented, diffuse, and somehow 'unreal.'" [8]

It was an audacious promise to satisfy Americans' yearning for fulfillment and identity that distinguished the new gospel of spending, to which the unprecedented flocks of buyers seemed to be eager converts. Beyond meeting tangible needs, consumption had long served to announce social status or ideological commitment. Never before, however, had such a profusion of goods promised to transform their purchasers. As society became increasingly impersonal, goods were correspondingly personalized, celebrated as amulets that empowered the individual holding them. Mass-produced goods paradoxically promised distinctiveness and identity; purchasers could restyle themselves at will.

As the inventors of the gangster explored the new consumerism, their most persistent message was that achievement could be measured by an inventory of goods. Possessions constituted the main rewards for whatever combination of ability, hard work, good fortune, and ruthlessness the gangster exploited. To a large extent, the glamour of consumption served to make the criminal an attractive figure enjoying the fruits of his labors. As such, the invented gangster served a role not unlike the film stars and other celebrities who came to prominence in the 1920s: he illustrated the possibilities for fulfillment and display offered by the new consumer society.

The gangster's status as a glamorous consumer was most apparent in his attire. Journalists routinely noted that bank robbers, hijackers, or racketeers were "well-dressed," and they often offered painstaking descriptions. [9] Recurring symbols of consumption—expensive suits, tuxedos, spats, jewels, precious-metal cigarette cases and lighters—were the rewards of success. A *New York Times* writer in 1928 summed up the accomplishments of bootlegger Frankie Yale with a catalog of "His new automobile, his tastefully furnished apartment, his diamond stickpin, his two diamond rings, his belt buckle ornamented with seventy-five brilliants, his fifty suits of clothes, his twenty-five pairs of shoes." Lest the numbers fail to impress, the reporter noted that the suits cost two hundred dollars apiece and hats twenty-five dollars.[10] Another gangster, a "particularly careful dresser," according to Edward Dean Sullivan, had "twenty business suits of fine materials, golf, riding and hunting costumes, and four outfits of evening clothes."[11] The latest styles marked the gangster as an avid consumer who invested the time and expense necessary to stay on the leading edge of fashion. A *Collier's* writer in 1929 described a color-coordinated racketeer who "wore a faultlessly tailored blue suit, a blue silk shirt of a texture almost as thick as flannel, a blue tie, blue collar, blue socks, and a wide-brimmed Panama hat of the $500 woven-to-order variety. The hat band was a wide, wrinkled and most carefully folded blue silk scarf. A lapis lazuli ring and tie pin completed the youth's ensemble." He appeared in similar outfits, tan and soft green, on later days.[12]

Hollywood matched these sartorial displays, notwithstanding the limitations of black and white. In *Playing Around* a switchboard operator offers an enthusiastic description of the stylish crook: "swell clothes, fit him like powder fits your face—the edge of a silk handkerchief sticking out of his pocket on the port side—high-class duco job on the shoes." In *The Finger Points,* a reporter who joins his mobster subjects immediately trades the drab style of his past for the slicked hair, flashy jewelry, and double-breasted suits favored by his underworld associate Clark Gable.[13]

Along with fashionable attire the gangster acquired other possessions that marked him as an exemplar of consumption. Whether he lived in a traditionally furnished mansion or an ultramodern penthouse, the gangster surrounded himself with a wealth of goods, from antiques or art deco furniture to Persian rugs and priceless works of art.[14] New automobiles appeared with iconographic regularity. While news reporters stressed the ability to elude local police that high-powered automobiles gave the gangster, films emphasized their sweeping contours and shining chrome. *Playing Around's* most prominent prop is the gangster's sporty roadster. An old woman describes the protagonist as "mister diamonds with automobile with fancy horn."[15] In *The Public Enemy* James Cagney's rise in gangdom is clear when he switches from riding in a truck to a gleaming convertible that turns the heads of envious pedestrians. The camera's admiring sweep of its graceful lines hints at the enjoyment such a fine automobile brings its owner.[16]

The excitement offered by the consumer society, and its urban focus, were most apparent in the commercial amusements central to the gangster's image. He and his companions enjoyed a fashionable downtown nightlife of expensive restaurants, theaters, and cabarets. The gangster's patronage received regular attention in news stories, but fictional accounts offered the most enthralled, voyeuristic portrayals. Films lavished attention upon banquets, theatrical opening nights, and spectacular cabaret reviews. When burglar Chick Williams, in an early scene in the 1929 film *Alibi,* stops his car in front of a rich canopy entrance, strolls past a uniformed doorman, steps over the name "Bachmans" embedded in the tile floor, and enters an elegant cabaret, he introduces movie viewers to an extravagant world of sensuous consumption.[17]

Like molls and machine guns, cabaret scenes were an almost obligatory element of late twenties and early thirties gangster films. Much of the action in *Sweet Mama* takes place in the Club Palmer, which includes a huge stage with a revolving floor on which seminude chorines perform elaborate routines. In *The Finger Points,* gangsters operate and patronize the Sphinx Club, an ornate casino in a mansion graced by exquisite chandeliers and an immense grand staircase. The Corsair nightclub, of *Murder on the Roof,* is a luxurious Manhattan roof-garden cabaret that features a tuxedo-attired orchestra and tabletop telephones to facilitate introductions. The interior of *Broadway*'s Paradise Club, one film historian quips, "was as high as a cathedral, possibly to accommodate the extravagant headgear of the chorus girls."[18] In these temples of consumption the gangster spent with appropriate abandon. *Weary River* opens with dashing Jerry Larabee—in tuxedo, white gloves, and white silk scarf—entering a fashionable cabaret and bestowing lavish tips on fawning employees. *Playing Around* begins with the gangster, played by Chester Morris, in a spectacular nightclub with a large orchestra and fifty costumed pirates dancing on a huge shipboard set. So exceptional is the night's entertainment that it is being broadcast by radio. On another night Morris's date worries that their show tickets are too expensive. "Only" ten dollars apiece, he replies smugly. "Say, who do you think you're out with—a soda jerker?"[19]

Again the gangster was illuminating changes in the lives of his respectable counterparts, for, since the 1890s, an increasing number of them had forsaken the decorous amusements of their forebears for the sensuous world of urban pleasure promised by institutions of commercial leisure. Around the turn of the century, satisfied customers of amusement parks included middle-class city dwellers who reveled in the opportunity to shake off the restraints of everyday propriety. In the 1910s middle-class Americans became enthralled, as had less affluent city folk before them, with the sensuous world of the moving picture. By the 1920s, recreation districts like New York's Times Square and Chicago's State Street had replaced governmental and business districts as the most central, publicized, and widely recognized urban spaces. In large cities like Chicago and New York the popularity of cabarets in the 1910s and 1920s typified the ascendance of commercial urban entertainment. Cabarets were successful because they celebrated spontaneity and sexual expressiveness. Dancing, syncopated music redolent with the supposed abandon of black performers, and the indiscriminate mixing of entertainers and audience offered an infusion of vitality to patrons eager to shed the constraining remnants of nineteenth-century respectable morality.[20] The gangster was an oversized projection of the urban American seduced by the promises of consumption.

In portraying the gangster as an exemplary spender, the genre often promoted the new consumer values. Fine clothing, new cars, and expensive nightlife frequently brought the pleasure and fulfillment they promised. As critics regularly pointed out, Hollywood's perfunctory moralistic endings did little to counter its approving depictions of the enjoyment of ill-gotten gains. Happiness, the gangster genre often announced, could come through carefree spending.

So, too, could spending bring the individual distinctiveness many craved. In several films, the gangster's fine automobile causes lesser characters to see him as important and worthy of notice.[21] Costly attire set the gang leader apart from his more commonly dressed counterparts on both sides of the law. In *Broadway*, Steve Crandall's elegant overcoat, hat, tuxedo, black tie, cane, white gloves, and carnation are more than sufficient to mark him as a dominating criminal leader.[22] A staple Hollywood scene most vividly made this association of fine clothing with individual recognition. In *Little Caesar*, *The Public Enemy*, and several of their imitators, a tailor's fitting marks the young gang leader's rise. The gangster stands on a small platform, looking down on the obsequious little man literally bent to his service. When he finally wears the sharp new suit the gangster has also donned a new identity.[23]

Significantly, the identity that stylishness created could be internalized as well as projected, an insight expressed in the recurring motif of the gangster's self-evaluation in a mirror. In *Quick Millions,* Bugs Raymond, played by Spencer Tracy, admires his tuxedoed image as he prepares for an evening at the opera. His pleasure with the transformation is evident: "You could never picture me in overalls now, could you!?"[24] In Charles Francis Coe's serial novel *The Other Half,* Antonio Scarvak admires himself in a full-length mirror. "The well-tailored clothes, the silk shirt and cravat, the lovely diamond on his finger—all these things bespoke success," Coe explains. Reflecting Scarvak's fine new clothes and jewels, the mirror confirms to Scarvak that possessions have remade him.[25]

As men and women used the criminal to explore the consumer society, they examined the shifting meanings of class in urban America. The gangster's extravagant consumption seemed to suggest that economic mobility had blurred class distinctions. Walter Green traced the mercurial rise of successful criminals in a *Saturday Evening Post* feature in 1926. "The coke peddler or white slaver who has done a stretch of ten years or so comes up from Atlanta to find a new and splendid world of criminal opportunity. His mind turns to the higher and finer things of crookdom. He decides to become a respectable bootlegger. In a few short months he is driving downtown in his car, talking to his customers across a mahogany desk, slipping a careless hundred here and a careful thousand there."[26] No longer were criminals unable to transcend their shabby origins. The members of a motley New York gang, according to a 1922 *Literary Digest* writer, soon after entering the alcohol business, "began to change in appearance. I saw and heard of diamonds, ultra-fashionable clothes, limousines, stories of nightly debauches, where fortunes were spent in an evening."[27] In another early report *Saturday Evening Post* writer Will Irwin explained that "Shifty-eyed boys of the slums who were before the war content to play extra men in pool-room swindles, to act as lookouts for an occasional second-story game, or even, in hard times, to snatch hand bags, suddenly began to wear two-hundred-dollar suits of clothes, to flash five-carat diamonds, to drive high-powered cars, to shoot craps for a hundred dollars a throw." Only the caps that accompanied their "Fifth Avenue" attire gave evidence of their working-class, ethnic origins.[28] "Conditions have changed," a feature on Chicago crime concluded in 1926. "Hoodlums that used to sleep on benches half the time have suites in lake-front hotels now. They have their hands manicured and dress for dinner."[29]

Innumerable films showed that once formidable class barriers were now easily vaulted. *Doorway to Hell* dramatizes gang leader Louis Ricarno's rise in a scene in which he drives by and reminisces about the fifth-floor tenement where he grew up. The drab street, vendors, and fluttering laundry are of a different world than the one he now inhabits, and the chauffeur-driven limousine in which he sits represents the distance between the two.[30] The spectacular rise of a young man from the lower ranks of criminality toward gang leadership, one of the genre's most popular story lines, provided the basis for the three most successful and critically praised gangster movies of the early thirties—*Little Caesar, The Public Enemy,* and *Scarface.* Each of these films emphasizes the humble origins of its magnificently successful antihero. *Little Caesar*'s Rico Bandello first appears as a small-town crook holding up a gas station, eating in a greasy-spoon diner, and dreaming about success in the big city. Tom Powers, in *The Public Enemy,* is the son of a hard-working woman and an Irish beat cop who provides more discipline than luxuries. *Scarface*'s Tony Camonte is a product of a poor Italian tenement district family. The origins of these gangsters, and of dozens of their celluloid contemporaries, could not have been farther from the world of tuxedos, jewels, cabarets, and shining automobiles they came to inhabit.[31]

The inventors of the gangster often suggested that the new criteria of stylish consumption threatened to undermine older categories of social classification. They highlighted modern society's apparent erasure of older class lines by placing the criminal in close contact with men and women from the highest echelons of respectable society. Crook and trustee most frequently mixed in stylish pleasure palaces. "For several years now," *Cosmopolitan* writer O. O. McIntyre noted in 1931, "gorillas have almost completely abandoned their lower East Side cellar haunts and moved up to Broadway, to sit in Tuxedoed elegance at the ring side of the supper clubs."[32] According to a *New York Times* feature, in earlier decades one interested in observing New York's underworld needed to travel to a gaslit, sawdust-covered Bowery saloon like "'Chick' Tricker's Fleabag." By 1930, though, it had become "a waste of time to journey so far from the haunts of supposed respectability."[33] As the reference to "supposed respectability" suggested, traditional social divisions seemed to be blurred not only by lower-status people laying claim to the rewards of the consumer society but by higher-status people abandoning the moral high ground for vaguely disreputable pleasures. As one concerned writer asked, "Has the racketeer leveled himself up or has society leveled itself down?"[34] In the Palais d'Argent nightclub, featured in William E. Weeks's novel *All in the Racket,* "college boys and big butter-and-egg-men, prostitutes and bankers, dancing mothers and politicians rubbed shoulders with racketeers and citizens of the underworld with the greatest joviality."[35] "Any one acquainted in the least with Broadway," *New York Times* writer James C. Young asserted with some irony, "knows that the city's 'best people' as well as the worst may be found in the night club."[36] No longer distinct species, the respectable and the disreputable were linked as consumers of the same expensive pleasures.

The shifting landscape of the consumer society's class relations was extraordinarily confusing social terrain to early twentieth-century Americans, especially those who counted themselves among the middle, respectable class. Never precise, "middle class" in the late nineteenth century connoted inclusion in several categories, generally linked, of occupation, income, ethnicity, religion, and public behavior. After the turn of the century disparate social changes combined to make the category more and more problematic—but no less important—than ever before. Some of the changes involved the working class, including immigrants. The widespread availability of inexpensive mass-produced clothing lessened differences in attire. During the First World War, the income gap shrank as unskilled workers enjoyed substantially increased real wages, while white-collar earnings stagnated. Families of skilled laborers often lived on a larger income than those of white-collar clerks. It was also change in the lives of those who considered themselves middle-class that made the category more problematic. "Middle class" became increasingly amorphous as new occupations displaced independent professions and small entrepreneurship as the typical pursuits of white-collar males. More important, Americans from across the class spectrum increasingly participated in the indulgent quest for gratification and pleasure that had once marked immigrants and the working class as different. Cabaret-going, joy-riding, and jazz dancing seemed to situate many of those who claimed middle-class status far beyond the borders of respect-ability.[37]

Just as the stylish gangster invited consideration of changing class relationships, he also offered an exploration of the meanings of eth-nicity, another vital cultural concern of urban Americans. In the 1920s and 1930s the social upheaval once occasioned by massive immigration had been replaced by tensions resulting from the ex-panding occupational and residential mobility of immigrants and their children. Prominently featuring Italians, Irish, and Jews,[38] the invented underworld offered guidance to urban Americans of all sorts as they negotiated the shifting ethnic terrain of their diverse society. Despite the continuation of the long-standing cultural association of ethnic otherness with criminality, the genre usually permitted a rela-tively tolerant assessment of the ethnic minorities it spotlighted. Three factors—the inclination to see criminals as essentially ordinary, the insistence on individual moral responsibility, and the desire not to offend large segments of a prospective mass audience—generally checked any outright attribution of criminal behavior to innate ethno-racial traits.[39] Instead, ethnicity was treated primarily as a mat-ter of style. As the gangster rose in crime and in society he came into his own as a consumer and usually shed the obvious markers of his ethnicity. He favored cosmopolitan downtown restaurants over the cheap neighborhood joints of his past; he moved away from the ghetto; he purged his clothing and his language of ethnic traces. In his suavity, as in his organization and planning, the ethnic gangster exhibited a range of stereotypical urban attributes. Observers saw him less as a member of an outside group than as a successful Ameri-can. The inventors of the gangster offered a useful lesson to their audience: for whites in a consumer culture, social categorization was less determined by ethnicity than ever before. Ethnicity was becoming more a signifier of background than a determinant of opportunity or behavior. The gangster's origins suggested how far an ambitious per-son might rise in society and how insubstantial old barriers had be-come. Ironically, the ethnic gangster, partly through his smooth style, contributed to the replacement of complex, progressive-era racial taxonomies with the emerging conception of a monolithic white race.

Casting the gangster as a stylish, successful American, and

suggesting that ethnicity had lost its former ordering power, did not preclude an ethnocentric reading of the images of the underworld. For one of the sources of the genre's success was that its multilayered symbols permitted alternate interpretations by different audience members.[40] Swarthy skin and Jewish or Italian surnames were among the recurring markers that might be seized upon by those inclined to racialist understandings, even in the absence of explicit ethnic condemnations. For some audience members the mere association of crime and particular ethnic groups justified more than a hint of racial determinism. Relatively benign mass-culture images probably fueled the hatred of one anonymous letter-writer to the Chicago Crime Commission: "There is no way to get rid of these Italians and Irish but extermination. . . . Why isn't someone big enough to put a gun to the head of that dirty Italian Capone?"[41] Any portrayal of Italian, Irish, and Jewish Americans as criminals undoubtedly fanned xenophobic fears of dangerous others.[42]

The ethnic gangster's rise from the slum to a life of lavish consumption, his mixing with refined men and women from the upper echelons of society, and their willingness to patronize sensuous palaces of commercial entertainment and to tolerate his presence there: all illuminated upheaval in a social order that, at least in memory, had seemed stable and enduring. "A new social strata is in the making," journalist Fred Pasley explained in his expose of racketeering. "The old order is being undermined and threatened."[43] In the view of an *Outlook and Independent* writer on "the new underworld" in 1929, "the old lines of demarcation are gone."[44]

Faced with the apparent disintegration of "the old order" of class and ethnicity, some observers suggested that the changes were more superficial than substantial. They used the criminal to contend that fundamental differences separated members of various, still distinguishable social groups. Though the gangster might come into close contact with respectable society, he would inevitably remain distinct from it. Stylistic uniformity was patently superficial. James C. Young, using the rhetoric of class distinction, wrote that "the 'gentleman crook'" was a product of the imagination. Though the gangster "indulges his fancy to live as the other half," wrote Young, "A dinner coat and a motor car cannot make the typical crook appear a 'gentleman.' He may learn how to comb his hair and where to put his hands at a dinner table, but he still remains a social pariah."[45] "Home Life of the Gunman," an editorial cartoon reprinted in *Literary Digest* in 1924, carried a similar message. The crook has acquired the trappings of respectability but his background pollutes everything around him. The framed family portraits are mug shots, the many books are about crime, guns, and death statistics, the vase of flowers and dainty, lace tablecloth are atop a beer barrel, and guns lie on the fold-out desk. His youngest child plays innocently, but with a loaded pistol, and two older children, a boy and a girl, compose their Christmas requests—for, respectively, "a nise new gat" and "lip stick and a pare of flesh colord stock[ings]."[46] Despite a few of the right purchases, this family would never be mistaken for the Astors. In *Scarface*, Tony Camonte's new tuxedo cannot hide his simian carriage.[47] *Little Giant*, a 1933 comedy in which Edward G. Robinson reprised his role from *Little Caesar*, culminated the occasional tendency in films to portray gangsters as laughable pretenders to respectability. After retiring from his career as a Chicago bootlegger, Robinson buys a California estate and vows "to mingle with the upper class. I'm going to be a gentleman." His attempts at playing polo, ordering from French menus, and choosing appropriate formal attire turn out disastrously.[48] Society need not fear unknown contamination by Little Caesars and their social peers.

This showcasing of gangster buffoons was a central component of many Americans' efforts to use the criminal to accommodate to the consumer society, because it represented a reconciliation of the new consumer values and the older urge to give order to society through definition, ranking, and exclusion. As many of these examples suggest, it was the gangster's misadventures in the realm of consumption itself that marked his real inferiority. The hopeful message was that style, which superficially shrouded social differences, on a deeper level—yet one readily apparent to discriminating eyes—provided the means for necessary social ordering. Style continued to provide crucial information because the gangster, in his frenetic pursuit of fashion, revealingly overstepped the boundaries of good taste. One writer noted that his gangster subject's suit was not only "expensive" but "perhaps a bit too obviously so to be in good taste."[49] In *Scarface* an understated upper-class moll tells Tony Camonte that his new apartment, with which he expects to impress her, is "kind of gaudy." "Ain't it, though!" he replies proudly.[50] The flamboyant gangster, highlighting the promise for self-expression at the heart of consumerism's appeals, served as a warning that overindulgence would lead to hideous excess. But he also suggested that the standards of tasteful consumption themselves could serve as a reliable tool for distinguishing the socially respectable from the disreputable. Respectability was manifested in refined consumption. The boldly striped suits and absurdly large diamonds of those aping their social betters betrayed a lower-class background and its attendant moral flaws. Sartorial excess revealed that despite lower-class pretensions there were real differences between groups of people. Far from hiding these differences, clothing and other consumer goods highlighted them. Accurate social classification merely required good taste, the preserve of respectable men and women. Moreover, the overadorned gangster buffoon carried a clear message to people from working-class and ethnic backgrounds: attempts to use possessions to rise above one's proper place in society are futile.[51]

Despite the sanguine suggestions that style itself might provide the basis for the essential task of social differentiation, many observers believed consumerism's blurring of important categories was not just superficially misleading but dangerously disorienting. Some critics, concerned about consumerism's effect on workers and immigrants, used the criminal to show that the pursuit of extravagance and unnatural mobility could result in a fearsome loss of moral bearings. William McAdoo, considering the "Causes and Mechanisms of Prevalent Crime" for the *Scientific Monthly,* blamed the enthusiasm for spending money of lower-class Americans. Crime originated in the pernicious new tastes of those who spent "recklessly in a style of living to which they ordinarily would not be accustomed."[52] A *Literary Digest* article, offering the same message, deplored the "extravagant living standards" and "newly acquired expensive tastes" that resulted from high war wages. Finding the falling real wages of the early twenties "insufficient to satisfy their desires," some workers turned to crime.[53] Embedded in these analyses were extraordinarily censorious attitudes about spending and mobility. For some Americans, the violent, bedazzled gangster showed that the new era's emphasis on purchasable pleasures undermined a proper class and ethnic order and threatened the morality and docility of groups now lamentably unwilling to recognize themselves as a lower sort.

Many who observed the new spectrum of spending rejected the notion that stylistic cues remained as important tools of social differentiation. Not only had the gangster come to Broadway, but once there he went unrecognized or, at the least, unremarked. The gangster's smooth exterior and fashionable leisure activities enabled him to blend with respectable society. Cabaret-going film gangsters partied alongside men and women of wealth and refinement. Anti-crime crusaders sat at cabaret tables adjacent to those of criminal leaders. "Gangsters now wear evening clothes," the *Saturday Evening Post* explained, "and mix unknown with decent citizens."[54] "In one instance in an intimate jazz mosque," a *Cosmopolitan* writer claimed, "I saw three reputed killers sitting at a table next to Vincent Astor and his party."[55] Ed X., a "typical criminal" featured in a *Saturday Evening Post* article by Richard Washburn Child, "could stand about at an afternoon tea on a Long Island estate without exciting the suspicions of some of the guests—or the butler."[56]

As Americans used the criminal to grapple with the impenetrability of the stylish exterior, they often emphasized the role of malleable, superficial behavioral traits. For the gangster often brandished a stylish "personality"—a combination of agreeable mannerisms and pleasant banter—that complemented his consumption. Superficial personal behavior, along with possessions, did much to establish identity in modern society. Child emphasized the personality of Ed X., whose polished facade concealed his slum origins and criminal career. Ed sported "well-tailored" clothes, a new straw hat, and manicured nails. His "graceful" gestures, unforced habit of looking straight into the eyes of a questioner, and easygoing demeanor gave him "the outward appearance of one who is used to good manners. There is nothing coarse or gross about him." Those who met Ed liked him. "How easy it would be," Child warned, to "develop, instinctively, a sympathy for some very likable and appealing personality." "I like this Ed X.," a friend of Child's proclaimed; "He is an impulsive but warm-hearted boy."[57]

The gangster genre, borrowing a page from contemporary advice books, taught that a successful personality could be achieved by the mastery of the art of small talk.[58] No longer were crooks "addicted to the 'Toity-toid Street and Toid Avenue' school of enunciation."[59] Ed X. spoke with "quiet restraint."[60] Another racketeer had made himself "a fine conversationalist."[61] Earning a reputation "as a regular fellow" in the underworld, an infiltrator wrote, required lavish spending and mastery of the art of amiable chatter: "Introduction followed introduction. 'Awf'ly glad to meet you'; 'Pleased to know you'; 'It is a pleasure, indeed'; 'Interesting to know you, I am sure, my dear fellow,' were some of my stock phrases." [62] A conversation among gangsters at a cafe, according to O. O. McIntyre, "was the persiflage of the average group of young fellows around a restaurant table." [63]

Writers and filmmakers linked the artifice of personality with the urban consumer society by showcasing the gangster's glibness in expensive arenas of commercial entertainment. It was in these highly theatrical environments that the gangster's front was most convincing. In Charles Francis Coe's 1932 novel *Payoff*, serialized in the *Saturday Evening Post*, racketeer Cut Cardozzi exudes "personal magnetism" after entering a swank downtown casino. "The gleam in his eye and the breadth of his smile were attractive. The gusto with which he did every little thing was almost magnificent." His smile, according to the narrator, "is worth a million dollars." Cut is soon on a first-name basis with new acquaintances, whom he addresses as old friends. He chats about his ineptitude at the gaming tables, buys drinks, and lights his companion's cigarettes. The narrator later comments, "I had been able to . . . feel the power of the man's personality." [64]

Americans' fascination with the charming gangster represented an effort to understand what Warren Susman has called the transition from a "culture of character" to a "culture of personality." In nineteenth-century bourgeois society, according to Susman, respectable folk based their evaluations of each other on character, a complex of traits that emphasized moral conformity and industriousness. A solid reputation depended on lifelong rectitude before an audience of vigilant community members. Recasting David Riesman's analysis of the other-directed personality, Susman contends that by the turn of the century new standards emerged that were geared to modern mobility, abundance, and corporate employment. Advice writers who had once counseled on the nurturing of character now publicized the requirements of personality. Positive evaluations from the ephemeral acquaintances of modern life, like success in corporate hierarchies, seemed to depend less on deep-seated qualities of character than on charm, good humor, and general attractiveness, which was in part a function of the careful assembly of consumer goods. By the 1920s, the external, malleable traits of personality had largely replaced character as key standards by which urban Americans evaluated their acquaintances.[65]

As these inventors of the gangster explored the leveling consequences of consumerism, they put forth an alternative set of values that sought to reestablish the primacy of social distinctions based on the standards of the old culture of character. For this vision of the consumer society did not include the comforting message that in the midst of change were the sources of a safe new order. Depictions of stylish criminals mixing with respectable citizens constituted a serious critique of the culture of consumption's new standards of social classification. The men who had achieved status and mixed with leading citizens on the basis of consumerism's new standards were exposed as untrustworthy and dangerous. Style offered no reliable guide to the individual's true nature, for men and women had a deep moral center unrelated to superficial display. Depictions of stylish gangsters implicitly urged a return to the exclusivity of the respectable folk in nineteenth-century society who had screened their acquaintances through the tight guidelines of the culture of character.

The smooth exterior, the gangster suggested, could be a powerful tool for deceit. Walter Davenport's description of a young robber's smile that "disarmed" reflected a common theme in portrayals of criminals.[66] Thus it was essential for Americans to learn, as had the heroine of Frank L. Packard's novel *The Big Shot*, a wise newcomer to the big city, "that appearances in Gangland, even to the extent of expensive and butler-equipped apartments on Park Avenue, might very easily be misleading and deceptive."[67] Although a violent or larcenous nature might be submerged by stylishness, it would eventually surface. The criminal inevitably exploited his contacts with respectability in ways that revealed his true moral nature. *The Whole Truth About Racketeers* developed the theme at length and emphasized the dangerously distractive quality of the new criteria for social status. "It is wise to remember that the greatest asset to the modern crook is a charming personality. Unlike his gorilla-like forebears in thugdom, he has abandoned his jimmy and his bludgeon for a winning smile and a suave voice." The careful assembly of consumer goods was essential to successful deceit. "The modern crook prefers donning slick attire, swinging a cane, driving a fast roadster, and trusting to his ingenuity and 'gift-o'-gab' to bundle up more 'sugar' than he

ever found in a night's ramble through a quiet apartment."[68] If respectability could be donned as easily as a suit jacket, no one was safe.

The realm of sophisticated urban leisure, the symbolic center of
the consumer society, seemed especially conducive to the fraudulence
of style. In this frontier of the upperworld and the underworld the
gangster revealed his real nature by preying on men and women lured
into complacency by his smooth manners and fine clothing. Accounts
of jewel thefts arranged by criminal carousers were a standard of the
gangster genre. One Chicago gang, according to the *Outlook and
Independent*, included a "spotter" who "dresses well [and] conducts
himself fashionably" in order to identify the best targets among
wealthy nightclub patrons.[69] In another account, the gangster host of
a party overheard an inebriated guest's excited description of another
woman's extravagant jewels and art collection. He "listened atten-
tively, smiling and courteous. . . . bade his guests a most gentlemanly
good-night," and arranged a burglary.[70]

This concern about the unreliability of the veneer of stylish sophistication was the central theme of a 1923 *Collier's* short story by
Octavus Roy Cohen, better known for his racist "darky tales" of life
in the Deep South. "There was nothing about Mr. Thomas Matlock
Braden to mark him as being other than a perfect gentleman," the
story began. It took place at a fashionable resort hotel, where Braden
"blended perfectly into the tinsel background." Distinguished in appearance, he had an "easy grace of bearing," spoke well, and "dressed
with scrupulous care" in "ultraconservative" attire. The consequences of the modern obsession with personality were among Cohen's key concerns. Though capable of icy haughtiness, Braden could
put an anxious stranger "instantly at ease." "He had an infectious
laugh, and he . . . injected the full radiance of a pleasing personality
into the laughter and good humored glance he bestowed upon" his
acquaintances. But Braden's facade was a carefully constructed sham,
and his true nature was better captured by the working-class
"Tommy" than the patrician "Thomas." "In cultivating this external
aspect . . . Tommy assumed a virtue he had not," Cohen wrote;
"Morally, Tommy was a total loss. He was courteous and suave and
cosmopolitan. And unscrupulous." Braden, who used this carefully
groomed personality to sell stolen goods, showed the deceptive power
of suavity, spending, and a ready smile.[71]

Writers emphasized the unreliability of social classifications based on style by portraying women—believed to be especially enthusiastic adherents of consumer values—as most susceptible to the gangster's trickery. Criminal gigolos, regularly exploiting their contacts with easily duped wealthy women, received considerable attention as perhaps the most accomplished manipulators of style. They operated "in the swankier night clubs and at times in the sedate surroundings of a good hotel or restaurant," according to the *New York Times Magazine.* "These highly polished individuals, with the latest in dress clothes, socks and ties . . . glib of tongue and wise in the ways of the world. . . . handle their teacups with feline grace and know the latest in dancing steps." Hapless women, embracing them and the consumer values they embodied, made for easy victims of the gigolos' criminal plots.[72]

The strongly anticonsumerist subtext of these cautionary tales was evident in their implication that it was the ostentatious display of affluent victims that provoked theft. Middle- and upper-class city dwellers who embraced the values of consumption seemed to bear some responsibility for the apparent upsurge in crime. Child, a staunch critic of luxury and spending, saw an "increase in temptation offered by the show of wealth used as personal adornment. The past ten years has seen much more display on the person—jewelry, expensive furs, and even large sums in folds of crisp new bills. Whatever good or bad taste may dictate this display, it is always crime bait."[73] The *Literary Digest* concurred that "lavish and unseemly display of valuables in public places has produced envy and resentment among the unfortunate and evil-minded."[74] The message was clear. Rampant crime testified to a crucial need for sobriety, modesty, and humility—the professed virtues of the nineteenth-century middle-class American untainted by the dawning age of extravagance. In sharp contrast to those who believed that style offered the means for differentiating the respectable from the disreputable, these writers indicted all the new extravagance as productive of terrible disorder.

While the gangster's disarming stylishness enabled him to execute specific criminal acts, its more pernicious consequence was to lure respectable citizens into dangerous complacency. The narrator of *Pay-Off* typically reported that Cut Cardozzi's personal magnetism not only impressed his observers but "dissipated suspicion."[75] Because their evaluations of others were clouded by the misleading criteria of consumption and personality, even civic-minded men and women failed to see or overlooked the criminal's nefarious activities. As a result, according to many observers, good citizens failed to unite in the righteous indignation necessary to purge the evildoers.

Charles Francis Coe's serial novel *The Other Half* focused on this confusion of identity in modern society. Bootlegger and killer Antonio Scarvak poses as a hardworking merchant who has amassed an honest fortune. Leading citizens of his unnamed city offer effusive praise for this immigrant whom they believe to be the embodiment of American opportunity. Scarvak's "palatial home," butler, moralistic pronouncements, and substantial contributions to the city's crime commission cause reporters, industrialists, and bank board members to see him as the victim rather than the perpetrator of gang outrages. Only when a tough newspaper editor sees through this facade and declares that Scarvak is "a wop gangster" does society begin to protect itself. Consumption and style were misleading guides to the true nature of Antonio Scarvak, and older guides, including ethnicity, seemed more reliable.[76]

Several writers, emphasizing the connection between stylishness and duplicity, suggested that only people blind to the dictates of style could see through the shroud covering men like Scarvak. Coe dwelled on the personal traits that enabled a detective finally to get to the bottom of Scarvak's criminal activity. Secret Service agent Lemuel Tobias Bekins lives up to his unfashionable name, which sounds as if it were lifted from an Horatio Alger novel. Bekins wears a grimy, battered hat, worn-out clothes, and thick glasses, smokes frayed cigars, speaks in a tremulous voice, ignores customary courtesies, and, to the annoyance of his listeners, continually "suck[s] his teeth." He is "a queer nut," Coe is at pains to establish. Reversing the message about men like Scarvak, a character wisely advises, "don't accept Lemuel Tobias Bekins on his mannerisms and outward characteristics alone."[77] A similar admonition appeared in Cohen's "Pink Bait." Only a slovenly detective, whose "grotesquely misfit . . . suit glistened with a sheen begotten of arduous wear," is able to expose the slick Tommy Braden.[78] Remoteness from consumer values made it possible to see through the veil of stylishness.

The seeming dangers of the consumer society included not only infiltration but moral contamination as well. The criminal showed that the lure of the consumer society's bounty might draw men and women from anywhere in the social order, even its supposedly virtuous middle, to immoral acts. More generally and thus more menacingly, the love of pleasure so weakened otherwise good citizens that they became accomplices in the criminals' misdeeds. The inventors of the gangster joined other recent social critics in suggesting that the deleterious moral effects of extravagance endangered the middle class as much or even more than they did the lower class previously perceived to be most at risk.[79]

In blunt parables, people resorted to crime so they could enjoy the luxuries and thrills of the big city. Youths, perceived as the vanguard of the pleasure seekers, seemed most susceptible to moral disaster. "Damned Young," a 1926 *Collier's* feature on young prisoners by William G. Shepherd, made the case with typical indignation. The up-to-date, mostly purchased pleasures of ordinary youth—movies, flashy clothes, jazz music, joyrides, dancing—easily led to moral corruption and criminality. "As clean cut a young fellow as you could want to see plays a saxophone in the band of one of our penitentiaries. He knew all about saxophones," Shepherd explained; "he was that kind of a pleasure lover." His criminality proclaimed a bleak message about the dangers of the all-too-common reckless pursuit of pleasure. "This boy had been a thrill seeker," Shepherd warned, and in his search for thrills he tried the heroin that led him to shoot a man. But "there was something more than drugs that made him a criminal. It was kick hunting that set him wrong." Another boy had stolen an automobile and had "joy-ridden in it nightly . . . with a short-skirted, painted, sixteen-year-old, dance-loving, movie-mad 'sweetheart.'" "For gasoline, dance and movie money" the boy and a companion held up gasoline stations, eventually killing a police officer. Looking at him, Shepherd wrote, "you could see his life" and, he implied, the consequences of the new ethos of pleasure:

the jazz, the girls, the parking, the hip bottles, the movies, the latest foolish songs, the latest comic strips, the latest slang, the crazy hunt for thrills, the gasoline that must be got by hook or crook for the nightly rides; the new suits, with the widest possible trousers; the new neckties; the latest hats with the gayest ribbons, that must come from somebody's pockets while he idled away his daylight hours in pool halls, drug stores or moving-picture theatres. . . . He was the new American criminal personified; the laughing, twentieth-century, thrill-hunting killer of our great cities.[80]

"A larger measure of leisure and a larger sphere of experience in which to spend it," a Chicago editor concurred, "have brought new perils to bear upon youth."[81] Youth was "drunk on thrills and excitement," Richard Washburn Child less soberly agreed.[82] The new purchasable pleasures, the criminal showed, could draw ordinary people to moral disaster.

While youths often seemed at greatest risk other Americans were far from immune from this moral contamination. Indeed, writers regularly contended that it was middle-class parents' pursuit of pleasure that spurred youthful criminality. Child, tying extravagance to the vogue of irresponsibility, contended the crime problem resulted from "boys and girls who are neglected, who are ruined by being given too much money to spend and altogether too little responsibility." Carousing parents failed in their moral duty to rear children with attentive discipline. More generally, acquisitiveness and pleasure-seeking seemed to have rotted Americans' moral fiber. For Child, the subject of crime offered the opportunity for a jeremiad about "a nation with too much money to spend, too much ease, too much excitement and too much restlessness."[83] Couching his critique of the moral dangers of consumption in medical terms, a neurologist quoted in the *New York Times* attributed criminality to "the tremendous growth of pleasure automobiles and moving pictures in this country . . . and the phenomenal sweep of jazz across the country [that] have drained off far more nervous vitality from our people than those of other countries without putting anything in the way of energy into the reservoir of our national strength."[84]

The new pleasure ethos, leading so-called respectable people to immoral acts, seemed to erase conventional distinctions between good and evil and replace them with a pervasive moral ambiguity. At cabarets, leading citizens enjoyed the same salacious entertainment and illegal alcohol that thrilled their gangster counterparts.[85] Especially for supporters of prohibition, the respectable purchaser's complicity with violent bootleggers provided the sharpest evidence that the pursuit of pleasure had triggered a deeply disturbing moral breakdown even at the top of the social hierarchy. As a *Woman Citizen* editorial suggested, the moral equivalents of the bootlegger were "men and women who think of themselves as the better element in the community."[86]

A bitter 1932 editorial reprinted in *Literary Digest* lambasted the moral laxity that seemed to accompany the modern pursuit of pleasure. The editorial, originally in the *New York World-Telegram,* expressed outrage and despair after the discovery of the body of the kidnapped infant son of Charles Lindbergh and his wife. For many, the kidnapping and murder had come to symbolize American lawlessness. The crime seemed to result from the duplicity that had become an accepted part of modern life:

> Much of the trouble we are in harks back to the illusionment that people can be crooked in certain respects and straight in others, that collateral is better security than character, that cleverness brings greater reward than reliability, and that success is not the real thing unless it can be measured by money. . . . Indirectly the wicked, wanton, causeless crime can be attributed to the wise-cracking, jazzed-up, hypocritical age in which we live.[87]

Once again, criminal and respectable citizen merged in a single crooked figure. The problem was not merely the duplicity of the dangerous other but that the insider, too, had been rendered amoral by the values of the consumer society. A return to the unyielding standards of character that had supposedly prevailed in a more upstanding era seemed the only possibility of redemption. The heinous crime showed that cleverness, wisecracking, and self-gratification, the stylish, valued activities of the new era, could result in nothing but fatal hypocrisy and "illusionment."

Many of the aspects of the consumer society that troubled journalists and genre novelists also concerned F. Scott Fitzgerald, whose Jay Gatsby was a close cousin to Coe's Antonio Scarvak. Gatsby—defined by his palatial home, fabled parties, gleaming motorcar, and wardrobe of expensive suits and thick silk shirts—was not the man he at first seemed to be. This bootlegger was a master of "personality," that "unbroken series of successful gestures." Gatsby's mastery of the superficial inevitably brings narrator Nick Carraway, like others, under his spell:

> He smiled understandingly—much more than understandingly. It was one of those rare smiles with a quality of eternal reassurance in it, that

you may come across four or five times in life. It faced—or seemed to face—the whole external world for an instant, and then concentrated on *you* with an irresistible prejudice in your favor. It understood you just as far as you wanted to be understood, believed in you as you would like to believe in yourself, and assured you that it had precisely the impression of you that, at your best, you hoped to convey.

Gatsby ascended from dull ordinariness to Olympian social heights on a fragile structure of elaborate illusions. Realizing "the unreality of reality," the great man "sprang from his Platonic conception of himself." [88] It little matters that Gatsby's veneer of refinement is paper-thin, transparent to one who listened to his cautious speech or considered his supposed boyhood in the "Middle West" city of San Francisco. The hordes who flock to his celebrated parties accept him as a great man.

Gatsby discovers, however, that the insubstantiality of modern identity is incompatible with substantial, meaningful relationships. Gatsby's motivating vision of his beloved Daisy Buchanan, itself a dream, is shattered when confronted by the hollow woman who plays the game of illusions even more brilliantly than he. Daisy, the respectable, "careless" society woman, turns out to be no more ethical than the bootlegger. The danger of superficial style and personality was not merely that decent folk would allow scoundrels to infiltrate their ranks. Gatsby and his associates, like countless other underworld characters, warned that modern Americans, seduced by the sirens of the artificial, were headed toward the shoals of moral disaster.

SCIENCE · AND · INVENTION

TESTING THE CRIMINAL'S MIND

THE IDEA of setting the psychologist to work to aid the courts in handling criminals is now familiar to the general public through the popular detective story, the stage, and the moving picture. Strange to say, the police authorities are slow to take it up. The classic detective-story situation, where the amateur, despised and hated by the professional sleuth, outwits him and catches the criminal, seems here to have its justification. From the police standpoint, the psychologist is an amateur. The police want nothing to do with him; and yet he appears to be making good. And now our biggest police department—that of New York—has its laboratory where there are facilities for testing the mentality of persons arrested before they are brought to trial. Says a contributor to *The Journal of Heredity* (Washington, June):

whose business it is to handle such instruments. Simple questions are asked, and the subject's reasoning power and other abilities tested, not only by his answer, but by the time it takes him to evolve it. Such questions have been asked as:

"'What difference would it make to people if the price of coal went up to twice what it is now?'

"'Why do people send their children to school instead of making them work?'

"'Which would be worse: to have all the money in the world disappear or to have all the steel in the world disappear? Why?'

"One of the tests used is the Trabue Language Scale D, which is given below. The subject is asked to write one appropriate word in each blank, and is given seven minutes for the task:

4. We are going.........school.
10. I.........to school each day.
11. The.........plays.........her dolls all day.
21. The rude child does not.......many friends.
63. Hard.........makes.........tired.
27. It is good to hear.........voice.........friend.

"There are still plenty of people to ...

F

With your pencil make a dot over any one of these letters F G H I J, and a comma after the longest of these three words: boy mother girl. Then, if Christmas comes in March, make a cross right here...... but if not, pass along to the next question, and tell where the sun rises .... If you believe that Edison discovered America, cross out what you just wrote, but if it was some one else, put in a number to complete this sentence: "A horse has.......feet." Write *yes*, no matter whether China is in Africa or not......, and then give a wrong answer to this question: "How many days are there in the week?" .... Write any letter except *g* just after this comma, and then write *no* if 2 times 5 are 10....... Now, if Tuesday comes after Monday, make two crosses here.........; but if not, make a circle here .....or else a square here...... Be sure to make three crosses between these two names of boys: George...........Henry. Notice these two numbers: 3, 5. If iron is heavier than water, write the larger number here......, but if iron is lighter write the smaller number here........ Show by a cross when the nights are longer: in summer?...... in winter?...... Give the correct answer to this question: "Does water run uphill?".......... and repeat your answer here .... Do nothing here (5 + 7 = ...), unless you skipped the preceding question; but write the first letter of your first name and the last letter of your last name at the end of this line:

Tool for identifying potential criminals, printed in *Literary Digest* (24 June 1916). Inherent differences, the psychological testers believed, separated the lawbreaker from the good citizen. Other sample questions, purportedly to evaluate intelligence, measured adherence to conventional values about hard work, etiquette, filial duty, and gender. Crime in this view represented the threat to decent society from dangerous, different outsiders.

Leading our Gallery of Ill Fame is Korbi, one of the new crop of stick-up artists and burglars

Kaplan (Kid Dropper), who was dropped himself

Gangsters, old style and new. Illustrations, like these from *Collier's* (28 May 1927), often compared contemporary bad men to their old-time counterparts. The mug shots, of notorious "old-type gangster[s]," evoked an era when rough outsiders seemed to pose the greatest threat to social order. Now respectable society faced corruption from within—from attractive, well-dressed, smiling insiders.

Monk Eastman, old-type gangster, war vet and feud victim

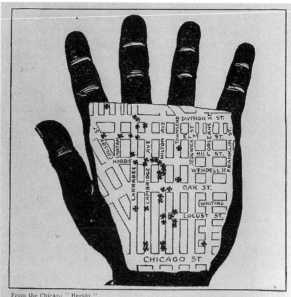

EACH BLACK CROSS A BLACK-HAND OUTRAGE.

Map of Chicago's "Little Italy," showing the scenes of bomb-throwings, shootings, and stabbings in the last eighteen months.

Another Abdication Needed
—Enright in the Milwaukee "Journal."

The shifting locations of urban crime. A 1915 cartoon (*Literary Digest*, 19 June) situated organized crime within a sharply delimited immigrant ghetto. In the following years, as a 1931 cartoon (*Literary Digest*, 11 July) suggest, middle-class Americans increasingly conceived of the gangster as operating in central, familiar urban territory. Seated on his downtown throne, the colossal racketeer personified developments at the very heart of the corporate-centered modern city.

The lavish Paradise nightclub, featured in *Broadway*. Crime movies introduced audiences to a sensuous realm of urban leisure.

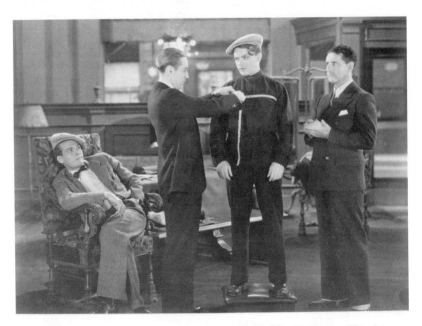

The young gangster (James Cagney in *The Public Enemy*), still in his working-class cap, being fitted for the tuxedo that will mark his rise. The underworld dramatized modern society's promise of self-transformation through spending.

The transformation of the working-class roughneck (Spencer Tracy in *Quick Millions*) into the elegant man-about-town. Audiences were invited to consider the social meanings of modern stylishness.

Making it big in *Scarface*. *Top:* The ambitious hoodlum (Paul Muni) sees the rewards of success. The boss's moll (Karen Morley) is the most desirable prize in an array of expensive commodities. *Bottom:* Raw power—and a flashy new suit—win her over.

Male-female relations were among the genre's central concerns. Spencer Tracy played the convicted gangleader released "to become a man again—for one night only!" The woman who waited—or did she?—was Bette Davis.

Underworld romances dramatized the pleasures and perils of modern sexual liberalism. "You're just a new kind of man in a new kind of world," the society girl (Norma Shearer in *A Free Soul*) tells heart-throb gangleader Ace (Clark Gable, in a role that propelled him to stardom as a romantic lead). Only after dwelling on her satisfaction as his mistress does the film show the cost of hedonism—Ace turns out to be a sadistic brute.

Tom Powers (James Cagney in *The Public Enemy*) smashes a grapefruit into the face of his nagging mistress (Mae Clark). Domination of women was an important part of the underworld fantasy of male power.

Posing as a moll, the virtuous young woman (Mary Astor in *Dressed to Kill*) plots to avenge her framed brother. The new sexual liberalism, the genre suggested, brought women considerable power, which might be used to manipulate weak men.

A model relationship in *Scarface*. *Left:* Cesca (Ann Dvorak) seduces Rinaldo (George Raft). *Right:* Their subsequent marriage and idealized domestic life validate her aggressiveness.

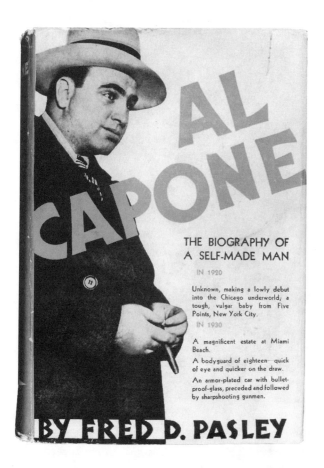

THE BIOGRAPHY OF
A SELF-MADE MAN

IN 1920

Unknown, making a lowly debut
into the Chicago underworld; a
tough, vulgar baby from Five
Points, New York City.

IN 1930

A magnificent estate at Miami
Beach.

A bodyguard of eighteen quick
of eye and quicker on the draw.

An armor-plated car with bullet-
proof-glass, preceded and followed
by sharpshooting gunmen.

BY FRED D. PASLEY

Publications of every sort capitalized on fascination with Al Capone in his heyday. Much of this literature, including Fred Pasley's popular biography (1930) and the cheap *Al Capone on the Spot* (1931), simultaneously celebrated and condemned a *public* enemy found to bear an uncanny resemblance to ordinary, non-criminal Americans. Businessman, competitor, patriarch, spender, playboy: each aspect of Capone's identity seemed to illuminate the lives of other urban Americans.

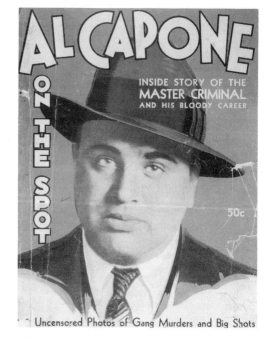

AL CAPONE
ON THE SPOT

INSIDE STORY OF THE
MASTER CRIMINAL
AND HIS BLOODY CAREER

50c

Uncensored Photos of Gang Murders and Big Shots

4 *Bad Men and Dangerous Women*

An advertisement for *The Public Enemy* exploited one of the genre's most compelling themes: "Come prepared to see the worst of women and the cruelest of men—as they really are!" Illustrations of the stars—handsome, stern-faced men and smiling blonde beauties—fleshed out the claim that the film was "a vital throbbing document of life today."[1] This promise of timely illumination of even the darkest corners of male and female nature pervaded the invented underworld. Countless images sought to distill masculinity and femininity down to their basic elements. Ambition, desperation, bravery and cowardice, strength and weakness, romance, sexuality, violence: these were the fundamental traits laid bare. Seeing them, the inventors of the gangster suggested, Americans could indeed understand men and women as they really were. The gangster illuminated meanings of masculinity in a society that seemed to deny the virtues on which traditional conceptions of male honor had been based. His wives and girlfriends brought to life a range of roles women might assume now that the relatively inflexible gender ideology of the past no longer seemed to circumscribe women's social, economic, and sexual aspirations. Loving and fighting, helping and competing, these men and women of the underworld explored the prospects for new relationships between the sexes in the modern world.

The creators of this genre were intensely concerned with the meaning of masculinity in modern urban society. In focusing on masculinity they reflected a cultural preoccupation whose origins extended back into the last two decades of the nineteenth century. The longevity of the simmering unease about masculine roles resulted from the gradual, incremental nature of the changes that fueled it. Broad economic and social transformations, pulsing outward from the large cities, had rocked the traditional foundations of middle-class masculine virtue. Independence and self-determination, linked since the Revolution to economic autonomy, now seemed beyond the grasp of men immersed in the structures of a newly complex corporate society. Few corporate employees could expect the control of their own destinies once enjoyed—perhaps more in memory than in fact—by their fathers or grandfathers. Traditional notions of masculine virtue clashed with the prospect of a career of taking orders from superiors. Moreover, in the new corporations qualities that seemed feminine, like cooperation and personableness, had become crucial to men's career advancement. Outside the work place old standards of masculinity faced similar threats. Women's mounting political activism, starting with reform campaigns and culminating in the attainment of suffrage, meant that politics was no longer a distinctly male domain. Perhaps equally important, the new scale of urban life put the manly distinction of the mantle of leadership beyond the reach of all but a few. Many American men lamented that the leading citizens of a fading village America, transported to the city, had become faces in the crowd.[2]

When the middle-class husband returned from the public world to his home he often perceived his position to be transformed there as well. Though the Victorians remembered by Americans in the twenties were two-dimensional foils, the caricatures did suggest the vastness of change in familial norms. Nineteenth-century middle-class marriage ideals emphasized affection and consensual decision-making, but they also conceived of the family as a hierarchical unit with ultimate authority reserved for male heads of households. The balance between hierarchical discipline and egalitarian companionship shifted around the turn of the century. By the 1920s, advice literature endorsed the ideal of companionate marriage which no longer recognized the ascendant authority of the male head of household. Moreover, familial authority in general eroded as the institutions and external experts of mass society—advertisers, commercial entertainment, and bureaucratically administered schools, to name a few—came to influence every facet of daily life. These changes in family life, as in so many other aspects of life, seemed most far-reaching in major urban centers.[3]

Most men probably welcomed the benefits of corporate employment and more egalitarian family roles.[4] Nevertheless the creation of new male roles, and the abandonment of old ones, was a wrenching process. Beginning around 1890 the resulting unresolved tensions fueled an urgent cultural discourse about the meanings of masculinity. Jeremiads found a particularly receptive audience. Middle-class Americans fastened on the warnings of many publicists, Theodore Roosevelt the most prominent among them, that modern society stifled individual achievement, promoted indolence and dependence, and, in the process, rendered men less than fully masculine. It was in the late nineteenth century that the pejorative "overcivilized" entered Americans' vocabulary in critiques of the feminizing influences of urban life. By the first decade of the new century Roosevelt and others castigated the softened, feminized male as the symbol of American weakness and decay.[5]

Some writers used the gangster to personify this declension. In the context of the erosion of the foundations of masculine virtue, the gangster occasionally confirmed the potential for male weakness in modern society and provided a powerful negative model of unmanliness. Male weakness ran rampant in the underworld. "The typical desperado preying upon jewelers, payroll messengers and women arrayed in strings of jewels is a poor kind of man," a *New York Times* writer scoffed.[6] The gangster's urbanity situated contemporary unmanliness in the city. Michael Fiaschetti, a former police detective writing in *Collier's,* dismissed one New York burglary gang leader as "a poor thing in all ways—a little, undernourished weakling."[7] Such weaklings required drugs to substitute for the manly bravery they so obviously lacked. Another New York crook, according to Fiaschetti, was "an undersized cocaine addict of a gangster."[8] A *Saturday*

Evening Post writer similarly seized on drug use to show that criminals were unmanfully dependent. "Nearly every" house prowler, he
explained, "is doped up with narcotics—a shot of coke or a sniff of
snow before he tackles a job—or he may tank up with some of the
present-day poison called hooch."[9] Deprived of their drugs, most
crooks reportedly could not stand the strain of police interrogation.[10]
Such victims of incapacitating nervous disorders seemed especially
unmanly because, since the nineteenth century, debilitating ner-
vousness had received enormous attention as a predominantly female
malady that seemed to confirm women's frailty and need of protection.[11] Dependent, nerve-ridden gangsters were poor excuses for men.

What gave the unmanly gangster alarming relevance as a cultural
symbol was not only his urbanity but his status as an enthusiastic
consumer. In many accounts, gangsters' effeminacy was manifested
by the stylishness they shared with men throughout urban society.
Since the middle of the nineteenth century, shopping had been a female task, and consumer indulgence had seemed a feminine trait.[12]
The gangster presented stylish swells as men so immersed in a world
of women that their gender identity had become uncertain. In the
process the inventors of the gangster provided grist for Americans'
anxious fascination with womanly men during this period of transformation in gender roles.[13] The underworld patrons of one nightclub, in a novel by Charles Francis Coe, were "overdressed and be-
jeweled almost like women."[14] A mobster in another account was a
"he-dainty."[15] Grizzled old yegg Whitey Igow, the subject of a nostalgic *Collier's* piece, dismissed a batch of finely dressed and manicured
young crooks as womanlike "cake eaters." One had "large, clear blue
eyes, soft wavy hair and the complexion women would go broke buying."[16] Compounding concerns about a decay of masculine fortitude
with concerns about the moral consequences of consumer indulgence, the inventors of the gangster used the underworld to condemn
the spending lives of his upperworld brethren.

Occasionally the disintegration of masculinity seemed to extend
into the sphere of sexuality. Voyeuristic portrayals of the underworld
hinted that male homosexuality was rampant in the modern city. In
both the film *Little Caesar* and the W. R. Burnett novel on which it
was based, Rico's aversion to women and devotion to his male pal—
who, significantly, deserts him for a woman—carried distinct homo-

erotic undertones.[17] "The New York gangster," wrote James C. Young, linking sexual deviance to consumerism, "frequently . . . is a pronounced degenerate. He wears flashy clothing and gaudy jewelry."[18] Other writers were more explicit. In Dashiell Hammett's 1930 novel *The Maltese Falcon*, the sallow-faced boy gunman is involved in a homosexual relationship with his effeminate criminal boss. Hammett draws a sharp contrast between the boy and virile Sam Spade, the enthusiastically heterosexual hero.[19] These presentations reflected prevailing understandings of homosexuality as inversion— male homosexuals were men acting out deep desires to be women— and extended the cultural use of the image of the homosexual, begun around the turn of the century and intensified after the Great War, as a powerful negative symbol of male surrender to female values. The "degenerate" gangster illuminated troubling cultural territory disturbingly proximate to the lives of men who spent freely, pursued pleasure, and lived in the city.[20]

Cosmopolitan contributor O. O. McIntyre summarized much of the underworld's indictment of modern urban men in a 1931 article, appropriately entitled "Bad Man," that compared contemporary crooks to the romantic outlaws of the previous century, desperadoes like the James brothers and Billy the Kid. Among the modern-day gangsters, according to McIntyre, "few have the natural bravado of the outlaws of the western plains—healthy, red-corpuscled men, quick on the draw and usually comparatively 'square shooters.'" Instead, "the 1931-model gunman is more often than not a chicken-breasted Broadway gigolo type—tubercular or otherwise diseased" who was dependent on alcohol and other drugs, traveled only in the safety of an armored car, machine-gunned his victims in the back, and was "at heart a miserable coward and a 'snitch.'" Perhaps worse, McIntyre suggested, modern bad men were stylish, pleasure-seeking, and overly sensitive—in a word, effeminate:

> They might be haberdashery clerks, song writers, song-and-dance men or any one of the slight and sleekly dandified fauna so peculiar to Broadway. Gaudy tips of kerchiefs flounce out of breast pockets; they swing canes; ankles are bespatted and hats are worn with a Prince of Wales dip.
>
> All are touched by a mawkish sentimentality. They have mama complexes and cry over little-ivy-clad-cottage songs.

For entertainment the typical "bad man in spats with a lisp" especially enjoyed a night-club performer who was "one of those female-impersonating and pathological hybrids we used to know as 'sissies' but who in the Broadway patois are 'pansies.'" No longer a red-blooded he-man, the gangster was indeed a "bad man," part of a netherworld in which old distinctions of gender did not exist.[21] A nation that once produced heroic red-blooded outlaws now put forth a sickly breed of effeminate cowards who bore disturbing resemblance to an array of standard urban types.

The kind of hand wringing represented by the image of the effeminate gangster was never the predominant cultural response to the fading of old male virtues. Instead, as manly independence became harder to achieve, American men beginning in the 1890s developed new standards of masculinity that sought to redefine the differences between men and women. The new standards celebrated what Theodore Roosevelt called "the great fighting, masterful virtues." Cultural spokesmen ranging from Roosevelt to Owen Wister to the founders of the Boy Scouts of America lauded aggressiveness, passionateness, and even a readiness for violence as the salutary traits that separated virile men from the weak sphere of women and "sissies." Proponents of imperialism, "muscular Christianity," and the vogue of bodybuilding equated strength and character and fueled the national obsession with forcefulness. As E. Anthony Rotundo has pointed out, the fighting virtues did not represent characteristics newly ascribed to men. Rather, they represented a revaluation of long-recognized "male" traits; destructive impulses in need of repression had become defining badges of virility.[22]

It is perhaps testimony to the intensity of men's need to develop affirming standards of masculinity that they settled on ones that so poorly fit with the actual circumstances of their lives. In 1922 novelist Sinclair Lewis offered a telling lampoon: for George Babbitt, the weak-willed, small-time realtor who dreamed of being a pioneer, successfully parking his automobile was "a virile adventure masterfully executed."[23] Men celebrated aggression at the same time that the ongoing organization of society rendered aggression increasingly counterproductive. When projected onto an international level, the new standards contributed to a war that ultimately brought not manly martial cohesion but divisive debates over the congruity of democracy and empire. Even though the primary thrust of economic consolidation was to limit competition, the valorization of struggle might provide a compelling rationalization for the conduct of corporations in the marketplace. But it provided little practical guidance for individual success within the corporation, which rewarded cooperation and personableness. Perhaps it was this disjuncture, this failure to develop cultural forms that adequately ordered the changing social experiences of men's lives, that underlaid men's enthusiasm for leisure activities, especially spectator sports and adventure fiction, that transported them from the feminized workaday world to idealized arenas of manly combat. Gridiron contests reinforced a conception of virile masculinity constantly eroded by the mundane realities of everyday lives.[24]

The gangster often resembled the other heroes of popular entertainment, for he was an exemplar of the fighting virtues. Many accounts trumpeted the durability of masculine values rather than confirmed their decay. No sickly, effeminate weakling, he was instead a tough guy whose position resulted from a commanding physical presence and exceptional prowess in the various arts of violence. Fictional accounts routinely explained that criminal bosses kept their subordinates in line with threats, glares, and fearsome punches. Challengers wilted in the face of awesome violence.[25] Louis Ricarno, the protagonist of *Doorway to Hell,* uses the threat of violence to persuade reluctant minor underworld bosses to allow him to put bootlegging "on a big business basis." Louis's small stature, shared by the gangsters played by James Cagney and Edward G. Robinson, adds to the heroic quality of his physical intimidation. When one boss continues to resist and pulls a pistol on him, Louis directs his attention to the machine guns he has placed and snaps, "Put that toy away—it's too small." Equipped with the bigger gun, Louis asserts his manhood as he consolidates his reign. His use of the technology of violence is an extension of the fierce aggressiveness that derived from his physical robustness.[26]

Contrary to the image of nerve-racked drug addicts, gangsters in many accounts possessed the coolness under pressure that complemented physical aggressiveness in the panoply of fighting virtues. Little Caesar's rise to gang leadership is in part a function of his implacability in the face of danger. While the vanquished former leader frets about being caught after a robbery that ended in murder, Rico calmly counts the loot and reassures the rest of the gang.[27] Bold gang-sters looked forward eagerly to the occasional mayhem that accom-panied their work and faced their own violent deaths with manly fortitude. In the Jack Lait novel *Put on the Spot,* the victims of a set-up modeled on the St. Valentine's Day Massacre react to their fate with such courage that the executioner has difficulty carrying out the deed:

> These damned rats acted so like men! He couldn't help hating them, but he couldn't help admiring them. No matter how badly a man needs killing, it is disconcerting if he doesn't . . . cooperate. He might at least show yellow so that there would be some pleasure in plugging him. He might whine and make a guy sore so that he would shoot in anger. But this mob!. . . . These Gorios knew how to die.[28]

The underworld served up male fantasies where masculine prow-ess brought awesome power. While women and weak men were ex-pected to exert commanding influence over only the small sphere of the home, if anywhere, strong men could determine the actions of multitudes of lesser persons throughout society. At its most benign this influence was apparent in the deferential treatment accorded gang leaders by the people around them. Illustrations of gangsters in cabarets often showed them magisterially seated and surrounded by admiring women and fawning servants.[29] Throughout *Playing Around* police officers offer Chester Morris matches or light his ciga-rettes, prompting an impressed young woman to ask, "Everybody knows you, don't they . . . ?"[30] Usually the big shot's power, of course, was not so innocuous: the inventors of the gangster endowed their subjects with a marvelous capacity for evil. In recognition of the ap-peal of these fantasies of male power, movie advertisements made especially succinct cases for the gangster's extraordinary abilities. "By his order men disappeared over night . . . gang wars started and ended. For Rico lived hard, ruled hard, fought hard," an advertise-ment for *Little Caesar* proclaimed.[31] "When he commands, the world obeys. Life, love, happiness are in his power," intoned an advertise-ment for *The Ruling Voice.* A tight close-up of the man's face super-imposed over an urban skyline indicated that his realm was, if not the world, at least a very large city. "Men are my prey! Women are my toys! None can live against my will," the villain proclaimed in another ad.[32] "He Stops at Nothing!" announced a somewhat less hyperbolic ad for *The Public Enemy:* "No man, no woman, no law, no power can change his mind."[33]

The presentation of the gangster as an exemplar of robust masculinity was most forceful in the roles played by the star of *The Public Enemy,* James Cagney. Cagney made his debut on film, as a bootlegger, in the 1930 *Sinners' Holiday* and first earned critical acclaim as a tough, wise-cracking gang lieutenant in *Doorway to Hell* the same year. His first leading role, as Tom Powers in *The Public Enemy,* catapulted him into stardom. Fans raved, and Warner Brothers, in customary Hollywood deference to success, offered him in variations on the same character, often as a gangster but also as a cabby, boxer, sailor, and G-man, in a rapid succession of profitable movies.[34] Cagney's characters were independent, confident, defiant of authority, and resolutely urban. His rapid-fire delivery and expressive face lent them an air of commanding intelligence. At the same time, his intensely kinetic acting style gave the characters an exuberant, intimidating physical presence.[35]

In Cagney moviegoers could see a model of pugnacious, swaggering masculinity. His insolent wit is always ready. Badgered by a police captain in *Doorway to Hell,* Cagney defiantly dismisses him, snapping, "I wouldn't plead guilty to having an appetite."[36] Cagney almost always seems physically tense and on the verge of a fight, and when conflicts do occur he rarely fails to rise to the occasion. Rivals soon regret their challenges to his authority. When a gang associate pulls a gun on him in *Lady Killer,* a 1933 comedy-adventure, Cagney grabs the man by the collar, pushes him down, and snarls, "Put that away or I'll jam it down your throat." Cagney prevails.[37] Later in the film he is in Los Angeles, on the lam from his underworld past. In need of a job, he is recruited by a studio agent "looking for types— new faces—tough guys for a gangster picture." After landing a role as an extra he incurs the director's wrath for failing to deliver a realistic-looking punch in a fight with a police officer. The cop, of course, is discovered to be unconscious.[38] Cagney's abilities give him great power, and he earns the respect and loyalty of those around him. In *Mayor of Hell,* also released in 1933, he plays a gangster and machine politician who has received a sinecure as the boss of a reformatory. Upon discovering the atrocious conditions there he bursts into the office of his surprised patron and demands reform. "I'll tell you what I want and I'm gonna get it or else," he exclaims in what could have been a generic gangster motto. When the boss's assistant attempts to interrupt, Cagney smashes his hand into the man's face and pushes him away. Again, the gangster was a powerful man who got his way.[39]

However compelling his performance, Cagney, like many of his underworld peers, dramatized a dilemma at the center of the new cultural constructions of masculinity: the irreconcilability of the fighting virtues with important aspects of men's actual lives. This was the dilemma that fueled Americans' passion for cultural representations of idealized, impossible male virility. Yet the images themselves suggested that the fighting virtues were unserviceable in the modern world. Independent masculine bravado seemed incompatible with modernity's great achievement, the efficient organization. In *The Public Enemy* the gang became more of an affectionate club than a passionless corporation. The ties that bound were of fraternity, not managerial rationality. Stenographers and filing cabinets were not to be found. Unlike his better organized—and less virile—fictional counterparts, Cagney relied upon his powerful fists and trusty gun rather than the efficient technology of hired killers.[40]

The inventors of the gangster thus relegated true masculinity to a sanctuary free of the feminizing influences of mundane modern society. In these accounts the underworld was a special male environment much like the gridiron, the cockpit, or the cattle ranges of western novels. Gangs in this version were exclusive clubs chartered on fraternity, bravery, and physical prowess. Members flouted the feminizing influences of the culture around them. Drinking, gambling, fighting, and oaths of unending loyalty were the rituals of a simultaneously attractive and dangerous mythic male world. But it was an unrealistic world that could imagine little if any role for women. The male world of the gang was a regular theme of *Saturday Evening Post* writer Charles Francis Coe. Like most regular *Post* contributors, Coe wrote in a single broad genre—in his case, the male adventure. Readers who started a Coe short story, serial novel, or even news article could anticipate a stirring tale about boxers, machine politicians, or, most often, gangsters, all of whom acted boldly in gritty spheres dominated by men. In a scene in the serial novel *Pay-Off* Coe offered a typical account of the gang as a sanctuary of male values. Holed up in a secluded hideaway, members revel in masculine pleasures. "There was always a card game in progress in this stag apartment, and during these card games the liquor would flow freely," Coe wrote.

Boasting, profanity, and competition were regular parts of this special world. As if recalling the primary rule of a boyhood tree house, Coe wrote that "there were inviolable rules against women sharing knowledge of [the hideaway's] location."[41] In another Coe novel the protagonist sends his wife and children away from his mansion and surrounds himself with gang underlings in anticipation of an impending attack. Free of feminine oversight, they drink, gamble, curse, smoke noxious cigars, soil the rugs, and let dirty dishes stack up around them. These were the vaguely rebellious acts inspired by a defiant working-class male ethic. Modern bourgeois consumerist values seemed incompatible with aggressive masculinity, even to its idealizers. Hardly he-dainties, these are men in a man's world, but it is clearly a man's world that could only exist in a few mythic realms.[42]

Despite the frequent presentation of the gang as a homosocial mythic male group, women did play integral roles in the gangster genre. At the same time that the genre dramatized the challenges facing men as men it explored the changes in women's roles since the late nineteenth century. The gangsters' female accomplices, mothers, wives, girlfriends, and casual lovers illustrated a range of possibilities for women in modern society. Journalists, fiction writers, and filmmakers did not restrict themselves, of course, to dispassionate observation of social phenomena; their works occasionally lauded and more frequently condemned the recent evolution of gender roles. In the process the inventors of the gangster attempted to fashion a new set of values to order women and men in modern urban society.

The gangster genre responded to the shifts in women's roles that had occurred since the late nineteenth century. Women's political activity elicited attention, and observers often noted sharp breaks between the behavior they saw and conventional notions of womanhood. National women's suffrage resulted in part from the marches and other flamboyant demonstrations of militant activists who used the mass media to publicize their defiance of the accepted norms of femininity. Militant suffragism overlapped with the feminist movement that emerged in the 1910s. In the late nineteenth century a small group of proto-feminist scholars had begun to undermine the intellectual foundation of the dominant ideology of separate spheres. In the 1910s feminism, with its broad-based critique of cultural and institutional limitations on women's opportunities, emerged as a widely discussed movement whose concerns ranged far beyond those of the older and more conservative woman's movement. While most suffragists hoped to extend the supposed innate, unique qualities of "woman" into the public world, feminists sought to obliterate the monolithic conception of "woman" by opening up political, economic, and sexual opportunities that would allow for the self-development of individual women. Agitation for causes like accessible birth control, legal equality with men, and disarmament highlighted the contested, changing notions of gender in public life.[43]

Women's changing participation in paid work and vocations also received considerable attention. The rate of increase in the percentage of women in paid employment dropped sharply after 1910, and the 1920s saw a tightening of opportunities for women in many high-status professions. Nevertheless, working women in the 1920s attained a new visibility and the public scrutiny that accompanied it. Much of this cultural prominence resulted from shifts in the types of women who worked and in the kinds of work they did. The proportion of employed women in clerical, managerial, sales, or professional jobs jumped from 18 percent in 1900 to 44 percent in 1930. Many of these highly visible jobs were filled by middle-class and married women whose predecessors a generation earlier had been much less likely to work outside the household. Female professionals, especially the few in predominantly male fields like law and medicine, became powerful symbols of women's new roles even as their own career prospects dimmed.[44]

According to many observers, women's physical appearances testified to the breaking of old barriers. Flapper fashions, even if more publicized than worn, were widely perceived to be a rebellion against conventional, confining styles. Cut for independence and activity, they celebrated a youthful, boyish aesthetic rather than the dependent femininity of old. Rejecting traditional notions of female passivity, the flapper highlighted women's heightened activity in the public world.[45] It was in the mass media that the new woman was omnipresent. "The new movie woman," Mary Ryan writes, "exuded above all a sense of physical freedom—unrestrained movement, confident gait, abounding energy—the antithesis of the controlled, quiet, tight-kneed poses of [earlier] heroines."[46]

Alongside the image of the new woman in the public world, women's changing expectations about marriages, families, and homes suggested a fundamental reorientation of their private lives. Popular ideas about marriage paralleled the shift in advice literature that occurred from the late nineteenth century to the 1920s. Middle-class women and men gradually abandoned the nineteenth-century ideals which had emphasized hierarchical gender-segregated obligations, innate female moral purity, and the function of the home as a redemptive sanctuary in a corrupt world. The rhetoric of courtship shifted in emphasis from love's spiritual and uplifting qualities to the pleasure it brought, and marriage and home life became similarly geared to gratification. To many alarmed observers, sober discipline seemed to have given way to modern hedonistic consumerism. The changes were most pronounced for women, whose special moral status had been intimately bound up with the older function of the home. Modern women from modern homes seemed to have renounced their most important role. Lending credence to this conclusion were rising divorce rates which, despite the rising marriage rate and declining age at first marriage, indicated to many observers that women were becoming alarmingly independent. So did the often-noticed, steadily expanding urban population of single women who opted not to live in a family setting.[47]

Though the inventors of the gangster responded to all these changes in women's lives, the modern transformation in sexual behavior received the most worried attention. In a process that began around the new century's start, accelerated in its second decade, and received greatest notice in the 1920s, some Americans developed a more liberal code of sexual morality that contrasted sharply with the stern absolutes of late nineteenth-century middle-class mores. Contrary to later stereotypes, most respectable Americans in the late nineteenth century regarded sexual drives of both men and women as legitimate, but they insisted that the only acceptable setting for sexuality, especially for women, was within marriage and the private home. Sexual expression increasingly occurred beyond the boundaries of home and marriage for urban middle-class men and women who followed the lead of bolder working-class counterparts. Because the old norms had weighed most heavily on women, the new patterns were most apparent among them. Observers correctly realized that the feminists of the 1910s who agitated for "sex rights" were the vanguard of a much larger movement. By the twenties a new morality had been taken up by a vastly larger group of women: teenage girls and young adults who regarded necking, petting, and, to a lesser extent, premarital intercourse as normal, appropriate behavior.[48]

Simultaneous with the changes in private activity, sexuality increasingly became a public phenomenon for middle-class urban Americans as it had been for working-class youths since the late nineteenth century. Media reticence faded, most rapidly in the 1910s, as discussions of the new behavior and relatively forthright campaigns against venereal disease and prostitution became commonplace. In the 1910s and 1920s, commercial establishments that celebrated heterosexual expressiveness, like dance halls and cabarets, proliferated and became accepted among respectable city dwellers. Movies, by the twenties the preferred entertainment of middle-class as well as working-class Americans, similarly cultivated and reaped the profits of the new sexual liberalism. The messages of the movie screen were evident on the street, where changes among women seemed most profound. To observers, whether sympathetic or alarmed, a host of suggestive activities adopted by middle-class women by the 1920s—smoking, public drinking, jazz dancing, wearing flapper dresses—symbolized the apparently carefree sensuality of the new age.[49]

The inventors of the gangster occasionally suggested that these changes in women's lives were unacceptable to strong, authoritative men. Women's apparent independence and sexual aggressiveness seemed to represent a serious threat to the male power already at risk in modern society. Outside their homes, gangsters reveled in the pleasures of the new sexual culture, but within the confines of the family many were obsessed that wives, sisters, and daughters abide by strict traditional codes of behavior. Male power seemed to rest on patriarchal domination, and some portrayals of the gangster offered a fantasy of that power intact in modern society. Few wives of gangsters ventured outside their homes to work. Male concern about, and regulation of, the sexual behavior of female family members received more attention. In Charles Francis Coe's serial novel *The Other Half,* Antonio Scarvak admires his wife's submissiveness and domesticity, particularly her "careful and industrious" homemaking, but his greatest satisfaction is that "when he held Rosy in his arms he knew he had the exclusive rights." Antonio's own promiscuity with modern, wanton women sets his control of Rosy in sharp relief.[50] Though young Louis Beretti's family lives in a vice-ridden slum, the illicit pleasures of which he regularly enjoys, he ensures his sisters' chastity more securely "than if they had been immured in iron cages on the top of distant mountains." "A woman's place is in the home," he teaches them forcefully.[51]

For the most part, however, the gangster genre offered little reason to believe that strong patriarchs could or should continue to force women into nineteenth-century roles. Even Coe suggested that Scarvak's success depended on Rosy's monumental stupidity.[52] In a 1930 *Liberty* short story a gangster father hopes to keep his daughter, "a white-faced, raven-haired virgin," safely at home but is reduced to ineffectual fretting about her "no good" beau.[53] The futility of the effort to control women was apparent in the inability of *Scarface's* Tony Camonte to keep his sister Cesca from the seductive world of urban nightlife, revealing fashions, and modern romance. As played by Ann Dvorak, Cesca is a sultry, flirtatious, sexually eager eighteen-year-old modern. Early in the movie Tony chases off a young man who had been kissing her in the hallway of their tenement. Commanded to "do what I say," Cesca retorts "Sure, and never have any fun." Later Tony is infuriated upon seeing her dancing, literally cheek to cheek, in the lush Paradise nightclub. Cesca's revealing dress and evident pleasure compound his anger. Regarding his flapper sister, the criminal is a defender of conservative gender values:

> *Tony:* Next time I catch you in a place like that again I'll kill you.
> *Cesca:* I'll do what I want, same as you. Understand?
> *Tony:* You're gonna stay home. Understand? . . . Running around with others! Letting them hold you! Letting them look at you! Dressing up like that for fellas to see!
> *Cesca:* What I do with fellows is my business!
> [Tony slaps her angrily.]

Despite this menacing violence Tony is unable to control his strong willed, sexually aggressive sister. Moreover, *Scarface* casts this defender of traditional morality as an incestuous monster. Her mother warns Cesca, "To him you're just another girl." The would-be patriarch's motivation is not morality, but sexual jealousy.[54] As important to male power as confining women to traditional roles seemed to be, these accounts suggested, such control was impossible and undesirable in modern society.

In their explorations of the interactions of men and women, most of the inventors of the gangster acknowledged that changes in gender behavior, though perhaps subject to modification, were irreversible. They focused on changes in women's behavior, but their purpose was neither to show men how to force women to follow old rules nor to persuade women to take up the dress and actions of stereotypical straitlaced Victorian predecessors. Rather, their portrayals of the underworld represented an effort to understand the new meanings of "male" and "female" and, based on that understanding, to shape men's and women's behavior. Often drawing on traditional notions of masculinity and femininity, the inventors of the gangster attempted to frame a new set of values appropriate to their modern urban society.

An advertising campaign for the 1933 Warner Brothers' melodrama *20,000 Years in Sing Sing* made clear the assumption that underlay much of the genre's discussion of new relations between men and women: expressive heterosexuality was a normal and even essential aspect of human behavior. The posters and newspaper advertisements for the film, an adaptation of warden Lewis Lawes's popular book, indicate the extent to which observations about male-female relationships suffused the genre. On the screen Lawes's account of his experiences working in the correctional system was transformed, one ad promised, into "a throbbing human love story." Ads featured remarks by Spencer Tracy, a convicted gangleader, to Bette Davis about such pressing concerns as the effects on an imprisoned man of her low necklines, tight dresses, and fragrant perfume. The film validated the importance of sexual behavior by considering the effects of its absence: "What happens to desperate men when love is locked out of their lives? What becomes of the love-starved women who wait—and the women who can't wait? Now at last you can get the answers to daring questions you must have asked yourself." Sexuality, the questions announced, was central to, and even constitutive of, individual identity. Released on furlough, Tracy, who as a convict was merely a number, "becomes a man again—for one night only!" Reformation or its absence no longer provided the most compelling theme for a drama about a convict. Instead, the central concern was the pernicious consequence of forced abstinence.[55]

The gangster genre's most insistent message about the new relationship between men and women was that openly expressive sexuality had become a nearly ubiquitous element of modern urban life.

Cabarets, penthouse apartments, and other paradigmatic big-city settings were infused with a sexual charge that energized behavior, dress, and entertainment. Men made bold advances, often successfully; women flirted and wore sensuous, revealing clothing. "The Payoff," a short story in the family magazine *Liberty,* typified the mass media's interest in the literal throwing off of old strictures in the new urban environment. At a fashionable downtown nightclub, a young woman from the audience begins a sensuous dance, finds her dress "too tight around her thighs," strips it off, and finishes in her lingerie. All the while "the music twitched and throbbed like the hands of a lover around her." [56]

The underworld showed that the new expressive sexuality offered excitement and gratification. Hollywood provided the most vivid accounts. So customary was the genre's attention to male-female relationships that critics lambasted those few releases that failed to present sufficiently "the love interest." [57] Trumpeting sexual themes, movie advertising usually depicted at least one attractive young woman in addition to the stern villain-hero. [58] The films often lived up to the billing, with characters venturing far beyond customary boundaries of sexual morality. Before the institution of Hollywood's Production Code Agreement on self-censorship in 1934, scenes in numerous movies carried unmistakable suggestions of non-marital sexual relations. Urban apartments seemed the appropriate settings for this relatively explicit sexuality. In the 1929 film *Weary River,* the gangster's girlfriend, in skimpy lingerie, listens dreamily as the romantic protagonist plays the piano in his art deco apartment. A close-up emphasizes her dark lips. She kneels before him and they kiss passionately; in the background the camera reveals his inviting bedroom. [59] A scene in *The Public Enemy* shows a pajama-clad James Cagney breakfasting with his mistress. They argue, and he soon spends his time with a voluptuous woman, played by Jean Harlow, whom he has picked up on the street. [60] In *Lady Killer* Cagney has stalked angrily from a gang meeting to his adjacent bedroom. Turning to a moll dressed in a loose house robe, another member commands, "Go take care of him—we need him." Her ministrations suffice to delay Cagney's departure from the gang. [61]

The inventors of the gangster, joining a widespread discussion, focused much of their exploration of modern sexuality on the behavior of women from respectable backgrounds. In an inversion of earlier stereotypes, ethnic, working-class women represented whatever sexual restraint persisted in modern society. Young women from middle- and upper-class backgrounds seemed most bold. In *Louis Beretti*, for example, Louis's working-class Italian sisters are models of chastity, but the daughter of "a good family in Boston" is his eager sexual initiator, and the daughter of "the Westchester Pedersens" dreams of being his moll.[62] In the novel *Little Caesar*, Olga Stassoff, the girlfriend of a gang member and gigolo, warns him off providing services beyond dancing: "Just do your stuff and leave it at that. I'm on to these society women. I know what they want."[63] Films regularly offered the same message, that the gangster was powerfully attractive to young women from "good" families.[64] In *Scarface* the haughty blonde moll played by Karen Morley is drawn to Tony Camonte, even though she deplores his brutish manners and atrocious taste.[65] The frequent use of blonde actresses to portray gangsters' molls—Joan Blondell and Jean Harlow were regulars—confirmed that "nonethnic" women were in the vanguard of the new sexuality. "The Payoff," the short story in which dancer Marie Starr flings off her tootight dress, elaborated on that insight by contending that Starr is from a good home and has taken up the expressiveness once the exclusive property of exotic nonwhites. She dances to "negroid" music of the "jungle." An astonished observer "had never seen a white woman dance like that."[66]

News accounts also encouraged Americans to use the underworld to explore the changing behavior of middle-class women. According to a 1929 feature in *Outlook and Independent*, the gangster had "dropped his underworld women. . . . 'moll buzzers,' female pick-pockets, shop lifters, badger-game workers and blackmailers" for honest working girls and even middle-class ladies, all of whom "talked another language" from that of the underworld.[67] Old stereotypes about sexually adventuresome women no longer held. A *New York Times* feature disputed the portrayal of criminals' women as "blatantly of the night world. . . . slangy, tough flappers, floridly dressed and hard boiled to the last degree." Instead, according to the *Times*, many were "girls . . . of modest dress and appearance, with anxious mothers in the background and an obvious urge to maintain respectability." One typical young woman continued to live with her hard-working parents in their suburban home while she became ever more deeply involved with "a notorious racketeer." Her appearance remained that of a typical high school girl. "Her face retains its beauty, her dress is simple, her voice low and her choice of words good." Though she knew her boyfriend to be a racketeer, she neither drank nor smoked and even "scorn[ed] make-up."[68] Such otherwise innocent, disturbingly unremarkable young women populated the realm of modern sensuousness.[69]

Those who used the underworld to understand middle-class Americans' new sexual behavior linked the revolution in manners and morals to the consumer values that had emerged at the same time. To many gangsters, women were exquisite possessions that marked one's taste and rise in the world. Tony Camonte's acquisition of his former boss's beautiful moll is the ultimate validation of his success. She personifies his new world of expensive pleasures.[70] Women were presented as articles to evaluate, acquire, and enjoy. A *New York Times* article explained that the gang leader's "woman-kind, for reasons which those familiar with the psychology of the sex may be left to fathom, are commonly very beautiful—he has an appraising eye and is able to take his pick."[71] Women welcomed the criminal's attention because he offered entrance into a world of exotic furs, fine automobiles, exclusive nightclubs, and luxury apartments. "Come on," one Warner Brothers gangster successfully urges a pretty young woman, "let's go spending."[72] Films regularly featured women who carefully appraise the gangster's possessions. That James Cagney's luxury convertible and well-tailored clothes win him the affections of the Jean Harlow character in *The Public Enemy* would not have come as a surprise to any fan of the genre.[73]

The connection between consumption and sexuality was explored in several films that told of women who dropped their virtuous sweethearts for slick, profligate villains. *Playing Around,* from 1933, focuses on a young woman's rejection of her childhood sweetheart, a soda jerk in her father's drugstore, in favor of a criminal playboy with fancy clothes and a roadster to match. In Sheeba's eyes, poor but honest Jack is no match for high-living Nick. Jack takes Sheeba to a nightclub, but after seeing the menu suggests they leave for a cheaper place where "they get this review on the radio, and plenty loud, too." "I can see I'm in for a big wild evening," she complains. Nick, a striking figure with a top hat, tuxedo, and cane, later offers them a ride home but Jack insists that they take the bus. The roadster's trick horn, Sheeba exclaims longingly, has "sex appeal." Her father sums up the difference between Jack and Nick: Jack is "a fine steady boy" while Nick is "this new sheik . . . I only know him by his flashy car and his trick horn." She resists her father's exhortations to marry Jack, who, she declares, is "not my idea of a big passionate moment." Sheeba knows little more about Nick than does her father, but his possessions, along with his expensive lifestyle, suffice to win her devotion. Romance and consumption were so closely linked as to be inseparable.[74]

The inventors of the gangster suggested that the fundamental link between modern sexual expressiveness and consumption was the pursuit of thrills. Like the craze for spending, the embrace of the new codes of sexual conduct seemed to result from a pervasive ethos of self-gratification and indulgence. The underworld's portrayers, reflecting deep-rooted cultural assumptions about aggressive male sexual nature, devoted little attention to men's willingness to become involved in sexually liberated relationships. But women's willingness demanded explanation. Numerous writers concluded that modern women were drawn by powerful appeals of adventure, excitement, and romance. "Night-club girls" fell for New York hood Jack Diamond, a *Liberty* article explained, because "he was dark, mysterious, bold" and had "the thrill of evil in him, the glamour of the gunman on him."[75] Writing in the *Saturday Evening Post,* Don Marquis commented that one young woman, a student in a renowned Eastern women's college, became involved with a mobster because "she saw something romantic in him."[76] Another young woman, whose "parents were prosperous, cultured people," fell in with a French-born gangster for similar reasons, according to a *Collier's* feature. "She was the victim of her active imagination and the false romance of the movies and the vaudeville theatre. It is probable that she would have avoided the common American gunman as she would disease, but to her the French apache represented something quite different."[77]

Some observers suggested that this pursuit of thrills was an understandable response to modern life. Orderly, routinized life created a demand for the intense experiences promised by spending and the new sexuality. Many filmmakers and writers, echoing the concerns articulated about shifting masculine roles, contended that women craved excitement because ordinary men had become insufferably dull. In the 1923 film *The Exciters,* a rich girl marries a gang member because he is "a real man."[78] This admiration is shared by Jean Harlow's hedonistic moll in *The Public Enemy,* who derides the namby-pamby civility of "the men I've known—and I've known dozens." Tom Powers is different.[79] When hoodlum Louis Beretti, trying to disabuse an infatuated aristocratic girl of her notions of underworld glamour, tells her, "it aint your kind of a world" she retorts, "It's probably a better one—at least it's more exciting." An affair with Louis "would have been a new thrill."[80] Conventional men, Walter Noble Burns explained in his book about Chicago crime, left vibrant women bored and restless. Women craved the vitality absent from modern society:

> If the lot of gangland women seems hard and woefully sad, they are far from viewing their situation in any such tragic light. Gangland has its fascinations. The women who breathe its tense atmosphere enjoy its thrill of danger and its raw drama and would not exchange it for the dull routine of more peaceful environments. They are like women of the old frontier who preferred the perils of the wilderness to prosaic existence in towns and cities. Or like the fair ladies of the days of chivalry, who were happiest when their knights were driving spears into the hearts of foemen or splitting skulls with battle axes. Gangland is romance, and the drab, stereotyped world beyond its dangerous borders is fit only for slaves of the typewriter, school teachers, or anemic feminine souls content to settle down with some white-collar clerk in dreary comfort and obscurity. Gangland women are satisfied with gangland.[81]

Burns and others like him undoubtedly provide more insight into men's anxieties than women's motivations. Nevertheless, they had developed a compelling explanation of the modern pursuit of thrills and women's enthusiastic participation in the chase.

As Americans explored how the ethos of pleasure reshaped relations between men and women, they often used the underworld to express serious concerns about the changes. Their invented underworld represented a harsh critique of important aspects of modern sexual liberalism. To many observers, the apparently unrestrained pursuit of gratification by many urban Americans seemed especially pernicious, and the gangster and his female associates showed its disastrous consequences. Indulgent men and women risked catastrophe. Yet even as women engaged in more "masculine," sexually aggressive behavior, that catastrophe took gender-specific forms that confirmed persistent, fundamental distinctions between the sexes.

The inventors of the gangster contended that women opened themselves to disaster when they recklessly pursued gratification. Most obviously, they risked physical harm. If a woman allowed a man to ignore standards of sexual conduct, many accounts suggested, he might also ignore standards of nonviolence. Many films portrayed mistreatment similar to that promised by a 1934 advertisement for *The Big Shakedown,* which proclaimed that the master criminal was "a tough gangster who doesn't hesitate to bump off his moll when he tires of her."[82] In the 1929 film *Alibi* a robber throws his moll to the floor when she fails to follow his orders. She whimpers ruefully, "I gave up a good husband fine and warm . . . for you."[83] Abuse of women became an important component of the Cagney gangster persona. In a much-discussed scene in *The Public Enemy* he angrily smashes a grapefruit into the face of his moll. In the aptly named *Lady Killer* he drags a woman across a room by her hair and literally kicks her out the door.[84]

The dangers of women's descent from the pedestal were more explicitly set out in the 1931 film *A Free Soul.* Norma Shearer plays a hedonistic society girl who becomes the mistress of the macho gangster Ace, brought to testosterone-saturated life by Clark Gable. Few movies offered more frank depictions of a woman's satisfaction in an illicit affair. Shearer reflexively wets her lips when the two characters first meet, and she soon slinks around Gable's penthouse wearing only a negligee and a satisfied grin. "You're just a new kind of man in a new kind of world," she tells him dreamily. But when she refuses to marry, Ace turns into a violent brute. "I thought I had the right to do anything I liked," she whines. The film's moral lessons also included a strong warning about breaching class barriers in the pursuit of gratification. Shearer's father, initially supportive of her carefree lifestyle, recoils upon learning of the affair. "The only time I hate democracy," he tells Gable, "is when one of you mongrels forgets where he belongs." "Only swine should travel with swine," Shearer finally learns.[85]

More frequently, the underworld announced that modern, sexually assertive women risked moral catastrophe. At a minimum they hazarded their feminine virtue: the gun moll, Arthur Reeve wrote, was "a girl who has forgotten how to blush."[86] From that loss utter corruption and even death as "a drug-crazed suicide" were predictable fates.[87] The nightclubs where gangsters and women met, a *Liberty* writer reported, were filled with "kids of seventeen or so, slim, peppy, laughing, seminude, girls born to dance and sing for a time—and then to sacrifice and suffer, or to cash in on their attractions."[88] In Marquis's *Saturday Evening Post* article, the eastern college woman attracted to the mobster first hopes to reform him but is instead converted to his values. She leaves him only because of his stupidity in committing a pointless crime and getting caught.[89] Even the seemingly innocent woman thrill seeker was in danger of moral corruption. In *Playing Around,* pleasure-loving Sheeba is an unwitting accomplice when her exciting sheik Nick shoots her father in a robbery to support their extravagant life of leisure.[90]

Men, the inventors of the gangster contended, faced different risks from excessive pursuit of sexual gratification. Some men, several accounts suggested, might be drawn to homosexuality. In *Louis Beretti,* a pleasure-loving young man who shunned work was intensely attractive to women but "had a queer streak of gallantry, and was not given to physical love making."[91] Like sexuality in general, accounts associated homosexuality with another manifestation of the modern pursuit of pleasure, lavish spending: extravagant clothing and expensive entertainment seemed to characterize the homosexual.[92] In its description of a high spending, womanizing racketeer as having "the profile of a faintly decadent Greek," one short story suggested that the risk was not merely to the kind of effeminate man described elsewhere as a "pansy."[93]

More generally, the genre warned that excessive sexual indulgence sapped men's drive and judgment. Some gangsters, like the sexually ambiguous Rico in W. R. Burnett's *Little Caesar,* recognized the danger and attempted to protect themselves. "What he feared most in women," Burnett wrote, "was not their treachery, that could be guarded against, but their ability to relax a man, to make him soft and slack."[94] In a regular plot line, men who failed to protect themselves suffered terrible consequences. In *Sweet Mama,* a young woman infiltrates a gang in order to exonerate her brother. After her duplicity is uncovered, an underling reminds his boss, "This isn't the first time a blonde has played you for a chump." "No? Well, it's the last time this one will do it," the boss replies. He is correct, for it is the last time she needs to do it: her efforts are already sufficient to put him out of business.[95] In *The Widow from Chicago* an attractive woman poses as the sex-starved widow of a famous gunman in order to prove that Edward G. Robinson murdered her brother. The Robinson character, falling for her ploy of insisting that she has no interest in a "cheap small-time crook," boasts about the killing and is implicated.[96] Sexual thrill-seeking made men act out of dangerous passion rather than the cool rationality that usually guided them. In *Louis Beretti,* one gangster is put on the spot for his habit of spilling confidential information to duplicitous women. Passion made him forget one of gangland's cardinal rules: "A guy wasn't supposed to tell a skirt anything."[97]

Two novels by Jack Lait, *Put on the Spot* and its sequel, *Gangster Girl,* explored the weakness that women induced in normally strong men. Precursors to a series of blue guides in which Lait extended this exploration of urban sexual geography, the novels featured Annie, "whose deadly red hair and tilted nose and adolescently ripe form" wreak havoc across the Chicago and New York underworlds.[98] Chicago mob leader Goldie Gorio ignores his rule against using violence for any reason other than business—"We're civilized" he tells his lieutenants—and secretly kills Annie's boyfriend in order to have her for himself. Later Goldie stages a spectacular but irrational assault to free her from the municipal jail. But Annie is "a red-headed hunk o' dynamite": Goldie's impulsive actions bring underworld turmoil, the decimation of his gang, and, eventually, his own death at her hand.[99] Annie has a similar effect on New York mob leader Silk Freeman, who before meeting her "made men do what he wanted and . . . made women do as he pleased."[100] Soon he is expressing unending, servile devotion. He too dies because of his infatuation.

Another examination of the enfeebling effect of male sexual indulgence was Charles Francis Coe's serial novel *Repeal.* Beautiful, manipulative Mary Marks brings catastrophe to a gang's four successive leaders who become her lovers. It is common knowledge in the underworld that love and business do not mix:

> Any mob always gets itself feverish over a dame that hooks a leader. . . . Running a mob is like running a factory. You got to be on the job to see that things are done. When a man starts strutting his stuff before a woman, he struts so much he forgets what keeps him up there. Then, pretty soon, he has no more reason to strut.

Abandoning himself to pleasure, gang leader Shoots ignores his business responsibilities. But the gang, faced with the repeal of prohibition, "needed strong leadership, not mellow romance." The gang becomes rife with dangerously disruptive questions: "Where were we going? What was in the wind? What would that lifting shoulder and slanting eye do to booze trucks, breweries, machine guns and mobsters?" Shoots's violent death inevitably follows, as do the downfalls of Mary's subsequent marks. In this story, as in others like it, the inventors of the gangster warned that modern sensuousness was corrosive of male power and ambition.[101] Like stylish consumption, the new sexuality was potentially emasculating. The message was clear: if men were to be strong and successful, they needed to resist the temptations of an overly indulgent society.

As many of the accounts of male enfeeblement reveal, writers and filmmakers often used the underworld to show that the new emphasis on sexual pleasure gave women vast potential power over men. Lait's "astonishing" Annie was a "girl who could betray and murder and sacrifice and love—this blend of passion and romance and treachery and manslaughter."[102] Thus the gangster genre, often the stage for fantastic representations of male potency, at times staged similar fantasies of female empowerment. Here was another instance where the invented underworld carried a multiplicity of sometimes contradictory messages, available for audience members to see or ignore as they were inclined. The best example is *The Public Enemy*'s Gwen, the voluptuous, hedonistic moll played by Jean Harlow. Undoubtedly some viewers saw Harlow merely as an object of male erotic fantasy. But the scenes of Harlow and Cagney together make it clear that her power in the relationship matches her substantial physical presence. Her extravagant, clinging wardrobe, her calculating physical display, her acute understanding of Tom's desires: all are in the service of fulfilling her own thirst for sexual pleasure. "You're a spoiled boy, Tommy. You want things and you're not content until you get them," she tells him. "Well, maybe I'm spoiled too."[103] Harlow and others like her staked out women's right to gratification.

Some observers, combining older notions of female sexual self-control with the newer acceptance of pleasure-seeking, contended that women drew strength from their rational channeling of the irrational forces of sexuality. Cunning, manipulative women used their sexuality to exploit gullible men. Donald Henderson Clarke's novel *Confidential* offered a typical account. Rhoda, a wise young new-comer to the city, meets a gangleader and recognizes he is a dangerous man. "But she could use him perhaps. She had nothing but confi-dence in herself. Men were so silly. She knew how to handle men. You controlled your own feelings and kept the upper hand. It was easy if you knew how." [104] Publicity material for *The Widow from Chicago* proclaimed about the woman who traps Edward G. Rob-inson: "Love is her racket. And she's got the market cornered!" [105] The aptly named Mary Marks, an expert in love, "understood just how it worked and just how to work it." Her power was a disturbing perversion of conventional female traits: "She was all feminine. There was not a thing about her that was not delicate and fragile and weak, yet she bent Shoots around her tiny white finger, drove him just as easy as she would the new roadster." [106] As Mary's new roadster sug-gests, such manipulation often aimed at gaining access to the hard-earned wealth of men. More generally, smart women could play on their feminine charms to take power in a world seemingly controlled by men. Yet the images, of course, were as restricting as they were liberating, for sexuality provided the only key for women's access to power. For men, ruthlessness, brilliance, wealth, or reputation might bring power. Women depended on the power of seductiveness.

As they considered the power of sexually aggressive women, many Americans clearly sympathized with male "victims." They used the underworld to fantasize that exploitative, manipulative women de-servedly paid a heavy price for their encroachments on male power. Violence toward women by Cagney characters was precipitated by the women's attempts to control male behavior. In *The Public Enemy*, Tom Powers assaults his moll when she nags at him during breakfast. No woman would tell him what to do. In *Lady Killer*, Cagney's brutal treatment of his former moll is in response to her efforts to use her sexual desirability to control him. Earlier in the film, she abandons him when her duplicity leaves him briefly broke and jailed. After he becomes wealthy she returns in hopes of capitalizing on his attraction to him. She breaks into his apartment, and he finds her stretched invit-ingly across his bed. Not to be exploited again, he kicks her out of the room. Strong men would not permit the usurpation of their power by conniving women. [107]

The usefulness of the underworld in establishing the justly dangerous consequences of powerful women's exploitation of men is apparent in "The Payoff." Marie Starr, the uninhibited dancer, poses as a naive innocent to win the affections of Denny, the racketeer impresario of a busy cabaret. In her first exercise of power over Denny, Marie "hooked him" with a glance. Her erotic dance melts his usual wariness: "Denny's knees turned to water; he fumbled in the dark, found the stool of the tiny floor piano, sat down heavily. His palms were sweating; he wiped his face until his handkerchief was sopping." Her scheming nature emerges when he offers her a job dancing and she accepts only after insisting on an even more generous salary. When she tells him to give her a cigarette, her true nature is confirmed: down-home origins notwithstanding, she is an independent modern woman. She becomes Denny's mistress to advance her career but refuses his ardent proposals of marriage. Eventually she leaves him for a movie producer who promises bigger opportunities and a chinchilla coat. Returning after Hollywood does not work out, she confesses, accurately, "I hurt you horribly, just because I was ambitious"—and plots to use him again. Denny implies that he will take her back, but after she breaks her contacts with her Hollywood patron he tells her to remember that "ambition has to be made of stern stuff" and commands her to leave—"to go straight to hell." The ambitious, manipulative, overly independent woman, the story proclaimed, justifiably receives her harsh reward.[108]

These lessons were part of a broader early twentieth-century campaign to limit women's assertions of power and independence from male authority. By the 1920s this reaction to women's new social roles had gained considerable force. Politicians and special interests who faced opposition from women's groups, especially pacifist organizations, launched effective demagogic attacks against the "spider's web" of feminist and radical organizations that allegedly plotted social revolution. Career women faced constant discrimination. Though animosity toward married middle-class working women did not peak until the Depression, it was formidable even during the prosperous years of the twenties. Psychologists suggested that career women became "hardened" and unattractive to men and that feminists were psychologically maladjusted. Experts and novelists, elaborating a new doctrine of heterosexual liberalism, hung the pejorative "repressed" on women who seemed insufficiently committed to male sexual pleasure. Extreme cases provoked the damning insinuation of lesbianism. Approving accounts of the imminent harm faced by independent, ambitious women were one aspect among many of the media's contribution to the continuing effort to channel women's lives so that they would not overwhelm male prerogatives.[109]

While the inventors of the gangster most often instructed with negative examples, they occasionally used the underworld to offer positive models of proper relationships between men and women. These depictions of commendable, mutually satisfactory relationships showed readers and moviegoers how to negotiate the difficult terrain of gender roles in modern society. Despite conservative unease with some aspects of the new roles, few advocated turning back the clock to an imagined past. Indeed, contributors to the genre joined in the caricature of desiccated, hypocritical Victorians so popular in the 1920s and 1930s. These images, as Christina Simmons has argued, powerfully endorsed a new liberal, pleasure-oriented sexual ideology.[110] The inventors of the gangster envisioned sexuality as a pent-up force that had broken the impossibly restrictive barriers of an earlier era. Their task was not to build new dams but to lay out a set of values that would channel sexuality, accepting it but preventing moral inundation.

Commendable relationships in the underworld simultaneously legitimated and circumscribed the new openly expressive sexuality. Sexuality brought legitimate fulfillment, but only in relationships that were heterosexual, at a minimum geared toward eventual marriage, and, especially for women, monogamous. *Little Caesar* focuses on two relationships, one vaguely homosexual between Rico and Joe Massara, his early partner, and the other between Olga Stassoff and Joe. With considerable difficulty Joe quits Rico and his gang in order to be with Olga, and the film dwells approvingly on their love affair. Their expensive surroundings, their career as professional dancers, Joe's perfect tuxedo, and Olga's tight-fitting, elegant dresses situate them in the sensuous urban realm of modern pleasure-seeking. Their embraces and shared dressing room leave no doubt about the nature of their relationship. Meanwhile Rico attempts vainly to force Joe away from Olga. "Nobody ever quit me," Rico stews. The moralistic ending passes judgment on the two relationships: Joe and Olga are together and successful, while Rico's supposedly unnatural feelings toward Joe cause his downfall.[111]

Scarface similarly contrasts the unnatural relationship of Tony and his sister Cesca with the legitimate relationship of Cesca and her lover, Guido Rinaldo, Tony's closest friend and underworld partner. Cesca and Guido are highly sympathetic characters, and the film offers a positive view of their love affair. The modernity of the relationship is evident in its roots in Cesca's aggressive pursuit of Rinaldo. When she first sees Guido, he is on the street and she flirts from her bedroom window. Later, when they meet at the Paradise nightclub, she playfully invites him to inspect her beauty ("I look pretty good from two stories up," she says; "Am I different now?"), asks him to dance, and, after his refusal, does a provocative solo shimmy. He resists only because he fears the reaction of the insanely protective Tony. Cesca is a model of the sexually aggressive modern young woman. When Guido tells her, without conviction, that as "only a kid" she should stop her suggestive talk, she responds, "I told you I had grown-up ideas." Just as Guido is attracted to the sensuous woman, so, the film indicates, are women appropriately attracted to sensuous men. As played by George Raft, Guido is handsome, debonair, and better dressed than any other man in the film. Here is the man fit for the new woman. The two marry and share an elegant apartment. In this happy setting Guido relaxes with the newspaper while Cesca, now domesticated, serenades him from the piano. The new pursuit of sensuous pleasure, the underworld again revealed, can bring true fulfillment. It is only the atavistic Tony's murderous jealousy that ends this bliss.[112]

Another message of the model couples was that while women had gained vast potential independence in modern society, successful relationships with men required a renunciation of that independence. In "The Payoff," Denny dumps "ambitious" Marie for Cherry Chase, whom he marries. Though Cherry also dances in Denny's club, she is "a brown-eyed bundle of bounce and biological urge," unblemished by career ambitions. Male authority was preserved, and conflicting goals would not mar the couple's sensuous pleasure.[113]

These messages about appropriate roles for women in modern relationships were at the center of Donald Henderson Clarke's popular 1929 novel *Louis Beretti*. Despite his success at forcing his sisters into sheltered, traditional roles, Louis marries a woman who is a paragon of modernity. Before their marriage, "sturdy, self-reliant" Margaret "had earned her own living without any difficulty." She is a virgin, but when she tells Louis she has never been kissed, it is "a white lie"; a kiss from an earlier suitor had left her "suffocated with ecstasy." Margaret's notions about sexuality are decidedly up-to-date, drawn from motion pictures and "many novels." She fantasizes about an ideal male, "a love slave," and "she would have liked very much to have done a bit of petting like the other girls." She finds their wedding night "most exciting and stimulating," and, despite having been taught that contraception is sinful, is "very happy and tremendously relieved" when Louis tells her to see the family doctor about birth control.[114] More new woman than stereotypical repressed Victorian, Margaret is an embodiment of modern values.

Clarke used the attractive character of Margaret to endorse women's new attitudes and roles, but only in the context of her dependent relationship to her husband. Margaret legitimated the new woman by rendering her harmless, showing that she represented no threat to male authority or prerogatives. In a telling detail, Margaret goes on excursions to movies and the theater with her girlfriends, like other modern young wives, but she never drives. Independence from her husband does not extend to taking the wheel, which neither she nor Louis contemplates. Moreover, Clarke assures his readers that women's acceptance of the ethos of sexual pleasure does not diminish their faithfulness. Louis's infidelity to her she passively accepts, much in the same way she makes no attempt to curb his belching and grunting. In general, Clarke explained, "she felt a vague satisfaction that she had married a man who wasn't going to be tied to a woman's apron strings." "Louis was the head of the family. And she knew it." Her influence over him is limited to the moral suasion long seen as women's most appropriate power.[115]

The 1933 film *Blondie Johnson* typified the efforts of the inventors of the gangster to explore the new territory on which modern men and women interacted and to fashion values that would guide others over that terrain. In an unusual plot variation, the eponymous heroine is a gang leader and thus a personification of women's potential independence. Trouser-clad Blondie, suggesting modern society's blurring of conventional gender categories, is sarcastic, strong, and defiant, and she professes to care about nothing except her own material advancement. The film centers on the problematic dynamics of power between men and women. Warner Brothers publicity boilerplate played up that enticing angle:

> In her long list of screen successes Joan Blondell has invariably been ruled by men. She's been slapped and cheated—often she's been the sacrificing girl who lets "her man" go to another—but throughout the string of pictures in which she has appeared, a man has dominated her. Now along comes Blondie Johnson. . . . As Blondie Johnson Joan not only refuses to allow the male to govern her, but she rules that species with a hand of iron.[116]

Blondie is an exciting, sympathetic embodiment of women's power. Nevertheless, at film's end, she reforms and recognizes not only the error of her criminal ways but, more important, the error of ignoring her female nature. Finally admitting her love for the man who has pursued her, she promises to be faithful. When he tells her, "you're a fresh dame," Blondie corrects him: "Sweetheart to you, Danny." The modern woman, the underworld again taught, could be and must be domesticated.[117]

I read one of those books on the market now and I don't think much of it. It's well-written—as far as I can see from the ten pages at the beginning—but it's about somebody else. I don't belong in this book any more than I belong in a book by Horatio Alger.

—Al Capone, 1931[1]

5 *The Invention in the Flesh: Al Capone of Chicago*

The next stage of cultural invention personalized the generic gangster by giving him a particular name, city, and career. In the late twenties and early thirties a colorful array of individualized criminals was paraded before the public: Dutch Schultz, Jack "Legs" Diamond, and, with the most fanfare, Al Capone. In Capone's own argot, the mass media had "the goods on him."

Fascination with Capone produced the most vivid and widely disseminated portrait of the gangster in twentieth-century American culture. Starting in the middle of the twenties a national audience received fragmentary glimpses of a violent, audacious young crime boss. After the St. Valentine's Day Massacre of 1929 Capone became among the most highly publicized of Americans. A smiling, celebrity-like portrait, polished down to the rose in his lapel, graced the cover of *Time* magazine in March 1930 on the occasion of his release from a short prison term he apparently sought to protect himself from dangerous enemies.[2] Americans marveled at Capone's wealth and power, built on an empire of prostitution, gambling, racketeering, and bootlegging. His career came to an abrupt end in October 1931 when he was convicted of failure to report income and pay taxes—the irony was not lost on contemporary observers—and was sentenced to eleven years' imprisonment. Perhaps because of this dramatically unsatisfactory downfall, fascination with Capone temporarily waned after 1931. Until then, however, Americans were transfixed by the boss of the Chicago underworld.

Though Al Capone lived in the realm of flesh and blood, for most Americans he existed only as a cultural invention. Foremost among the inventors was Capone himself. By all accounts, he was a man who welcomed the limelight and worked constantly to manipulate public perceptions. This was the concern that lay behind his famous formulation of contradictory labels for him and his most notorious activity—racketeer or businessman, bootlegging or hospitality. In press conferences, interviews with reporters, and a highly theatrical social life, Capone worked as hard as any movie star to create a favorable public image. Nevertheless, the same producers of mass culture who had created the generic gangster ultimately presented Al Capone to the American public. He was the subject of popular books, numerous pulp publications, movies, and feature articles in newspapers and magazines ranging from *Master Detective* to *Collier's* and *The Outlook*. The most important group in the production of this material was big-city newspaper reporters, who not only churned out daily stories but wrote most of the more substantial accounts. Newsmen or former newsmen wrote all in a succession of high-selling Capone books that appeared from 1929 to 1931.[3] Though the pulps—cheap, brief picture books sold on newsstands—were published either anonymously or under the name of a prominent police officer, much of their structure and even language came from the full-length books. Former *Chicago Daily News* columnist Ben Hecht wrote the screenplay for *Scarface,* Hollywood's most unabashed venture into Chicago gangland. In all these media, journalists took a leading role in inventing Al Capone: sifting known facts, conjuring up others, and, perhaps most important, choosing the defining metaphors.

In inventing Al Capone, newsmen were capitalizing on their essential skill of explaining the big city to a fascinated public. Americans seized on his story because it offered important lessons to people struggling to live in and with the modern city. As Capone himself recognized, his cultural role ironically mirrored those of other exemplary urban success stories, Alger heroes included. Fred Pasley understood the connection when he subtitled his successful Capone book *The Biography of a Self-Made Man.* Like the stories of Benjamin Franklin, Ragged Dick, and Andrew Carnegie, the Capone legend was a uniquely American success story that instructed in the possibilities and perils of life in the big city. Both softening and reinforcing the hortatory spirit of those earlier tales was the promise of intimate understanding so persuasive in the new age of the mass media celebrity. Close-up photographs and inventive journalism set up "Al" as a knowable personality, mass culture's equivalent of a peculiar neighbor or distant relative periodically the focus of others' attention. That the Capone legend simultaneously performed the cultural work of another venerable genre—the expose of urban corruption—testifies not only to continuing ambivalence about the city but to many Americans' discomfiting perception of the hopeless intertwining of good and evil. At once attractive and repulsive, Capone illuminated the lives of urban Americans.

In addition to providing the gangster genre with its archetype, the Capone legend consolidated the position of Chicago at the geographic center of the underworld. Since the late nineteenth century Americans had used Chicago lawlessness to symbolize urban disorder.[4] In 1916 Henry Barrett Chamberlin, soon to be a founder of the Chicago Crime Commission, wrote of gunmen's "Crimes of Violence That Have Made Chicago (In)famous."[5] "Chicago's 'Wildest' Crime Orgy," screamed a 1919 headline in the usually sedate *New York Times.*[6] Yet the imagery of chaos was already giving way to the new Chicago Crime Commission's antithetical portrayal of regularized, businesslike criminality. The Commission's public statements received considerable attention in the national media and contributed significantly to the city's criminal reputation. This ironic role of civic leaders in building the city's bad reputation culminated in 1926, when the local Better Government Association petitioned the United States Senate for a federal investigation of the link between criminals and corrupt city politicians. Americans outside the city offered little help, but they could not have failed to see Chicago as a crime capital, a reputation that soon became international. As R. L. Duffus wrote in

insights into the paths to success, both in the underworld and in the legitimate society it modeled.

The central theme of the Capone narrative was an individual's escape from obscurity to wealth, power, and fame. The narrative began, in standard fashion, with the arrival of the young hero in the city where he was to make his name. Born of immigrant parents in a Brooklyn slum, the hero had dropped out of school in the fourth grade to help his family in an assortment of difficult, unremunerative jobs on both sides of the law.[16] He arrived in Chicago with little more than an ugly scar, variously attributed to combat in Europe or a barroom brawl precipitated by his offensive remarks about a young woman.[17] He had come to the city in 1920 to help protect Big Jim Colosimo, leader of a corrupt labor union and proprietor of opium dens, houses of prostitution, gambling resorts, and a popular cabaret. Troubled by the extortion attempts of Black Hand kidnappers, Colosimo had earlier imported Capone's eventual mentor, John Torrio, from the Brooklyn Five Points gang to serve as his bodyguard. Torrio possessed unusual management skills and soon oversaw Colosimo's operations. After a particularly threatening Black Hand demand Torrio recruited the young strong-arm from his old Brooklyn gang. Despite these precautions Colosimo was shot to death in his cabaret in May 1920. The murder merited little attention outside Chicago when it happened, but grew to near-epic proportions in the next ten years. By then the killing at the dawn of the decade seemed to illuminate an inevitable transition from quaint old ways to a new order.[18]

Serving as a milestone against which the developments of the twenties could be measured, Colosimo's story showed the transformative effect of the infusion of modern business values into the underworld and invited its mass culture audience to consider the changes wrought by new corporate values on the society as a whole. In the fading world of Big Jim, success depended less upon grand visions, extraordinary intelligence, or careful organization than upon modest, attainable goals and hard work, and achievement occurred within the tight confines of a local community. For these reasons the story of Colosimo became an important counterpoint to the rise of Al Capone.

The quaint tale of Jim Colosimo's rise, steeped in nostalgia, marked as ludicrously out-of-date the Alger-like model of success it paralleled. After arriving as a ten-year-old immigrant boy he sold newspapers, shined shoes, and learned the trade of the pickpocket. Despite his efforts he "often didn't have the price of a flop." [19] Opportunity came in the forms of jobs as a railroad crew water-boy and, later, as a street sweeper. One writer noted incredulously that "it was five years before he could rise from the distinction of a city street cleaner." [20] Yet through dint of hard work and luck this immigrant youth parlayed "the exalted position of whitewing" into the foundation of his eventual wealth. [21] "His was a gradual but sure and steady rise." [22] "More cunning than intelligent . . . and, above all, peculiarly talented in the art of making friends," Colosimo eventually became recognized as a leader of the whitewings and the larger local Italian community. [23] The two "picturesque" aldermen of the old levee vice district, Hinky-Dink Kenna and Bath-house John Coughlin, patronized him "because they saw in him a future political power, small but nevertheless influential." [24] In exchange for the block of votes he controlled, Kenna and Coughlin helped Colosimo attain a considerable but highly localized success. His career was built on traditional crimes, limited to a long-standing old vice district, rooted in a village-like community, and supported by patrons reminiscent of a colorful but fading past.

Colosimo's demise showed that mere pluck and good fortune, however, were no longer sufficient for success. For nothing in this background prepared him for leadership of the modern corporate gang. "Big Jim Colosimo, though he had built up the machine for which he was famous, didn't know how to handle it on a fast track," one pulp book explained. [25] Compounding his lack of up-to-date skills, Colosimo lacked the passion for continual expansion that drove the modern businessman-gangster. Unaware that the only alternative to entrepreneurial growth was stagnation, he was content to relax and enjoy his modest prosperity. Big Jim's advancing age, girth, and indolence marked his difference from younger, leaner, and more aggressive counterparts. "Colosimo, fat and prosperous and nearing forty," Pasley wrote, "was smugly content with things as they were, satisfied to operate within the Twenty-second Street district." [26] "He took things easy," according to another account, and "spent most of his days just sitting in his huge ornate cafe dreaming contentedly." [27] "Play took the place of work in the life of Big Jim Colosimo," [28] who entrusted his daily operations to the care of Torrio and Capone. When he failed to respond to assaults by vice crusaders on his operations, and when he proved reluctant to exploit the opportunities presented by new prohibition laws, Colosimo became "a nuisance to his lieutenants" and a hindrance to "progress."[29] His murder validated the judgment that "a slow-thinking, slow moving man such as Colosimo had no place" in the modern underworld.[30] Nor did such a dinosaur have a place, the Capone legend implied, in the corporate order the underworld so closely paralleled.

In John Torrio, Colosimo's antipodal successor, audiences received a respectful lesson in the capabilities of the efficient, up-to-date businessman. Torrio embodied the relentless drive that Colosimo fatally lacked, and the story of his gang celebrated the replacement of small, local enterprises by diversified, far-ranging, and highly organized corporations in the larger economy. "Within a brief time after his arrival," Edward Dean Sullivan wrote, "the bawdy houses of Chicago were organized as never before, new prices and standards were established and the foul business had become a 'syndicate.' It was a business in every detail except in reliance on court or police protection."[31] Many, of course, would dispute the exception. This publicizing of the advantages of replacing small gangs with a single organization constituted a primer on the corporate order's economies of scale.[32] Realizing the opportunities presented by prohibition, Torrio bought idle breweries, organized a distribution system, and arranged for political protection. "He simply saw another business opportunity" that would complement his "multiplicity of interests." Unlike the complacent Colosimo, Torrio "looked far beyond the confines of the First Ward to the latent opportunities throughout metropolitan Chicago."[33] So completely did he transcend Colosimo's localism that when crusading mayor William Dever attempted to clean up Chicago in 1923 Torrio simply moved the center of his operations to neighboring Cicero. Even his use of violence illuminated a business executive's calculations. When the need arose "he issued an order to his gunmen as to so many counter-jumping clerks."[34] The mayhem he directed "wasn't personal. It was a system. It was efficient; he was proud of it."[35]

Accounts of the skills and values Torrio brought to the management of this criminal enterprise represented a simultaneously appreciative and critical assessment of the make-up of the leading executive. It was because "the cash register was all that counted with him," as Walter Noble Burns wrote, that Torrio succeeded so magnificently.

Scruples presented no obstacle to profits. Within a brothel where women were despoiled around the clock, Burns wrote, Torrio

> sat in an upholstered office, as neat as a pin, at a mahogany desk. . . . A calm, poised, efficient business man was Torrio. No bluster, no lost motion, no wasted words. Weighing his business chances, figuring his margin of profit. Shrewd, far-seeing, unscrupulous, of relentless energy. Square—that was his reputation—his word as good as his bond.

These, Burns concluded, were "all the qualities of a great financier and a great business man."[36]

As the description of Torrio's office indicates, the Chicago mythologists suggested that business success depended almost as much on a particular personal style as on the use of modern corporate methods. Failure seemed inevitable for Big Jim Colosimo because, as the nickname indicates, he never developed the essential cosmopolitan outlook and instead remained tethered to his working-class, ethnic origins. In Howard Hawks's classic film *Scarface,* filmed in 1930 and released in 1932, the Colosimo character is dark complected, disheveled, and unlike his successors speaks with a thick Italian accent.[37] Pasley wrote that he attired himself and decorated his home "without taste or refinement but on a scale of barbaric magnificence."[38] This egregious bad taste seemed to testify to innate limitations that belied any attempts at improvement. Survival depended on assimilation to the dominant, nonethnic culture.

By contrast, Torrio's lifestyle was that of a refined middle-class American. Success came to the dignified, well-mannered executive who dressed with understated good taste, kissed his wife goodbye in the morning, detested profanity, and enjoyed nothing more than a quiet evening at home in his favorite easy chair. Aside from his love for Italian opera, few traces of ethnicity marked him as distinct from what many Americans took to be an undifferentiated nonethnic norm. His speech was soft but commanding and "without trace of foreign accent." In contrast to Colosimo's first wife, an immigrant brothel-keeper, Torrio's wife was a respectable Kentucky woman "with generations of American ancestry back of her."[39] In every respect except for a few details of his occupation, here was a model of American middle-class respectability.

Nevertheless, Torrio did not long reign atop the Chicago underworld, and his downfall, like the murder of Colosimo, provided a text for important lessons about success and failure in a competitive society. He stepped down after a nearly successful attempt on his life in January 1925. Driving in the city with his wife, Torrio was intercepted and pursued by enemy gunmen. He made it to the curb in front of his South Side house but while scrambling to get inside received a shotgun blast to the jaw and was left for dead. "Utterly terrified"[40] after his release from a guarded hospital room—Torrio insisted on one far from windows and fire escapes—he welcomed sentencing on a prohibition conviction and thereby acquired the security of a bulletproof cell. While in prison he fretted about his safety, and upon his release ten months later he fled the city and, according to some accounts, the country. In recounting this transfer of leadership from Torrio to Capone writers showed the limitations of efficiency. In the social mirror that was the underworld, the struggle for success required not just brains but guts—boldness, courage, a willingness to fight. Torrio was a scared "rabbit," "a coward . . . at heart," "the Big Boy who wasn't quite big enough."[41] "One close call was enough for him," the *Literary Digest* explained. "As they say of a fighter, 'he can dish it out, but he can't take it.'"[42] The unmanly man would inevitably fail as a leader.

In recounting Capone's replacement of Torrio, their chroniclers endorsed a vision of business competition that rewarded aggressive masculinity. For in temperament and physique Capone personified the raw virility that Torrio so obviously lacked. "Nerveless fearlessness," as one writer put it, set him above his predecessor.[43] Despite his eventual refinement, Capone could be "crude, tough, profane, bellicose, domineering, a swashbuckler and a bully," Burns wrote. "Physically he was impressive—lithe, muscular, with good shoulders and hard fists: a husky roughneck; a typical gangster as of old the public pictured gangsters."[44] Pasley concurred that he was "stout-muscled [and] hard knuckled," attributes appropriate to his early work as a bouncer and all-around thug.[45] Writers went to great lengths to reconcile Capone's putative physical prowess with his undeniable girth. Pasley conceded that Capone was "ponderous of movement till engaged in action, [but] then as agile as a panther."[46] The "great bulk of his is not all fat," Enright agreed; "great bulges of muscle . . . enable him at times to move with the speed and power of a tiger."[47] This "burly" thug presented a stark contrast to "Little Johnny Torrio."[48] A "face of strength," with "lines of bulldog determination" completed the profile.[49] Enright summarized the effect:

> You can imagine this man facing an enemy and shooting it out with him in armed conflict. You can imagine his stubby hands throttling a traitor in his ranks or smashing into the mouth as fists to halt a denunciation or a threat. You might even imagine him striking down a pistol arm and countering with the thrust of a long knife.[50]

At least in the underworld, the fighting virtues reigned supreme.

Capone's inventors proclaimed that aggressive masculinity and modern business organization could coexist, for they linked this toughness with business acumen exceeding even that of Torrio. "Not the ordinary gangster," according to *Does Crime Pay?*, Capone was "a shrewd, brainy, quick thinking, cool tempered man."[51] "No desperado of the old school is 'Scarface Al,' plundering or murdering for the savage joy of crime," *Time* concurred; "He is, in his own phrase, 'a business man' who wears clean linen, rides in a Lincoln car, leaves acts of violence to his hirelings."[52] He became "the John D. Rockefeller" of the underworld because he understood the imperative of the modern economy: organize or perish. According to Pasley, "Capone was to revolutionize crime and corruption by putting both on an efficiency basis, and to instill into a reorganized gangland firm business methods of procedure."[53] These writers accepted Capone's own description of his affairs: "Everybody calls me a racketeer. I call myself a businessman. When I sell liquor, it's bootlegging. When my patrons serve it on a silver tray on the Lake Shore Drive, it's hospitality."[54]

The equation of success and executive sagacity resulted in a remarkable interview and related editorial in an October 1931 issue of *Liberty* magazine. In "Two Mighty Men—H. G. Wells and Al Capone," the editor asserted that Capone was "a true philosopher" whose "clear, constructive reasoning" about contemporary problems invited comparison to that of the celebrated author, a contributor to the issue.[55] The interview fit in a standard mold: that of commentary on national concerns from a respected leader. "How Al Capone Would Run This Country" served as a forum for a successful executive to put forth his vague solutions for the Depression and, yes, lawlessness that plagued the nation. This businessman-savant's interviewer was none other than celebrity journalist Cornelius Vanderbilt, Jr., presumably by birth a competent judge of such authorities. Like countless other executives, Capone fretted that "Bolshevism is knocking at our gates" and fulminated that the worker needed protection "from red literature, red ruses; we must see that his mind remains healthy." Like Richard Washburn Child and other conservative businessmen he believed that the disintegration of the traditional home had corrupted American society. His predictable solution was that important men needed to work together to solve contemporary problems. The performance of Herbert Hoover, the engineer-businessman made president, had fallen far short of expectations. "Isn't it a peculiar thing that with one of the world's greatest organizers as our chief executive we lack organization more now than ever in our history?" he asked. "An American Mussolini," Capone opined, offered the best hope. Al Capone, master criminal and paragon of success, was an executive worthy of consultation, and his vacuous proclamations perfectly echoed those of many of his legitimate counterparts.[56]

Capone's far-flung organization, described in the jargon of the corporation, provided the invented underworld's most intense illumination of the capabilities of modern business methods. In Michigan Avenue headquarters, large accounting and clerical staffs facilitated the operation of "a supertrust . . . with the efficiency of a great corporation."[57] But the activities of this wonderfully efficient business meant that descriptions of it constituted not just an appreciation of corporate methods. For Capone's organization showed a disturbing proximity between ordinary, amoral business objectives—the pursuit of corporate profits—and those that generated terribly immoral and destructive acts. It was an ordinary board of directors that oversaw the firm's wide-ranging interests in bootlegging, vice, narcotics, and diverse forms of racketeering. Hijackings, bombings, and murders were among "the dry-as-dust affairs discussed in the matter-of-fact routine" of their typical meeting. "As far as appearances were concerned, it was like a board meeting of some big wholesale house or La Salle Street financial firm," Burns wrote. "Fashionably garbed, immaculately groomed, a flower in a buttonhole here and there, the directors puffed at their cigars unconcernedly, yawned now and then, and sometimes nodded. Their daily board meetings were something of a bore. They sat through them from a sense of business duty."[58]

Always exerting commanding influence was the Big Boss, Al Capone, whose "genius for organization and . . . profound business sense" insured the success of the enterprise.[59] During Capone's heyday—years of shaky national prosperity followed by years of contraction—Americans continued their long struggle to come to terms with the power of the corporation. The new ways of understanding crime suggested, of course, new ways of understanding business. The Capone legend offered Americans a subversive set of metaphors for rethinking their business society.

Along with the story of Capone's rise in his own organization, conflicts with rival gang leaders formed a key element of his legend. Popular accounts lavished great detail upon his struggles against a series of capable foes, especially the successive leaders of the rogue North Siders, Dion O'Banion, Hymie Weiss, and Bugs Moran. Central to each narrative episode was a careful weighing of the strengths and weaknesses each enemy brought to the fight. In tracing Capone's victory—for he invariably possessed the advantage—his chroniclers offered parables about the path to success in modern society. The fundamental metaphorical lesson was that business competition was a series of violent conflicts, war waged by any available means and ending only with total victory and mortal defeat. Counterbalancing this bleak, potentially subversive lesson was a powerfully conservative message that success came to those who deserved it. Merit alone underlay Capone's supremacy in gang wars that reportedly brought the deaths of five hundred lesser men. Gangland, and the society it modeled, inevitably rewarded the strongest competitor. Here the underworld served a metaphorical function very similar to Darwinian biology in the late nineteenth century. Survival of the fittest, whether due to natural selection or machine guns, alternately justified celebrating the victors and damning the system.

The first of these conflicts, which pitted Capone and Torrio against Dion O'Banion, highlighted the necessity of rational, carefully moderated behavior in the new world of business. O'Banion had risen to prominence on the strength of opportunism coupled with a "quick brain [and] iron nerve." His first specialty was safe-blowing, for which he used "very little care and plenty of explosion." Early on he recognized the opportunities opened up by prohibition and made a name for himself hijacking the trucks of illegal beer and liquor distributors who had no recourse to the law. "What O'Banion lacked in care or comprehensive planning," Sullivan wrote, "he made up in stark courage and the faculty of instantly seizing a chance."[60] These were valuable attributes, essential to gangland success, and Capone and Torrio, who believed O'Banion "was capable of going far under the direction of a cool, wise leader," offered him an alliance and prepared to enjoy the fruits of ever-larger organization.[61]

O'Banion accepted the offer but defects of temperament precluded long-term success, for he never could learn the value of controlling his temper or of weighing short-term expediency against long-term interests. In one well-publicized incident, he shot a rival whom he happened to see standing nearby outside a crowded theater lobby. In another, he planned to murder policemen who detained a beer truck when they were not paid a small bribe. Torrio prevailed and paid the bribe. "That was the difference between Torrio and O'Banion," Burns wrote. "A cool head made Torrio all powerful; a lack of it left O'Banion even at his best a superior sort of ruffian."[62] "Where Dion was spontaneous and ruthless," a pulp explained, "Capone was deliberate and machinelike."[63] While Capone and Torrio built alliances, O'Banion and his gang remained hijackers at heart, and the trucks of allies were no safer than those of enemies. "Torrio was a business man first and a gangster second," another pulp explained. "O'Banion was a gangster."[64]

It was the inability to cooperate, Capone's chroniclers taught, that brought about O'Banion's death on 19 November 1924. His fatal error, most accounts contended, was the sale of the Sieben Brewery to Torrio and Capone after O'Banion learned that it was about to be raided by federal prohibition agents. Torrio and Capone realized that they had been double crossed and arranged a brilliant execution. Audacity, bravery, and opportunism were not sufficient for success. Indeed, these qualities needed at times to be held in check in the highly organized modern society. As Sullivan summarized, "In a business requiring cold courage he was perhaps too coldly courageous."[65] He failed to recognize that in the new economy immediate individual desires must frequently be suppressed in favor of the needs of larger groups. "Civilized existence, with its restraints and taboos, oppressed him."[66] Restraint, structure, and regularity were essential.

Accounts of O'Banion's successors as head of the North Side gang expanded on the perils of indiscipline. Louis "Two-Gun"

Alterie was run out of town by more sensible peers after he publicly challenged O'Banion's killers to a gunfight at high noon on the busy downtown corner of State and Madison. The incident surprised few aware of Alterie's previous claim to notoriety: "executing" the horse that had killed partner Nails Morton in a riding accident.[67] Such was not the stuff of greatness. O'Banion protege Hymie Weiss suffered from similar shortcomings. "Hymie's chief fault," according to *Does Crime Pay?*, "was that he was too fiery and spontaneous and as a result was always getting himself into hot water."[68] Overly loyal to the memory of his slain leader and friend, Weiss "devoted less time to business than to revenge . . . [and] went to lengths of sheer bravado never before approached," Sullivan wrote.[69] "His relentlessness," Burns wrote, "was untouched by motives of business expediency."[70] The ensuing conflict between Capone's gang and the North Siders seemed to be one between two systems, the former mercenary and businesslike, the latter based on "friendship, loyalty and affection."[71] Scoffing at calls for a truce, Weiss led a daylight raid of a dozen automobiles that swept down the main street of Cicero and riddled the Capone headquarters with weapons fire. In the same month he ambushed Torrio. According to *The Morgue: The Gangster's Final Resting Place*, a uniquely gruesome pulp, Weiss's "forays were not well planned, but were led purely by instinct, and were brutal and reckless in the extreme." He was "totally lacking in judgment, diplomacy, and finesse."[72] Torrio lived and the Cicero bombardment injured no one except an innocent woman walking on the street. Though courageous, intelligent, and charismatic, Weiss succumbed to passion that reduced his actions to mere blustering. The message of this ineffectiveness was clear, according to *Does Crime Pay?* "Hymie's failure to get Al proved he was not the man to rule the gangs in Chicago."[73] Chance played no role in the determination of underworld leadership; order prevailed through the apparent chaos of gangland conflicts and merit inevitably triumphed.

In this instance, the validation of business methods came from the muzzles of machine guns, "Chicago typewriters" in aptly commercial slang. The Capone gang set up gun nests in the windows of a boarding house across the street from Weiss's headquarters—the same flower shop in which O'Banion had met his death. Accounts reveled in the Capone gang's efficiency:

They sat all day by the windows, smoking cigarettes, their guns in their laps, waiting patiently, like jungle beasts watching a trail. Weiss had been tried, convicted, and sentenced to death. His executioners were ready. No more chance for life was left him than to the condemned murderer who stands on the trapdoor of a gallows with the rope around his neck. The tragedy was now only a question of time and opportunity.[74]

Weiss's 11 October 1926 death in the inevitable hail of bullets—and his admission into the pages of *The Morgue*—was the final resolution of an utterly fair competition.

As they waxed lyrical about especially well planned slayings, gangland's chroniclers offered a reconciliation of the values of efficiency and individualism that might otherwise seem at odds. For the aesthetic of violence with which they evaluated the performance of various killers celebrated both efficiency and the expression of individual creativity. Marvelously precise, the Weiss killing was a "gala drama of murder."[75] Masterful technique seemed to promise individual fulfillment as well as professional success. O'Banion and Weiss, according to one pulp book, were "picturesque," but "it is quite plain that nothing either of them ever achieved in Gangland history possessed finish and perfection in the same degree as did the deft and artistic method by which they were eliminated and laid away."[76] Faced with Weiss's blundering challenges, Capone was "the master killer" practicing "the fine art of murder."[77]

Perhaps it was the terrible combination of audacity, efficiency, and creativity expressed in the St. Valentine's Day Massacre of 1929 that so captured Americans' fascinated attention. According to one enthusiastic pulp, it "was without a doubt the most perfectly planned and executed deed ever heard of."[78] Several men in police uniforms entered a beer garage on Chicago's North Clark Street and ordered the seven men inside to line up with their hands against the wall. Under the impression that this was a routine shakedown, the seven complied. Then two men carrying machine guns entered the garage and killed them with several sweeps of fire. The killers left the garage impersonating police officers and suspects in custody and drove away in a car with police markings. Their employer, Al Capone, was far from the scene—as one pulp put it, "in his white pants at Miami."[79] Like many another businessman, he from afar directed other men's use of powerful technology. The North Side gang was decimated. The crime, Pasley gushed, "was precision engineering. The five assassins might have been robots, wound up and synchronized, every movement clicking concurrently and reciprocally."[80] According to *Al Capone on the Spot*, "the exquisite planning and execution of the master mind were again in evidence." A cascade of metaphors suggested that business and art need not be distinct. The killings were "murder dramatized and staged in the perfect production." They were "gang murder raised to one of the arts. This is execution under efficiency engineers. This is the handiwork of the master mind of murder."[81]

The audacity behind acts like the St. Valentine's Day killings constituted a major source of fascination with the Chicago gangster. For all their attention to the self-control of careful businessmen like Torrio and Capone, writers gloried in the exploits of men who seemed willing to try anything, no matter how daring, and almost always succeeded. Dion O'Banion's robbery of the Sibley warehouse, during which he substituted water for 1,750 barrels of bonded Kentucky whisky, was recounted with folkloric enthusiasm.[82] Torrio and Capone's sweeping takeover of Cicero, including its polling places, was described, though somewhat more grimly, with a similar tone of awestruck appreciation.[83] Central to the Capone legend was that when he embarked upon a mission, whether the corruption of a town or the murder of a rival, he never failed. Al Capone seemed marvelously capable of flouting law and authority, overcoming any obstacle, and imposing his will on a resistant world. As much as the invented underworld bulwarked the values of personal responsibility, it was the focus on particular criminal celebrities that ensured the individual would not be lost in "gangsterism," yet another impersonal social phenomenon. Perhaps this explains why so much of the recounting of Capone's exploits glistened with awestruck appreciation barely dulled by a coating of moralistic censure. Living in an age of complexity and restraints, Americans were grateful to this exemplar of the individual triumphant.

In its portrayal of the ascendant individual the legend of Al Capone bore striking resemblance to that of another paragon of success: Charles Lindbergh. On the surface the public images of the two men could hardly have been more different. Indeed, the media reacted with bitter incredulity as their public paths crossed in 1932 when the imprisoned Capone offered to aid in the search for the hero's kidnapped infant son. Yet the two figures, each a product of the media, represented many of the same concerns. Like Capone, Lindbergh seemed a holdover of that endangered species, the self-sufficient man. His solo flight across the Atlantic in May 1927 was the act of a courageous "pioneer" who succeeded where more advantaged teams of lesser men had failed. Yet, as John W. Ward argues in his classic article on "The Meaning of Lindbergh's Flight," the public not only worshiped the self-sufficient "Lone Eagle" but also gloried in the technology and corporate productivity that made his feat possible. Al Capone performed equally wondrous, if less universally celebrated, acts of individual will and creativity while immersed in a corporate world whose bureaucratic organization and multi-layered restraints on behavior might seem antithetical to individual autonomy. Both men proclaimed that the individualism of the traditional success mythology could be reconciled with the impersonal institutions of mass society. The individual and the organization need not be at odds.[84]

For all its emphasis on violent episodes of gangland succession and competition, the Capone story was not limited to these events. Americans were also fascinated with the personal life of Al Capone. Not only was he the boss of the Chicago underworld and mastermind of the St. Valentine's Day Massacre; he was also renowned as a devoted family man, an affable host, a connoisseur of urban nightlife, and the owner of an Edenic Miami estate. These other roles were fundamental to Capone's status as a compelling cultural symbol. For in lifestyle as in business, he instructively negotiated difficult social terrain traversed by millions of urban Americans. Here too it was Capone's ironic adherence to accepted standards of conduct, rather than his transgressions, that most captivated his public audience.

A large portion of the Capone story concerned his identity as a voracious consumer—as one writer put it, "perhaps the greatest spender in gangland history."[85] He was celebrated as the owner of hundreds of fine suits, a thirty-thousand-dollar limousine, and an eleven-carat diamond ring. Widely reproduced photographs showed the half-million-dollar Florida estate and an appropriately relaxed, silk-robed Capone fishing from the deck of his yacht.[86] Capone personified the pleasure, excitement, and self-transformation that the consumer society promised. His inventors at once offered an eager audience vicarious thrills and an invitation to consider the meanings of consumption in their own lives.

Among the central messages of the Capone story was that consumption could bring remarkable individual transformations. In his progression from tasteless hoodlum to fashion template, Capone spanned the stylistic gap earlier defined by Colosimo and Torrio. Accounts of the hero's impoverished early life, unlike those in conventional success stories, did not focus on how hardship had forged an unyielding character. Instead, the salient feature of Capone's background was its lack of refined consumption. His nickname upon arrival in Chicago, according to one writer, was "Boxcar Tony," the first part a reference either to his mode of travel or to the large, dated, yellow-buttoned shoes he wore, and the second a denigrating rhyme upon the un-Americanized version of his surname, Caponi.[87] In his "loud clothes, red neckties, gaudy shirts, and much flashy jewelry," wrote Burns, the young Capone "might have been mistaken for a prosperous race-track tout or tin-horn gambler."[88] The Capone who made "a lowly debut into the Chicago underworld . . . was ostensibly just one of the bourgeoisie; loud of dress, free of profanity; . . . a vulgar person."[89] But people changed with their clothes, and soon Capone had landed in the aristocracy of consumption. As hinted by Pasley's odd use of "bourgeoisie," social categories were remarkably fluid. Capone's rise confirmed that modern commercial society awarded to the worthy the chance to remake themselves. Any person, even from the lowest stratum, had the opportunity to earn the purchasable pleasures that marked success in modern society.

Moreover, Capone's inventors taught that it was high living, perhaps even more than audacious deeds or unparalleled skills, that brought recognition. The yacht and Miami estate were impressive stages for the display of power and achievement. Confirmation of Capone's exalted status came from the reported reactions of ordinary men and women who encountered him during his rituals of consumption. Chicagoans craned their necks to see his limousine pass by on warm summer evenings. Theatergoers devoted their attention to him when he appeared in all his glory in their midst. Baseball fans noted with pleasure his attendance in a front-row seat at Wrigley Field. His appearance at a heavyweight championship fight in Miami overshadowed a sizable contingent of movie stars and other entertainers. Socialites clamored for invitations to his parties. Extravagant consumption, Capone demonstrated, attracted the public attention that constituted greatness. The spender was the individual singled out from, and by, the crowd.

Writers often offered a fundamentally conservative view that individual identity and fulfillment could be achieved through adherence to the dictates of stylish consumption embraced by the dominant American culture. The Big Shot was a conformist. Among his closetful of fine suits, according to Enright, "not one of them is of conspicuous weave or of a cut that would attract attention except for its excellence." His appearance had become "for the most part . . . that of the perfectly groomed business man."[90] Similarly, Capone developed the smooth behavior that conventionally accompanied stylish consumption. No longer a vulgar boor, he exuded the suavity appropriate to his new status. He mastered the fine art of "personality."[91] According to Pasley, he became "a reverent handshaker, with an agreeable, well-nigh ingratiating smile, baring a gleaming expanse of dental ivory; a facile conversationalist; fluent as to topics of the turf, the ring, the stage, the gridiron, and the baseball field."[92] In an oddly conservative fashion, writers upheld a Babbitt-like gangster as a model of fulfillment in the culture of consumption.

Nevertheless, the Capone legend expressed considerable unease with the realm of superficial images that modern society had created. Style allowed the successful person to present a front dangerously at odds with his or her true nature. Such potential disingenuousness was the point of Pasley's recounting of Capone's introduction to polished manners at the hands of John Torrio. When he arrived in Chicago Capone's nature was evident in his tasteless clothes, rough manners, and vulgar speech. But "the urbane Torrio" "instructed him in the social graces and in the art of dissembling to conceal one's thoughts. He taught him the commercial value of the bland smile and the ready handshake."[93] Several writers, grappling with these distortions, contended that they had difficulty imagining the personable Capone as a cold-hearted killer.[94] The incongruity of image and essence was clear in a pulp's list of highlights in Capone's life. Ranging from "Has a palatial estate at Palm Island, Miami Beach Florida" and "Is famed as a host" to "Employs gangland's most skilled machine-gunners" and "Won a ten-year war of gangs that cost 500 lives," the list testified to Capone's frighteningly convincing facade.[95] So did two facing pages of photographs in another pulp, *Does Crime Pay?* One page featured him as a man of leisure with a silk robe and a large cigar, fishing from the deck of his yacht. On the next page, two grisly pictures showed some of his murdered enemies.[96] Symbolized by the expensive-looking "radio" in Capone's apartment that detectives discovered to be a hollow storage space for handguns,[97] the veneer of style seemed to cover the truth.

Many of the non-business aspects of Capone's life that received greatest attention clustered around the theme of morality. Americans were fascinated with the soul of the racketeer. The Chicago mythologists relished biographical details that might seem irrelevant to the stories of violent criminal entrepreneurs: acts of charity, home life, small manifestations of basic human decency. Here, as in so many other aspects of their lives, Capone and his peers defied expectations. Perhaps it was the audience's involvement in the "revolution in manners and morals" discerned by Frederick Lewis Allen and millions of other Capone contemporaries that made the gangster's erratic moral compass so compelling. The underworld dramatized a generalized moral inconsistency.

The putative generosity of the Chicago gangster received regular examination for the surprising revelations it offered about his moral nature. Though some writers discounted good deeds as self-serving public relations stunts, most accepted them as genuine. "Having known adversity," O'Banion supported widows, kept old people out of the poorhouse, and funded a crippled child's trip to the Mayo Clinic, Burns reported. He "relieved distress wherever he found it" and could often be seen "dropping in at tenements and hovels to make poor people happy with his gifts."[98] Capone received considerable good press for similar philanthropic acts, among them paying the medical bills of a woman injured in an attack on him. In some accounts he came across as a candidate for beatification. His "heart is as big as all outdoors," Pasley wrote; his "way through life has been strewn with deeds of kindness for the sick and needy."[99] During the early years of the Depression, his soup kitchens and gifts of coal, clothing, and groceries won appreciative attention. "His generosity," wrote Burns, "was princely, and his heart warmed and his purse opened to anyone in distress, white or black, Jew or Gentile."[100]

Discussions of these acts of generosity carried important messages. Like attention to the gangster's conventional spending habits

and business techniques, they worked to compress the distance between the lawbreaker and the upstanding citizen, the "deviant" and
the "normal." Al Capone and his peers were not freaks in whom few
observers could see anything of themselves. Instead, the Chicago
gangster was an ambiguous figure, riven with contradictions. In his
fundamental make-up he mirrored his audience, as no less an authority on normal psychology than Dale Carnegie understood when he
used Capone as one of many exemplars of basic human nature. Like
Washington, Lincoln, and the Roosevelts, the mobster was at once a
great and representative man.[101] That this exemplary bad man mixed
his violence with acts of charity encouraged his audience to confront
the inseparability of good and evil. For if Al Capone had such a capacity for good, surely his audience shared at least some of his capacity for evil.

It was in the reported domestic lives of the Chicago gangsters
that their ambiguous moral status was most striking. Some earned
reputations for debauchery and the corruption of innocent women.
But most of the gang chiefs reportedly chose to live quiet home lives
arranged along the lines of conventional propriety. Killers and pan-
derers on the job, at home they headed the harmonious families pop-
ularly believed to be the embattled bulwarks of traditional morality.
One consequence was to bring the gang leaders closer to audience
members whose lives more or less conformed to conventional standards. Another was to encourage audiences to ponder the fracturing
of identity that characterized urban social life. The violent, home-
loving gangster epitomized the century-long differentiation of distinct spheres of work, recreation, and home life. He showed how a
person could construct extraordinarily different lives in the various
worlds he or she inhabited.

The first example in the Chicago narrative of surprising domestic
morality was Jim Colosimo. His businesses as pimp and drug seller,
among others, might have been taken as evidence of utter ruin. So
too his first marriage—to a brothel-keeper. But the underworld
chroniclers presented Colosimo's love affair with Dale Winter, a
singer in his cabaret, as evidence of latent decency. Winter, who came
to the city hoping to sing in musical theater, was a model of feminine
purity. "She neither drank nor smoked," Burns wrote; "No indelicate
word ever passed her lips. No whisper of scandal touched her." She
ignored a multitude of debauched suitors and after sing-

ing—"garbed in simple, shimmering white, a red rose across her bo-
som"—went home every night to her mother. Somehow "this Mona
Lisa of the Red Lights" fell in love with her employer and they married.[102] "Colosimo was in love with her and, for the first time in his
life, decent impulses began to stir in his curious and contradictory
nature," a pulp explained; "she seemed to renovate Colosimo himself.
More and more absorbed did Colosimo become in his love for the
tiny flower of a woman."[103] "Rooted in bottom slime as he was,"
Burns mused, Colosimo nevertheless "had many kindly human qualities—charity, open-handed generosity to those in distress and poverty, a capacity for loyal friendships. . . . Deep within him a tiny spark
of fine manhood survived."[104] "Every decent trait in this heretofore
vicious and unsentimental underworld leader was brought to the
fore," Sullivan wrote.[105] Criminal though he was, he retained the
moral sense to respond to a virtuous woman.

Fittingly, Colosimo's up-to-date successors more fully arranged
their lives along the modern pattern of distinct spheres. Their fickle
morality allowed them to construct radically fragmented lives. Torrio's love for quiet evenings at home received regular notice.[106] As a
child Dion O'Banion had served as an altar boy and sung in the choir
at Holy Name Cathedral, and he remained a devout Catholic. He was
also a cold-hearted killer and was eventually shot down in his flower
shop across the street from Holy Name. A pulp reveled in the contrasts: "He loved flowers. He loved killing. He would have nothing to
do with traffic in women and would not touch alcohol in any
form."[107] Widely reproduced wedding photographs presented the
gangster as a beaming model of domestic bliss.[108] "His domestic life
with his wife was the life of a perfect middle-class florist," a *Literary
Digest* article commented after his death. Tinkering with the family
radio and player-piano were his favorite pastimes. His grieving widow
presented him as "not a man to run around nights."[109] "It is strange
the peculiar twists that can find lodgment in a character," Sullivan
mused; "O'Banion, vengeful, unfeeling and desperate in the dangerous field in which he moved, was a genuine home lover when not
active in his outlawed affairs."[110]

It was Al Capone who best exemplified the multiplicity of lives
one might lead in modern society. Photographs of the modest two-
flat where he lived with his wife, son, mother, sister, and two brothers
appeared regularly in pulps and drew attention to his devotion to

family life.[111] Fred Pasley, like others, played up the considerable irony:

> He who is editorialized as 'by common repute and common police knowledge head of a murderous gang' selected for his domestic fireside a locality securely remote from the scene of his professional activities. No gang shootings occur hereabouts. No aliens infest it. There are no alky-cookers, no gambling joints, no blind pigs. Life is tranquil, orderly, reposeful. It is a nine o'clock neighborhood—a refuge to which the tired business man may repair, certain of soothing easement from all . . . care.

The Capones were good neighbors, and Al enjoyed nothing more than "puttering about in carpet slippers," fiddling with the radio, and playing with his son, whom he professed to "idolize."[112] Capone reportedly came home every evening for dinner and spent most of his evenings in a favorite easy chair with a cigar.[113] Sentimental music brought tears to his eyes.[114] So far did this benign domesticity extend that, according to *Time,* the Big Shot was wearing a pink apron and carrying a pan of spaghetti when he greeted reporters at his home.[115] Most accounts included Capone's fervent wish that he could retire from the rackets; only the certainty that enemies would kill him kept him from a life of relaxation. Otherwise he "would be the happiest man in the world," free to devote himself to the family that he loved.[116] From such a villain even the most sanctimonious readers might have had a difficult time distinguishing themselves.

That Americans were intrigued by this chasm between domestic and professional identities explains the regular inclusion of an otherwise irrelevant episode in the life story of the nation's greatest criminal. A couple who rented out their Florida estate while they went on a Egyptian tour discovered that the Capone family, using a front, had become the tenants, and they steeled themselves for the wreckage they would discover upon their return. But once again the mobster and his family defied expectations. Not only was the house in perfect order; Capone had left as a gift the many settings of silverware and china he had purchased to augment the owners' supply. When the couple received a large telephone bill for calls to Chicago, they thought it a small price to pay for the safe return of their home. That afternoon, however, Capone's wife Mae—"a quiet little woman in the simplest of clothes"—appeared at their front door with a thousand dollar bill to cover the charges. The mastermind of the St. Valentine's Day Massacre was a perfectly responsible, well-mannered tenant.[117]

A 1929 *New York Times* feature, "Chicago in New War Against Gang Rule," ended with a discussion of the victims of the St. Valentine's Day Massacre, which, though it had occurred only ten days earlier, had already come to symbolize the depredations of Chicago gangland. Unlike most writers, who elaborated upon the brilliance of the killers, reporter R. L. Duffus wrote about the seven dead men. "The identities of the men killed," he wrote, "throw a glaring light on what a gang is like." By omitting the names of the victims he suggested that each was representative of a broad type. Three were longtime professional criminals with records. "They lived in sporting hotels and led a fast life." Another "was, or seemed to be, a respectable married man with a family who had probably been drawn into the circle" to perform a specific task that required an innocent-looking outsider. The fifth victim, probably "a fashionable bootlegger," was "the son of a respectable widowed mother." Another was a mechanic, "uneducated and obscure." The final victim was an optometrist, "a young hanger-on" from a good family. "Except the first three," Duffus wrote, "the group had nothing in common but the money-making enterprise in which they were jointly engaged. They came from widely different homes, moved in widely different grades and kinds of society and could not have been in any sense companions." Complex in background, they were probably also complex in character. "There are all kinds of gangsters, and Chicago knows them all," Duffus wrote; "Yet it is hard to find the human wolf of criminal fiction—at least, it is hard to find a gunman who acts the part twenty-four hours a day." The only sure conclusion to be drawn from "this assortment of humanity" was that "the amazing contradictions of human nature" defied easy explanation.[118]

The article typified Americans' use of Al Capone and his peers. Ultimately, the underworld demanded attention not so much for its uniqueness as for its representativeness. The gangster's trappings of difference served not to set him apart but to focus attention on him as an outstanding member of the urban crowd. In Duffus's account, the violent deaths of seven formerly obscure men told of the bewildering fragmentation of identity possible in the modern city. For others,

Capone and his dead enemies in the Clark Street garage highlighted the promises and perils of a competitive, highly organized, urban consumer society. In all these accounts, the true subject of the inventors of the gangster was human behavior in a new urban environment.

Epilogue

Around 1934, as Al Capone languished on Alcatraz, important changes occurred in the larger cultural invention to which he belonged. Throughout the thirties, some gangster images continued to offer familiar messages about consumption, gender roles, organization, and individual responsibility. Nevertheless, underworld imagery became less prominent in the mid and late 1930s. One reason was the 1933 repeal of national prohibition, which decriminalized the activity most associated with underworld lawlessness. Perhaps equally important was Hollywood's imposition of strict self-censorship in 1934, which muted the uncritical screenplays and graphic violence central to the gangster genre. More generally, in the depth of the Great Depression audiences probably found that conventional elements of the gangster genre, developed a decade earlier, no longer addressed urgent cultural issues. Underworld imagery would remain compelling only to the extent it grappled with problems that mattered to millions of Americans.

Though attention diminished, the public enemy did continue to play important cultural roles. One new role involved the criminal's relationship to governmental authority. In the twenties and early thirties criminals highlighted official weakness, ineptitude, and corruption. Powerful, technologically sophisticated mobsters blithely ignored stereotyped backward Irish flatfoots, underpowered patrol cars, and a toothless federal government. This relationship changed dramatically after the media coronation of J. Edgar Hoover and his G-Men as the nation's crime busters. A series of highly publicized outlaws, John Dillinger the most important, served as foils to the newly potent federal crime fighters. Cast as supporting characters in modern morality plays, these criminals contributed to a timely, hopeful message about a new federal effectiveness in responding to urgent national problems.[1]

The gangster genre also adapted by shifting emphasis among its elements. That the underworld's subversive messages about business seemed especially apt as the Depression wore on is suggested by films like *Bullets or Ballots,* which traces the control of a predatory gang to the directors of a large bank, who meet in its imposing, columned capitalist temple.[2] A different cycle of films, epitomized by *Angels with Dirty Faces* and *Dead End,* inverted genre conventions and explored the environmental roots of criminality. These sympathetic portrayals of helpless men and women caught up in circumstances beyond their control perhaps offered consolation to audiences struggling with the incomprehensible forces of an economy in chaos.[3]

The most striking change in underworld imagery was that the gangster was increasingly situated outside the city. Hoover's FBI helped concentrate the nation's attention on bandits like Dillinger and Pretty Boy Floyd, who targeted poorly protected small-town banks. Hollywood joined in this expansion of the geography of crime from the major urban centers to the distant countryside as well. Filmmakers placed the criminal in desolate environments worlds apart from the vibrant cities of his recent past. An extended chase in *Public Enemy's Wife* takes place in Florida, but not in Capone's Miami. Now the gangster's territory covers remote, dusty back roads. From the rugged mountains of *High Sierra* to the isolated desert service station of *The Petrified Forest,* the gangster has entered a new realm that often seems, as a character in *Heat Lightning* laments, "a thousand miles from anywhere."[4]

In moving the public enemy to a harsh natural landscape, writers and filmmakers placed him against the backdrop that Depression-era Americans used to produce their most powerful images of contemporary troubles. The explanatory imagery of the twenties had been

overwhelmingly urban—filled with skyscrapers, bustling businessmen, and new women, all set to a jazz score. Beginning in the early
1930s writers and photographers often turned to the countryside to
capture the hardships of a people mired in economic depression. Rural people once seemed quaint and dated. Now hopeless farmers and
dejected migrants epitomized contemporary hard times.[5] The gangster, patterned after the men and women of those other rural images,
lost his city swagger. His clothes, now less stylish, were often covered
in dust. No longer surrounded by an efficient organization, he was
often a loner, perhaps assisted by a few dubiously reliable confeder-
ates. Most strikingly, the rural gangster lacked the cocky self-
assurance once rooted in the vitality of the prosperous city. As *The
Petrified Forest*'s Duke Mantee, brilliantly played by a worn-out, battered Humphrey Bogart, grumbles, "I spend most of my time since I
grew up in jail. It looks like I spend the rest of my life dead."[6] Where
urban settings had reveled in human accomplishments, the prehistoric mountains and unchanging deserts of later films overawed the
puny deeds of mere men and women.

The outlaw's return to the countryside signalled that in the
depths of the Depression Americans' social concerns no longer centered so exclusively on the city. More or less reconciled to urbanism,
Americans had turned their attention to a different set of social
problems.

Coincident with Capone's deterioration from neurosyphilis, gangster
imagery faded during the Second World War. Capone died in 1947.
Nevertheless, he was not forgotten, and Americans have continued
to use his cultural progeny to understand their social worlds.
Through the Cold War, shadowy images of nefarious criminal syndi-
cates instructed Americans about the terrible powers of extensive
subversive networks. Crime films in the fifties and sixties explored
youthful rebellion in new and powerful ways. The *Godfather* cycle
and its imitators reconsidered familiar themes, again problematic, of
individual responsibility, familial obligation, corporate greed, and
sexual morality. In the eighties and nineties, for many Americans images of African-American and Hispanic gangs have become bound
up with perceptions of irremediable urban pathology. At the end of
the century as at its beginning, some observers are using crime to

mark large groups as fundamentally different, dangerous, and unworthy. Meanwhile, disaffected youths see in the video images of "gangsta" rappers a violent message of identity and empowerment. Underworld imagery and its messages have changed, but their potency remains.

Notes

Introduction

1. See "List 28 as Public Enemies," *Chicago Tribune* 24 April 1930; Warner Brothers, *The Public Enemy,* 1931.

2. Joseph R. Gusfield, *Symbolic Crusade: Status Politics and the American Temperance Movement* (Urbana: University of Illinois Press, 1963) remains persuasive, though more recent scholars have properly corrected the tendency to isolate the prohibition movement as a moralistic throwback only distantly related to pragmatic concerns.

3. For more on the relationship of genre and values, see Richard Slotkin, *Gunfighter Nation: The Myth of the Frontier in Twentieth-Century America* (New York: Harper Perennial, 1992), 5–10; John G. Cawelti, *Adventure, Mystery, and Romance: Formula Stories as Art and Popular Culture* (Chicago: University of Chicago Press, 1976). For a provocative discussion of the development of a national commercial culture from local roots, see William R. Taylor, "The Launching of a Commercial Culture: New York City, 1860–1930," in *Power, Culture, and Place: Essays on New York City,* ed. John Hull Mollenkopf (New York: Russell Sage Foundation, 1986), 107–33. Discussions of the gangster genre have focused on films and include, most usefully, Carlos Clarens, *Crime Movies: From Griffith to the Godfather and Beyond* (New York: Norton, 1980); Eugene Rosow, *Born to Lose: The Gangster Film in America* (New York: Oxford University Press, 1978). Robert Warshow, "The Gangster as Tragic Hero," chap. in *The Immediate Experience: Movies, Comics, Theatre and Other Aspects of Popular Culture* (New York: Anchor

Books, 1962), 83–88, is a thoughtful, though one–dimensional, rumination on the genre as a bleak critique of the success ethic.

4. The classic account is Emile Durkheim, *The Division of Labor in Society* (New York: The Free Press, 1964), 70–110. Also see Kai T. Erikson, *Wayward Puritans: A Study in the Sociology of Deviance* (New York: John Wiley, 1966).

5. I have found the following useful. Jerrold Seigel, *Bohemian Paris: Culture, Politics, and the Boundaries of Bourgeois Life, 1830–1930* (New York: Viking, 1986); Martin J. Wiener, *Reconstructing the Criminal: Culture, Law, and Policy in England, 1830–1914* (Cambridge: Cambridge University Press, 1990); Paula S. Fass, "Making and Remaking an Event: The Leopold and Loeb Case in American Culture," *Journal of American History* 80 (December 1993): 919–51; Judith R. Walkowitz, *City of Dreadful Delight: Narratives of Sexual Danger in Late-Victorian London* (Chicago: University of Chicago Press, 1992); Karen Halttunen, *Confidence Men and Painted Women: A Study of Middle–Class Culture in America, 1830–1870* (New Haven: Yale University Press, 1982); Karen Halttunen, "Early American Murder Narratives: The Birth of Horror," in *The Power of Culture: Critical Essays in American History,* ed. Richard Wightman Fox and T. J. Jackson Lears (Chicago: University of Chicago Press, 1993), 66–101; Ruth Rosen, *The Lost Sisterhood: Prostitution in America, 1900–1918* (Baltimore: Johns Hopkins University Press, 1982); James Gilbert, *A Cycle of Outrage: America's Reaction to the Juvenile Delinquent in the 1950s* (New York: Oxford University Press, 1986); Elaine S. Abelson, *When Ladies Go A-Thieving: Middle-Class Shoplifters in the Victorian Department Store* (New York: Oxford University Press, 1989); David J. Rothman, *The Discovery of the Asylum: Social Order and Disorder in the New Republic* (Boston: Little, Brown, 1971); Charles E. Rosenberg, *The Trial of the Assassin Guiteau: Psychiatry and Law in the Gilded Age* (Chicago: University of Chicago Press, 1968); William Howard Moore, *The Kefauver Committee and the Politics of Crime, 1950–1952* (Columbia, Mo.: University of Missouri Press, 1974); Estelle B. Freedman, "'Uncontrolled Desires': The Response to the Sexual Psychopath, 1920–1960," *Journal of American History* 74 (June 1987): 83–106.

6. Jack Katz, "What Makes Crime 'News'?" *Media, Culture and Society* 9 (1987), 47–75 (quotation from p. 74). Katz argues persuasively that consumers understand that journalistic accounts do not depict typical crimes or criminals. Though media portrayals of a crime wave do influence public perceptions of the overall amount of crime, popular notions of the composition of that increase conform more closely to reality—as measured by statistics of reported crime—than to journalistic accounts.

7. Warner Brothers, *Blondie Johnson* pressbook, 1933, Warner Brothers Pressbook Collection, State Historical Society of Wisconsin, Madison.

8. Clarens, *Crime Movies,* 53.

9. Gunther Barth, *City People: The Rise of Modern City Culture in Nineteenth-Century America* (New York: Oxford University Press, 1980), 58–62.

10. In addition to United Artists' *Scarface,* 1932, Hecht also wrote the basis for Paramount's *Underworld,* 1927, much revised by director Josef von Sternberg and often called the first of the gangster genre.

11. See Peter J. Schmitt, *Back to Nature: The Arcadian Myth in Urban America* (Baltimore: Johns Hopkins University Press, 1990), xix–xx; T. J. Jackson Lears, *No Place of Grace: Antimodernism and the Transformation of American Culture, 1880–1920* (New York: Pantheon, 1981), 57.

12. William R. Taylor, *In Pursuit of Gotham: Culture and Commerce in New York* (New York: Oxford University Press, 1992) 17–20, 31–32.

13. Richard Wightman Fox, "The Discipline of Amusement," in William R. Taylor, ed., *Inventing Times Square: Commerce and Culture at the Cross-roads of the World* (New York: Russell Sage Foundation, 1991), 84–86.

14. James Gilbert, *Perfect Cities: Chicago's Utopias of 1893* (Chicago: University of Chicago Press, 1991), 78.

15. Sinclair Lewis, *Babbitt* (New York: New American Library, 1980 [1922]), 45.

Chapter One

1. Charles Frederick Carter, "The Carnival of Crime in the United States," *Current History* 15 (February 1922): 756, 753. Comparisons of American and international criminality were offered by scores of writers, few of whom granted even the slight consolation of Communist preeminence in crime. See "America's High Tide of Crime," *Literary Digest* 67 (11 December 1920): 11; "The Permanent Crime Wave," *New Republic* 25 (5 January 1921): 156–57; "Wanted: A New Crusade," *Current Opinion* 70 (February 1921): 148–51; Edwin Grant Conklin, "Some Biological Aspects of Immigration," *Scribner's* 69 (March 1921): 355; Raymond B. Fosdick, "The Crime Wave in America," *New Republic* 26 (6 April 1921): 150–52; "Accounting for the 'Crime Wave,'" *Literary Digest* 70 (27 August 1921): 30; George S. Buck, "The Crime Wave and Law Enforcement," *Outlook* 131 (3 May 1922): 16–17; Basil Thomson, "The Crime Wave and How to Deal with It," *Saturday Evening Post* 195 (24 February 1923): 9; Rupert Hughes, "Cross Country Crime," *Ladies Home Journal* 41 (June 1924): 21; Evans Clark, "U. S. Indicted as the Most Lawless Country," *New York Times,* 2 November 1924; Wesley W. Stout, "Fingerprinting Bullets," *Saturday Evening Post* 197 (13 June 1925): 6; Richard Washburn Child, "The Great American Scandal: Our Crime Tide," *Saturday Evening Post* 198 (1 August 1925): 7, 149–50; "The Rising Tide of Crime," *Literary Digest* 86 (15 August 1925): 5–7; Mark O. Prentiss, "War on the Growing Menace of Crime," *Current History* 23 (October 1925): 1–2; "More Advertising Against Crime," *Literary Digest* 87 (17 October 1925): 34; Theodore E. Burton, "Curbing Crime in the United States," *Current History* 23 (January 1926): 470–75; "Why There Is Less Crime in Europe," *Literary Digest* 94 (3 September 1927): 14; Frederick L. Hoffman, "Murder and the Death Penalty," *Current History* 28 (June 1928): 408–10; Francis Bowes Sayre, "Crime and Punishment," *Atlantic* 141 (June 1928): 735.

2. This publicizing of scientific theories about criminality was part of a larger popularization of scientific knowledge in the 1920s. See Warren I. Susman, "Culture and Civilization: The Nineteen-Twenties," chap. in *Culture as History: The Transformation of American Society in the Twentieth Century* (New York: Pantheon, 1984), 107–08.

3. Sayre, "Crime and Punishment," 745.

4. On the eugenicists' understandings of crime, see Mark H. Haller, *Eugenics: Hereditarian Attitudes in American Thought* (New Brunswick: Rutgers University Press, 1963), 95–110; Daniel J. Kevles, *In the Name of Eugenics: Genetics and the Uses of Human Heredity* (New York: Knopf, 1985), 46–47, 70–73. One study found that from 1910 to 1914 "the general magazines carried more articles on eugenics than on the three questions of slums, tenements, and living standards, combined." See John Higham, *Strangers in the Land: Patterns of American Nativism, 1860–1925* (New York: Atheneum, 1963), 150–51.

5. Wesley O. Howard, "Why Must I Judge These People?" *Collier's* 72 (4 August 1923): 19.

6. "Exploring the Criminal Mind," *Literary Digest* 96 (24 March 1928): 24.

7. Howard, "Why Must I Judge These People?" 19.

8. Conklin, "Some Biological Aspects of Immigration," 356.

9. Honore Willsie, "American Race-Control," *Woman Citizen* 7 (3 June 1922): 15.

10. French Strother, "The Cure for Crime: Stop the Breeding of Mental Defectives," *World's Work* 48 (August 1924): 396.

11. Conklin, "Some Biological Aspects of Immigration," 352–53.

12. "Exploring the Criminal Mind," 23.

13. Strother, "Cure for Crime," 395–96; "Exploring the Criminal Mind," 23–24.

14. "Exploring the Criminal Mind," 23.

15. Max Schlapp quoted in Edward H. Smith, "Jail Can't Cure Them, Doctors Can," *Collier's* 72 (11 August 1923): 22.

16. Edward H. Smith, "Origins of Young Criminals Are Studied," *New York Times*, 15 August 1926.

17. Winthrop D. Lane, "Curbing Crime by Scientific Methods," *Current History* 24 (September 1926): 887.

18. Fred E. Haynes, "What Is Crime Today?" *Independent* 114 (28 March 1925): 345.

19. "Crime Cures, What Have You?" *Literary Digest* 87 (26 December 1925): 24.

20. Harry Elmer Barnes, "The Crime Complex: Modern Methods in Treating Criminals Scientifically," *Current History* 21 (December 1924): 360–61.

21. Max Schlapp quoted in Smith, "Jail Can't Cure Them, Doctors Can," 22.

22. French Strother, "The Cause of Crime: Defective Brain," *World's Work* 48 (July 1924): 276.

23. Edward H. Smith, "Science Finds Causes of Tendency to Crime" *New York Times*, 31 January 1926.

24. Barnes, "Crime Complex," 362.

25. Strother, "Cure for Crime," 393.

26. Sayre, "Crime and Punishment," 745.

27. Barnes, "Crime Complex," 361.

28. Smith, "Science Finds Causes."

29. Smith, "Science Finds Causes."

30. Barnes, "Crime Complex," 361.

31. Strother, "Cause of Crime," 277–79.

32. Walter Lippmann, "The Underworld: A Stultified Conscience," *Forum* 85 (February 1931): 66.

33. See T. J. Jackson Lears, *No Place of Grace: Antimodernism and the Transformation of American Culture, 1880–1920* (New York: Pantheon, 1981), 32–38; Alan Trachtenberg, *The Incorporation of America: Culture and Society in the Gilded Age* (New York: Hill and Wang, 1982), 42–47; Gerald F. Linderman, *Embattled Courage: The Experience of Combat in the American Civil War* (New York: The Free Press, 1987), 17–18; Susan Curtis, "The Son of Man and God the Father: The Social Gospel and Victorian Masculinity," in *Meanings for Manhood: Constructions of Masculinity in Victorian America* (Chicago: University of Chicago Press, 1990), 71–72, 232n; Paul Boyer, *Urban Masses and Moral Order in America, 1820–1920* (Cambridge: Cambridge University Press, 1978), 284–92; Roland Marchand, *Advertising the American Dream: Making Way for Modernity, 1920–1940* (Berkeley: University of California Press, 1985), 268–69.

34. Joseph Gollomb, "Meeting the Crime Wave: A Comparison of Methods," *Nation* 112 (January 1921): 80.

35. Fred L. Holmes, "Making Criminals Out of Soldiers," *Nation* 121 (22 July 1925): 114.

36. Strother, "Cure for Crime," 396.

37. "America's High Tide of Crime," 12.

38. Smith, "Jail Can't Cure Them, Doctors Can," 22. Also see "Rising Tide of Crime," 5.

39. Strother, "Cure for Crime," 396.

40. Clark, "U. S. Indicted as the Most Lawless Country."

41. Harry Elmer Barnes, "The Scientific Treatment of Crime," *Current History* 27 (December 1927): 309.

42. Edgar A. Doll, "The Control of Crime," *Scientific Monthly* 26 (June 1928): 551.

43. Barnes, "Crime Complex," 360. Also see Strother, "Cure for Crime," 389–97; Watson Davis, "The Nation-Wide Campaign to Reduce Crime," *Current History* 27 (December 1927): 303; Haynes, "What Is Crime Today?" 343; Barnes, "Scientific Treatment of Crime," 309–13; Lane, "Curbing

Crime by Scientific Methods," 886–92; Smith, "Jail Can't Cure Them," 22, and "Science Finds Causes"; George W. Kirchwey, "Crime Waves and Remedies," *Nation* 112 (9 February 1921): 206–8; E. S. Hitchcock, "What Is Prison For?" *Atlantic* 134 (November 1924): 612–15.

44. "Murderous Maniacs at Large," *Literary Digest* 86 (19 September 1925): 9.

45. Barnes, "Crime Complex," 368.

46. Watson Davis, "Psychiatry and Crime," *Current History* 28 (August 1928): 830.

47. Davis, "Nation-Wide Campaign to Reduce Crime," 304–5.

48. Barnes, "Scientific Treatment of Crime," 311.

49. Strother, "Cure for Crime," 394.

50. See Boyer, *Urban Masses and Moral Order*, 189–219; Higham, *Strangers in the Land*, 158–263; Roy Rosenzweig, *Eight Hours for What We Will: Workers and Leisure in an Industrial City, 1870–1920* (Cambridge: Cambridge University Press, 1983), 93–168; Kathy Peiss, *Cheap Amusements: Working Women and Leisure in Turn-of-the-Century New York* (Philadelphia: Temple University Press, 1986), 163–88; Egal Freedman, "Prostitution, the Alien Woman and the Progressive Imagination," *American Quarterly* 19 (Summer 1967): 192–206.

51. See, for example, two ambiguous accounts: Sir Basil Thomson, "Popular Fallacies About Crime," *Saturday Evening Post* 195 (21 April 1923): 8, 72; George S. Dougherty, "The Criminal as a Human Being," *Saturday Evening Post* 196 (15 March 1924): 182.

52. See Jan Cohn, *Creating America: George Horace Lorimer and the Saturday Evening Post* (Pittsburgh: University of Pittsburgh Press, 1989), 190–91, on Lorimer's rejections of several articles that ran counter (predictably in the case of one by Clarence Darrow) to *Post* orthodoxy on crime.

53. James L. Ford, "Crime and Sentimentality," *Scribner's* 78 (October 1925): 407; Richard Washburn Child, "The Great American Scandal: Turning Back the Crime Tide," *Saturday Evening Post* 198 (14 November 1925): 30; Richard Washburn Child, "The Great American Scandal: Why We Have Crime," *Saturday Evening Post* 198 (15 August 1925): 154, 157; Richard Washburn Child, "The Great American Scandal: Our Criminal Goes to Court," *Saturday Evening Post* 198 (31 October 1925): 177.

54. For similar characterizations of the experts, see Carter, "Carnival of Crime in the United States," 760–61; Richard Washburn Child, "On the Criminal Side," *Saturday Evening Post* 202 (5 April 1930): 25; "Causes of Crime," *New York Times*, 6 January 1929; "Meddler's Mischief," *Saturday Evening Post* 198 (19 December 1925): 24; "Rising Tide of Crime," 6; Charles Francis Coe, "Why Crime Waves?" *Saturday Evening Post* 200 (17 March 1928): 153; Louis E. Bisch, "The Inside of the Criminal Mind," *Saturday Evening Post* 198 (12 June 1926): 14–15, 165; William McAdoo, "Causes and Mechanisms of Prevalent Crimes," *Scientific Monthly* 24 (May 1927): 415–17; "Unpunished Crime," *Independent* 115 (29 August 1925): 226–27; Charles C. Nott, Jr., "Coddling Criminals," *Scribner's* 79 (May

1926): 540–43; Charles C. Nott, Jr., "The Juror's Part in Crime," *Scribner's* 79 (January 1926): 94–96; Charles C. Nott, Jr., "Old Adam: The Criminal is a Natural Man," *Scribner's* 80 (December 1926): 686–88; Prisoner No. 4000X, "A Criminal Looks at Crime and Punishment," *Scribner's* 81 (January 1927): 86–89; Don Marquis, "The Crime Situation: Interviews with Divers Authorities," *Collier's* 88 (28 November 1931): 19, 45; "'I Never Had a Chance,'" *Literary Digest* 84 (14 March 1925): 36; Burton, "Curbing Crime in the United States," 470–75.

55. Coe, "Why Crime Waves?" 153.

56. Nott, "Old Adam," 687.

57. Richard Washburn Child, "The Great American Scandal: Punishment and Pacifists," *Saturday Evening Post* 198 (7 November 1925): 32; Child, "Great American Scandal: Why We Have Crime," 20; Prentiss, "War on the Growing Menace of Crime," 2.

58. Prisoner No. 4000X, "Criminal Looks at Crime and Punishment," 86. For other accounts drawing on the commonsense views of actual lawbreakers, see Number 13, "The Background of Prison Cruelty," *Atlantic* 126 (August 1920), 214–21; An Ex-Convict, "Take a Criminal's Advice on How to Protect Yourself in the Present 'Crime Wave,'" *Independent* 105 (12 February 1921): 155–56; Child, "The Great American Scandal: Our Criminal Goes to Court," 178, 181–82; Edward H. Smith, "Pardon the Intrusion," *Collier's* 77 (27 March 1926): 12; Don Marquis, "As Crook Sees Crook," *Saturday Evening Post* 201 (27 October 1928): 14–15.

59. S. Tee Bee, "With the Gangsters," *Saturday Evening Post* 198 (26 June 1926): 54.

60. William G. Shepherd, "Damned Young," *Collier's* 77 (27 March 1926): 8–9.

61. Dougherty, "Criminal as a Human Being," 20. Also see "Virtue in Blackjackers," *Literary Digest* 80 (29 March 1924): 34.

62. Nott, "Old Adam," 687.

63. Thomson, "Popular Fallacies about Crime," 74.

64. Shepherd, "Damned Young," 8–9.

65. James M. Hepbron, "Local Crime Commissions; Their Origin, Purpose and Accomplishments," *Scientific Monthly* 24 (May 1927): 429.

66. Bisch, "Inside of the Criminal Mind," 166.

67. See John Knight, "Difficulties in Enforcing Criminal Law," *Current History* 27 (December 1927): 325.

68. See Hepbron, "Local Crime Commissions," 429; Dougherty, "Criminal as a Human Being," 182, 185; S. T. Bee, "High Rollers of Crime," *Saturday Evening Post* 198 (17 April 1926): 60

69. See Eugene Rosow, *Born to Lose: The Gangster Film in America* (New York: Oxford University Press, 1978), 85–88.

70. Dougherty, "Criminal as a Human Being," 186.

71. Child, "Great American Scandal: Our Crime Tide," 153.

72. Bee, "High Rollers of Crime," 56.

73. Shepherd, "Damned Young," 9. Also see Richard Washburn Child,

"The Great American Scandal: Take This Case," *Saturday Evening Post* 198 (26 September 1925): 6, 7, 182.

74. Child, "Great American Scandal: Take This Case," 6, 7, 186. Also see Rayner Seelig, "One Fine Day," *Liberty* 5 (15 February 1930): 24, 26, 28.

75. William G. Shepherd, "Damned Comfortably," *Collier's* 77 (3 April 1926): 9.

76. Quoted in "Virtue in Blackjackers," 34.

77. Bisch, "Inside of the Criminal Mind," 165. Also see Smith, "Pardon the Intrusion," 12; Charles W. Wood, "There's Honor Among Gunmen," *Collier's* 74 (26 July 1924): 15.

78. George S. Dougherty, "The Stick-Up and House Prowler," *Saturday Evening Post* 196 (7 June 1924): 70.

79. Shepherd, "Damned Young," 9.

80. Child, "Great American Scandal: Take This Case," 185. Also see Dougherty, "Criminal as a Human Being," 20.

81. Morris Markey, "Gangs," *Atlantic* 141 (March 1928): 305.

82. See Rosow, *Born to Lose*, 124.

83. Jack Grey, "The New Underworld," *Outlook and Independent* 151 (20 March 1929): 444–45.

84. Child, "Great American Scandal: Why We Have Crime," 20.

85. On the changing values about work and leisure, see Daniel T. Rodgers, *The Work Ethic in Industrial America, 1850–1920* (Chicago: University of Chicago Press, 1978), 233–34,

86. "Our Lawless Age," *Literary Digest* 71 (8 October 1921): 30.

87. Child, "Great American Scandal: Why We Have Crime," 154.

88. "Home-Made Thugs," *Literary Digest* 83 (27 December 1924): 32.

89. "Church Warfare Against Crime," *Literary Digest* 86 (5 September 1925): 32.

90. "Home-Made Thugs," 31.

91. Child, "Great American Scandal: Why We Have Crime," 154.

92. Richard Washburn Child, "The Great American Scandal: Youth and Felony," *Saturday Evening Post* 198 (29 August 1925): 19, 133. Margaret Marsh, "Suburban Men and Masculine Domesticity, 1870–1915," in *Meanings for Manhood: Constructions of Masculinity in Victorian America*, ed. Mark C. Carnes and Clyde Griffen (Chicago: University of Chicago Press, 1990), 123–24, notes the spreading notion that urban residence, especially in apartments, rendered impossible appropriate middle-class family life.

93. For more on the role of defective homes in causing criminality, see "Rising Tide of Crime," 7; Bisch, "Inside of the Criminal Mind," 166; "Our Share in the Murderer's Guilt," *Literary Digest* 80 (22 March 1924): 32–33; "Why Children Cheat and Steal," *Literary Digest* 80 (15 March 1924): 31–32.

94. For a perceptive survey of changes in middle-class families, see Paula S. Fass, *The Damned and the Beautiful: American Youth in the 1920s* (New York: Oxford University Press, 1977), 53–118. Also see Elaine Tyler May,

Great Expectations: Marriage and Divorce in Post-Victorian America (Chicago: University of Chicago Press, 1980), 49–72.

95. Assertions of the lack of respect for law usually contained a strong condemnation of unnecessary laws, among them business regulations and, especially, prohibition—even before the mid-twenties when business leaders organized a repeal movement partly on the grounds that prohibition set a dangerous precedent for government intervention in private matters and bred disrespect for law. See "America's High Tide of Crime," 12; Carter, "Carnival of Crime," 760; William B. Swaney, "What Shall We Do to Stop Crime?" *Current History* 16 (September 1922): 917–26; "Accounting for the 'Crime Wave,'" 30; Buck, "Crime Wave and Law Enforcement," 16–17; "Church Warfare Against Crime," 33; Bisch, "Inside of the Criminal Mind," 166; Coe, "Why Crime Waves?" 9; Hoffman, "Murder and the Death Penalty," 410. On the repeal movement, see David E. Kyvig, *Repealing National Prohibition* (Chicago: University of Chicago Press, 1979), 71–97.

96. Hoffman, "Murder and the Death Penalty," 410.

97. Child, "Great American Scandal: Why We Have Crime," 21.

98. Ibid., 154; Child, "Great American Scandal: Youth and Felony," 134.

99. On hopes that wartime crises would bring a purifying social discipline, see David M. Kennedy, *Over Here: The First World War and American Society* (New York: Oxford University Press, 1980), 39–92; Daniel Horowitz, *The Morality of Spending: Attitudes toward the Consumer Society in America, 1875–1940* (Baltimore: Johns Hopkins University Press, 1985), 114; and my article on the ideological response to the influenza epidemic of 1918, "Don't Shake—Salute!" *Chicago History* 19 (Fall and Winter 1990–91): 4–23.

100. Burton, "Curbing Crime in the United States," 472.

101. Dougherty, "Stick-Up and House Prowler," 70.

102. "Crimes, 'Crime Waves,' Criminals, and the Police," *Literary Digest* 60 (18 March 1919): 62. Also see Seelig, "One Fine Day," 22–23.

103. George W. Kirchwey, quoted in Clark, "U. S. Indicted as the Most Lawless Country."

104. Coe, "Why Crime Waves?" 9. Also see "Church Warfare Against Crime," 33.

105. Child, "Great American Scandal: Youth and Felony," 18, 134; Child, "Great American Scandal: Why We Have Crime," 158; Child quoted in "Gary and Smith Join National Crusade to Diminish Crime," *New York Times*, 30 July 1925.

106. For other accounts of a general failure to accept responsibility, see "Home-Made Thugs," 31; Swaney, "What Shall We Do to Stop Crime?" 917–22.

107. "Our Lawless Age," 30.

108. See, for example, Strother, "Cure for Crime," 389–97.

109. Davis, "Nation-Wide Campaign to Reduce Crime," 303.

110. "Let the Treatment Fit the Criminal," *Independent and Outlook* 150 (7 November 1928): 1119.

111. Haynes, "What Is Crime Today?" 343. For additional articles calling for criminal justice reforms based on deterministic understandings, see Barnes, "Crime Complex," 360–68, and "Scientific Treatment of Crime," 309–13; Lane, "Curbing Crime by Scientific Methods," 886–92; Smith, "Jail Can't Cure Them," 22; Smith, "Science Finds Causes"; George W. Kirchwey, "Crime Waves and Remedies," *Nation* 112 (9 February 1921): 206–8; E. S. Hitchcock, "What Is Prison For?" *Atlantic* 134 (November 1924): 612–15; "Psychiatry and the Criminal," *Literary Digest* 85 (16 May 1925): 25; Sheldon Glueck, "Reformers and Crime," *New Republic* 44 (23 September 1925): 120–23.

112. Dougherty, "Stick-Up and House Prowler," 17.

113. "Advertising Against Criminality," *Literary Digest* 86 (11 July 1925): 30. Also see Frank Dorrance Hopley, "The Cop Will Get You—If You Don't Watch Out!" *Independent* 115 (12 September 1925): 292–93.

114. See, for example, "Wanted: A New Crusade," 150; Swaney, "What Shall We Do to Stop Crime?" 917–22; R. M. Wanamaker, "The Campaign Against Crime: The Judge's Part in It," *Saturday Evening Post* 195 (28 October 1922): 46; Clark, "U. S. Indicted as the Most Lawless Country"; "To Put the Gunman Away for Life," *Literary Digest* 86 (15 August 1925): 32; Child, "Great American Scandal: Our Criminal Goes to Court," 29; Richard Washburn Child, "Criminals, Prosecution, et al.," *Saturday Evening Post* 202 (3 May 1930): 20–21; Burton, "Curbing Crime in the United States," 473–74; "Amateur and Professional Crime," *Outlook* 143 (25 August 1926): 561–62; "Common-Sense Legal Reforms," *Saturday Evening Post* 199 (28 August 1926): 24; Prentiss, "War on the Growing Menace of Crime," 4–5; "America's High Tide of Crime," 12; "Sandbags Versus Machine Guns," *Saturday Evening Post* 199 (20 November 1926): 32; Oliver P. Newman, "Stop Helping the Criminal: An Authorized Interview with the Chief Justice, William Howard Taft," *Collier's* 79 (22 January 1927): 8–9; "California's Great Opportunity," *Saturday Evening Post* 199 (26 February 1927): 26; "Honors Even," *Saturday Evening Post* 199 (1 June 1927): 30.

115. Quoted in "To Tighten Up the Screws on Criminals," *Literary Digest* 89 (26 June 1926): 14.

116. Nott, "Coddling Criminals," 541. For additional criticisms of the supposedly lenient treatment of convicts, see Carter, "Carnival of Crime in the United States," 757; Child, "Great American Scandal: Why We Have Crime," 157; "Meddlers' Mischief," 24; Nott, "Juror's Part in Crime," 96; "Darlings of Society," *New York Times* 29 April 1926; Boyden Sparkes, "Rubber-Stamp Parole," *Scribner's* 80 (July 1926): 27; Ford, "Crime and Sentimentality," 407–11; Prisoner No. 4000X, "Criminal Looks at Crime and Punishment," 86–89; "Rising Tide of Crime," 6; Bisch, "Inside of the Criminal Mind," 166, 169.

117. "Amateur and Professional Crime," 561.

118. Thomson, "Crime Wave and How to Deal with It," 9, 146.

119. Child, "Great American Scandal: Our Criminal Goes to Court," 170.

120. Nott, "Coddling Criminals," 543.

Chapter Two

1. Arthur Pound, "The Sunny Side of Crime," *Independent* 116 (19 June 1926): 708.

2. Richard Washburn Child, "The Great American Scandal: Crime and Our Police," *Saturday Evening Post* 198 (10 October 1925): 27.

3. William E. Leuchtenburg, *The Perils of Prosperity, 1914–32* (Chicago: University of Chicago Press, 1958), 178–82, 185–86, 192; William Leach, *Land of Desire: Merchants, Power, and the Rise of a New American Culture* (New York: Pantheon, 1993), 272–75. See Lizbeth Cohen, *Making a New Deal: Industrial Workers in Chicago, 1919–1939* (Cambridge: Cambridge University Press, 1991), 106–9, 116–20, for an account of resistance to and then acceptance of chain stores in Chicago ethnic neighborhoods in the twenties. On the proliferation of corporate sales agents in rural areas, see Olivier Zunz, *Making America Corporate, 1870–1920* (Chicago: University of Chicago Press, 1990), 151.

4. Louis Galambos, *The Public Image of Big Business in America, 1880–1940* (Baltimore: Johns Hopkins University Press, 1975), 8.

5. Leuchtenburg, *Perils of Prosperity*, 189–93; Galambos, *Public Image of Big Business*, 8.

6. Robert H. Wiebe, *The Search for Order, 1877–1920* (New York: Hill and Wang, 1967), 111–32. On the integration of women into clerical employment, see Lois Scharf, *To Work and to Wed: Female Employment, Feminism, and the Great Depression* (Westport, Conn.: Greenwood Press, 1980), 10–14; and Zunz, *Making America Corporate*, 103–24.

7. Wiebe, *Search for Order*, 164–95; Samuel P. Hays, "The Politics of Reform in Municipal Government in the Progressive Era," *Pacific Northwest Quarterly* 55 (1964), 157–69; Martin J. Schiesl, *The Politics of Efficiency: Municipal Administration and Reform in America, 1880–1920* (Berkeley: University of California Press, 1977), 114–15.

8. David M. Kennedy, *Over Here: The First World War and American Society* (New York: Oxford University Press, 1980), 94, 113–42; Ellis W. Hawley, *The Great War and the Search for a Modern Order: A History of the American People and Their Institutions, 1917–1933* (New York: St. Martin's, 1979), 20–27.

9. Hawley, *Great War and the Search for a Modern Order*, 45–48, 52–55, 66–71, 100–107; Ellis W. Hawley, "Herbert Hoover, the Commerce Secretariat, and the Vision of an Associative State, 1921–1928," *Journal of American History* 61 (June 1974): 116–40; Leach, *Land of Desire*, 349–72.

10. Bruce Barton, *The Man Nobody Knows: A Discovery of the Real Jesus* (Indianapolis: Bobbs-Merrill, 1925), 1–31.

11. Frederick Lewis Allen, *Only Yesterday: An Informal History of the 1920's* (New York: Harper and Row, 1964), 148. On adulatory attitudes towards businessmen, see Leuchtenburg, *Perils of Prosperity*, 186–89, 201–3; George E. Mowry, ed., *The Twenties: Fords, Flappers and Fanatics* (Engle-

wood Cliffs: Prentice-Hall, 1963), 3–42; Warren I. Susman, "Culture Heroes: Ford, Barton, Ruth," chap. in *Culture as History: The Transformation of American Society in the Twentieth Century* (New York: Pantheon, 1984), 122–49; Jan Cohn, *Creating America: George Horace Lorimer and the Saturday Evening Post* (Pittsburgh: University of Pittsburgh Press 1989), 30–39, 86, 136. For businessmen's own self-congratulatory attitudes, see James Warren Prothro, *The Dollar Decade: Business Ideas in the 1920's* (Baton Rouge: Louisiana State University Press, 1954). Lawrence W. Levine, "Progress and Nostalgia: The Self-Image of the Nineteen Twenties," chap. in *The Unpredictable Past: Explorations in American Cultural History* (New York: Oxford University Press, 1993), 204, perceptively detects a note of anxious defensiveness in businessmen's public self-sanctification.

12. Richard Washburn Child, "The Great American Scandal: Our Crime Tide," *Saturday Evening Post* 198 (1 August 1925): 153.

13. Frederick Arnold Kummer, "Why Men Go Wrong," *Collier's* 78 (6 November 1926): 11.

14. Bruce Rae, "Will-O'-The-Wisps of the Underworld," *New York Times Magazine*, 18 August 1929, 7.

15. These generalizations are based on a review of newspaper cartoons reprinted in the *Literary Digest*, cartoons accompanying articles in popular magazines and the *New York Times*, and a collection of Chicago newspaper cartoons preserved at the Chicago Crime Commission. For specific examples, see "Big Business," cartoon accompanying Edward H. Smith, "Crime Has Now Evolved As a Big Business," *New York Times*, 5 September 1926; "Many-Fisted," cartoon reprinted in "Gangsters and Prohibition," *Literary Digest* 109 (30 May 1931): 10; "Another Abdication Needed," cartoon reprinted in "The Tiger Roars at Racketeers," *Literary Digest* 110 (1 July 1931): 10.

16. See, for example, "Uncle Sam to Fight the Black Hand," *Literary Digest* 45 (19 June 1915): 1454. Also see Thomas M. Pitkin, *The Black Hand: A Chapter in Ethnic Crime* (Totowa, N.J.: Littlefield, Adams, 1977). In contrast the 1931 *Illustrated Gangland Map of Chicago* (Chicago: Bruce-Roberts, 1931) depicted the entire city. See "Latest Books Received," *New York Times Book Review*, 23 August 1931, 20.

17. "Wanted: An Exterminator," reprinted in "Church Warfare Against Crime," *Literary Digest* 86 (5 September 1925): 32; "Another Abdication Needed," cartoon reprinted in "Tiger Roars at Racketeers," 10.

18. Child, "Great American Scandal: Our Crime Tide," 153.

19. See also F. Raymond Daniell, "The Big Business of the Racketeers," *New York Times Magazine*, 27 April 1930, 4; Walter Green, "Who's Who in Hooch," *Saturday Evening Post* 198 (12 June 1926): 22; Jack Lait, *Gangster Girl* (New York: Grosset and Dunlap, 1930), 7; William E. Weeks, *All in the Racket* (New York: Charles Boni, 1930), 136.

20. See, for example, Universal, *Traffic in Souls*, 1913; American-Mutual, *Sign of the Spade*, 1916; Famous Players, *Poor Little Peppina*, 1916;

Universal, *Outside the Law,* 1921; Cosmopolitan, *Boomerang Bill,* 1922; Paramount, *Underworld,* 1927.

21. Warner Brothers, *The Finger Points,* 1931. Also see Universal, *Broadway,* 1929; Warner Brothers, *Special Agent,* 1935.

22. Henry Barrett Chamberlin, "Crime as a Business in Chicago," speech printed in *Bulletin of the Chicago Crime Commission,* no. 6 (1 October 1919): 1; "10,000 Follow Crime as a Business in Chicago, Says Civic Official, Appealing for Help," *New York Times,* 26 February 1921. For additional favorable publicity, see, for example, "Says Crime in Chicago Is Highly Organized," *New York Times,* 6 November 1919; "Drink and Crime," *New York Times,* 8 January 1920; "Controlling Crime: How Chicago's Commission of 150 Citizens Has Brought About Heavy Reduction in Offenses—New Methods Employed," *New York Times,* 16 April 1922; "The Rising Tide of Crime," *Literary Digest* 86 (15 August 1925): 5–7; "Church Warfare Against Crime," 32–33; Child, "Great American Scandal: Crime and Our Police," 63; James M. Hepbron, "Local Crime Commissions: Their Origin, Purpose and Accomplishments," *Scientific Monthly* 24 (May 1927): 426–31.

23. Arthur B. Reeve, *The Golden Age of Crime* (New York: Mohawk Press, 1931), 13.

24. Child, "Great American Scandal: Our Crime Tide," 154.

25. "To Put the 'Fence' on the Shelf," *Literary Digest* 95 (3 December 1927): 16.

26. James C. Young, "Crime Gangs Organized as Big Business," *New York Times,* 4 April 1926. For more on the scale of operation of fences, see S. Tee Bee, "With the Gangsters," *Saturday Evening Post* 198 (26 June 1926): 54.

27. Daniell, "Big Business of the Racketeers," 4. Also see "Chicago Problem, No. 2," *Outlook and Independent* 155 (30 April 1930): 699; and Fred D. Pasley, *Muscling In* (New York: Ives Washburn, 1931), 104.

28. Robert Warshow, "The Gangster as Tragic Hero," chap. in *The Immediate Experience: Movies, Comics, Theatre and Other Aspects of Popular Culture* (New York: Anchor, 1964 [1962]), 88.

29. United Artists, *Scarface,* 1932; Warner Brothers, *Little Caesar,* 1930; Warner Brothers, *The Public Enemy,* 1931.

30. See, for example, "The Story of Crime in Chicago," *Bulletin of the Chicago Crime Commission,* no. 8 (20 November 1919): 1–6; Henry Barrett Chamberlin, "Report of the Operating Director," *Bulletin of the Chicago Crime Commission,* no. 17 (31 January 1921): 5–7.

31. See, for example, Jack O'Donnell, "Running the Booze Blockade," *Collier's* 71 (2 June 1923): 9, 27–28; "Hijackers—The Bane of the Bootleggers," *Literary Digest* 78 (4 August 1923): 52–55; Fred C. Kelly, "How Crooks Can Be 'Respectable,'" *Collier's* 74 (2 August 1924): 30; Fred F. Sully, "Industry, the Subterfuge," *Saturday Evening Post* 197 (27 September 1924): 79–80.

32. "Church Warfare Against Crime," 33.

33. The inclusion of bootleggers in the accounts of the nation's most threatening criminals resulted in part from a resurgent discourse about the merits of national prohibition. Expressions of opposition to prohibition became more common in the national media after the middle of the twenties as elite activists began to voice strong dissatisfaction with the Volstead Law. Journalists publicized the arguments of those who blamed prohibition for a national epidemic of crime. See David E. Kyvig, *Repealing National Prohibition* (Chicago: University of Chicago Press, 1979), 71–97.

34. R. L. Duffus, "Philadelphia Bares a Bootleg Kingdom," *New York Times,* 9 September 1928.

35. Daniell, "Big Business of the Racketeers," 4.

36. Warner Brothers, *Doorway to Hell,* 1930.

37. Daniell, "Big Business of the Racketeers," 5.

38. Raymond Moley, "Behind the Menacing Racket," *New York Times Magazine,* 23 November 1930, 1.

39. *The Whole Truth About Racketeers* (New York: Macfadden, 1930), 63.

40. Moley, "Behind the Menacing Racket," 1.

41. Child, "Great American Scandal: Our Crime Tide," 153.

42. Alfred D. Chandler, Jr., *The Visible Hand: The Managerial Revolution in American Business* (Cambridge: Harvard University Press, Belknap Press, 1977), 484–500.

43. Smith, "Crime Has Now Evolved As a Big Business."

44. Smith, "Crime Has Now Evolved As a Big Business."

45. Forrest Crissey, "Beating the Bandits," *Saturday Evening Post* 198 (20 February 1926): 19.

46. Smith, "Crime Has Now Evolved As a Big Business."

47. Smith, "Crime Has Now Evolved As a Big Business."

48. On the development of middle management see Chandler, *Visible Hand,* 411–14. In his content analysis of middle–class periodicals Louis Galambos discovered that by the 1920s faceless managers replaced high-profile financiers as the personifications of business. See *Public Image of Big Business,* 181–83. The "new perception of the large firm reflected the fact that bureaucratic consolidation . . . was replacing the titans with less colorful leaders," he writes (183).

49. Child, "Great American Scandal: Our Crime Tide," 153.

50. S. Tee Bee, "High Rollers of Crime," *Saturday Evening Post* 198 (17 April 1926): 66.

51. Warner Brothers, *Little Caesar,* 1930.

52. See, for example, Universal, *Traffic in Souls,* 1913; American-Mutual, *Sign of the Spade,* 1916.

53. Bee, "With the Gangsters," 54.

54. "The Tyranny of Crime," *Saturday Evening Post* 206 (30 September 1933): 22.

55. Young, "Crime Gangs Organized as Big Business."

56. Smith, "Crime Has Now Evolved As a Big Business."

57. Crissey, "Beating the Bandits," 18–19.

58. On the changes in selling, see Zunz, *Making America Corporate,* 176.

59. O'Donnell, "Running the Booze Blockade," 27.

60. Warner Brothers, *The Big Shakedown,* 1934.

61. R. L. Duffus, "The Gunman Has an Intercity Murder Trade," *New York Times,* 8 July 1928.

62. Chester T. Crowell, "The Criminal's Lawyer," *Saturday Evening Post* 198 (29 May 1926): 24. Also see Warner Brothers, *The Mouthpiece,* 1932.

63. Smith, "Crime Has Now Evolved As a Big Business."

64. See, for example, "The Battle to Disarm the Gunman," *Literary Digest* 92 (19 February 1927): 9; "How the Gangster Goes Into Battle," *Literary Digest* 99 (17 November 1928): 42.

65. "Sandbags Versus Machine Guns," *Saturday Evening Post* 199 (20 November 1926): 32.

66. Louis McH. Howe, "Uncle Sam Starts After Crime," *Saturday Evening Post* 206 (29 July 1933): 5–6.

67. John R. Chamberlain, "Gangsters Have Lost Their Last 'Big Name,'" *New York Times,* 30 October 1927. Herbert Asbury, *The Gangs of New York: An Informal History of the Underworld* (New York: Paragon House, 1990 [1928]), was a popular, nostalgic account. Also see Young, "Crime Gangs Organized as Big Business."

68. Daniell, "Big Business of the Racketeers," 5.

69. Chamberlain, "Gangsters Have Lost Their Last 'Big Name.'"

70. Daniell, "Big Business of the Racketeers," 5. Also see Reeve, *Golden Age of Crime,* 32.

71. Duffus, "Gunman Has an Intercity Murder Trade."

72. Chamberlain, "Gangsters Have Lost Their Last 'Big Name'"; Daniell, "Big Business of the Racketeers," 5.

73. Daniell, "Big Business of the Racketeers," 5.

74. Walter Davenport, "Whitey Was a Piker," *Collier's* 79 (28 May 1927): 16–17.

75. On gangsters' education in violence in the service of businessmen, see "Chicago's Racketeers," *New York Times,* 29 May 1928; Reeve, *Golden Age of Crime,* 43.

76. Charles Francis Coe, "Statistical Law Enforcement," *Saturday Evening Post* 203 (18 October 1930): 146.

77. R. L. Duffus, "Chicago in New War Against Gang Rule," *New York Times,* 24 February 1929.

78. Rayner Seelig, "One Fine Day," *Liberty* 5 (15 February 1930): 22.

79. See, for example, Warner Brothers, *The Public Enemy,* 1931; United Artists, *Scarface,* 1932; Lait, *Gangster Girl,* 169.

80. Warner Brothers, *The Star Witness,* 1931.

81. Daniell, "Big Business of the Racketeers," 5.

82. "'Taken for a Ride' Gunman Epitaph," *New York Times,* 18 August 1929.

83. Duffus, "Gunman Has an Intercity Murder Trade." Also see "Bootlegging and Murder in Detroit," *Literary Digest* 78 (29 September 1923): 52.

84. Duffus, "Gunman Has an Intercity Murder Trade."

85. Chamberlain, "Gangsters Have Lost Their Last 'Big Name.'"

86. "Ex-Bandit Assails New Crime Ethics," *New York Times,* 18 May 1930.

87. Duffus, "Gunman Has an Intercity Murder Trade." Also see Asbury, *Gangs of New York,* xvi.

88. Edward H. Smith, "Machine Guns and Gas Are Easy to Purchase," *New York Times,* 21 November 1926.

89. See, for example, "Accounting for the 'Crime Wave,'" *Literary Digest* 70 (27 August 1921): 30; Jack Lait, *Put on the Spot* (New York: Grosset and Dunlap, 1930), 107.

90. Ernest Hemingway, *A Farewell to Arms* (New York: Scribner's, 1929), 177–78.

91. Theodore E. Burton, "Curbing Crime in the United States," *Current History* 23 (January 1926): 472.

92. Bee, "High Rollers of Crime," 60.

93. Charles Francis Coe, *Ransom* (Philadelphia: J. B. Lippincott, 1934), 73–74. The novel first appeared in *Saturday Evening Post* 206 (5 May–9 June 1934).

94. Warner Brothers, *Doorway to Hell,* 1930. Also see Pasley, *Muscling In,* 259–60.

95. Kummer, "Why Men Go Wrong," 35.

96. Jack Grey, "The New Underworld," *Outlook and Independent* 151 (20 March 1929): 444.

97. For more on the complicity of supposedly respectable citizens, see, for example, Kelly, "How Crooks Can Be 'Respectable,'" 30; "The Bootlegger's Partner," *Woman's Citizen* 8 (5 April 1924): 14; Lloyd Lewis, "On the Chicago Front," *Outlook and Independent* 154 (19 February 1930): 288; Grey, "New Underworld," 444.

98. Raymond Moley, "The Racket: Most Elusive of Crimes," *New York Times,* 9 August 1931.

99. Gordon L. Hostetter, "The Growing Menace of the Racketeer," *New York Times Magazine,* 30 October 1932, 3. Also see Gordon L. Hostetter and Thomas Quinn Beesley, *It's a Racket!* (Chicago: Les Quin Books, 1929).

100. "Chicago's New Use for Gunmen," *Literary Digest* 97 (16 June 1928): 9.

101. Moley, "Racket: Most Elusive of Crimes."

102. William G. Shepherd, "What's the Racket?" *Collier's* 87 (11 April 1931): 11. See also Anon., *Whole Truth About Racketeers,* 63.

103. Hostetter, "Growing Menace of the Racketeer," 3.

104. R. L. Duffus, "The Function of the Racketeer," *New Republic* 58 (27 March 1929): 167.

105. Walter Lippmann, "The Underworld: Our Secret Servant," *Forum*

85 (January 1931): 3. Also see Walter Lippmann, "The Underworld: A Stultified Conscience," *Forum* 85 (February 1931): 65–69.

106. Nearly exclusive attention to the role of the Depression as a wellspring of the genre has resulted in rather one-dimensional analyses, a tendency often compounded by the extrapolation from the two or three films widely viewed and remembered in the decades after the 1930s. See Robert Warshow, "The Gangster as Tragic Hero," chap. in *The Immediate Experience* (New York: Doubleday, 1962), 83–88; Andrew Bergman, *We're in the Money: Depression America and Its Films* (New York: Harper, 1971), 3–17; Robert Sklar, *Movie-Made America: A Cultural History of American Movies* (New York: Vintage, 1975), 179, 181; Richard Gid Powers, *G-Men: Hoover's FBI in American Popular Culture* (Carbondale: Southern Illinois University Press, 1983), 3–32; Richard Slotkin, *Gunfighter Nation: The Myth of the Frontier in Twentieth-Century America* (New York: Harper Perennial, 1992), 260–65; Lawrence W. Levine, "American Culture and the Great Depression," chap. in *The Unpredictable Past*, 224–26.

107. On the economic hard times faced by gangsters in the early thirties, see, for example, Coe, *Ransom* 129, 277; Charles Francis Coe, "Percentage," *Saturday Evening Post* 206 (26 August 1933): 32; Damon Runyon, "The Twilight of the Gangster," *Cosmopolitan* 92 (June 1932), 54–55, 178; Frank J. Loesch, "Coping with the Kidnappers: The Problem and a Proposal," *New York Times,* 30 July 1933.

108. On the gangster's desperate turn to kidnapping and other risky ventures, see, for example, "Our Racketeer Reign of Terror," *Literary Digest* 104 (11 January 1930): 12; Lewis, "On the Chicago Front," 288–90; "Kidnaping—A Growing Racket," *Literary Digest* 109 (23 May 1931): 11; Loesch, "Coping with the Kidnappers"; Charles Francis Coe, "Kidnapping Wave a New Gang Phase," *New York Times,* 16 July 1933; Edward Dean Sullivan, *The Snatch Racket* (New York: Vanguard Press, 1932), 242.

109. On increasing vilification of the gangster as a threat to American families, see, for example, Sullivan, *Snatch Racket,* 186; "The Kidnaper's Threat to American Homes," *Literary Digest* 112 (26 March 1932): 38, 42; "Everybody's Problem," *Saturday Evening Post* 206 (16 September 1933): 22; Mary Roberts Rinehart, "Can Women Stop Crime?" *Saturday Evening Post* 206 (18 November 1933): 8–9, 98, 100–101; Edward Doherty, "The Twilight of the Gangster," parts I and II, *Liberty* 8 (24 October 1931): 5–9, and (31 October 1931): 46–50.

Chapter Three

1. Edward Dean Sullivan, *Chicago Surrenders* (New York: Vanguard, 1930), 132.

2. *Dressed to Kill* was a gangster movie from the Fox studio in 1928.

3. See William Leach, *Land of Desire: Merchants, Power, and the Rise of a New American Culture* (New York: Pantheon, 1993), esp. 15–38; Alfred

D. Chandler, *The Visible Hand: The Managerial Revolution in American Business* (Cambridge: Harvard University Press, Belknap Press, 1977); Daniel J. Boorstin, *The Americans: The Democratic Experience* (New York: Vintage, 1974), esp. 101–29 and 137–56.

4. Leuchtenburg, *The Perils of Prosperity, 1914–32* (Chicago: University of Chicago Press, 1958), 180–81, 186, 196; Boorstin, *The Americans,* 330; Leach, *Land of Desire,* 269–72, 299–300.

5. Winifred D. Wandersee, *Women's Work and Family Values, 1920–1940* (Cambridge: Harvard University Press, 1980), 36–45; Daniel Horowitz, *The Morality of Spending: Attitudes toward the Consumer Society in America, 1875–1940* (Baltimore: Johns Hopkins University Press, 1985), 135, 153–54; Scharf, *To Work and to Wed: Female Employment, Feminism, and the Great Depression* (Westport, Conn.: Greenwood Press, 1980), 149–50; Leach, *Land of Desire,* 382.

6. See Leach, *Land of Desire,* 308–13; William R. Leach, "Transformations in a Culture of Consumption: Women and Department Stores, 1890–1925," *Journal of American History* 71 (1984): 328; Roland Marchand, *Advertising the American Dream: Making Way for Modernity, 1920–1940* (Berkeley: University of California Press, 1985), 117–53.

7. Marchand, *Advertising the American Dream,* 6–7, 153–55.

8. T. J. Jackson Lears, "From Salvation to Self-Realization: Advertising and the Roots of the Consumer Culture, 1880–1930," in *The Culture of Consumption: Critical Essays in American History, 1880–1980,* ed. Richard Wightman Fox and T. J. Jackson Lears (New York: Pantheon, 1983), 4. Also see T. J. Jackson Lears, *No Place of Grace: Antimodernism and the Transformation of American Culture, 1880–1920* (New York: Pantheon, 1981), 32–47; John Higham, "The Reorientation of American Culture in the 1890s," chap. in *Writing American History: Essays on Modern Scholarship* (Bloomington: Indiana University Press, 1970), 73–102; Elaine Tyler May, *Great Expectations: Marriage and Divorce in Post-Victorian America* (Chicago: University of Chicago Press, 1980), 49–51.

9. See, for example, Chester Crowell, "A State of War," *Saturday Evening Post* 198 (21 November 1925): 31, 160, 163; Gordon L. Hostetter, "The Growing Menace of the Racketeer," *New York Times Magazine,* 30 October 1932, 3; Frank L. Packard, *The Big Shot* (New York: P. F. Collier, 1929), 3.

10. R. L. Duffus, "The Gunman Has an Intercity Murder Trade," *New York Times,* 8 July 1928.

11. Sullivan, *Chicago Surrenders,* 64.

12. William G. Shepherd, "Meet the Colonel," *Collier's* 83 (2 March 1929): 8. Also see Arthur B. Reeve, *The Golden Age of Crime* (New York: Mohawk Press, 1931), 101–2.

13. Warner Brothers, *Playing Around,* 1930; Warner Brothers, *The Finger Points,* 1931.

14. See, for example, Charles Francis Coe, *The Other Half* (New York: Cosmopolitan, 1930), 18–21.

15. Warner Brothers, *Playing Around,* 1930.

16. Warner Brothers, *The Public Enemy,* 1931.

17. United Artists, *Alibi,* 1929.

18. Carlos Clarens, *Crime Movies: From Griffith to the Godfather and Beyond* (New York: Norton, 1980), 43.

19. Warner Brothers, *Playing Around,* 1930; United Artists, *Alibi,* 1929; Warner Brothers, *Sweet Mama,* 1930; Warner Brothers, *The Finger Points,* 1931; Columbia, *Murder on the Roof,* 1930; Warner Brothers, *Weary River,* 1929.

20. John Kasson, *Amusing the Million: Coney Island at the Turn of the Century* (New York: Hill and Wang, 1978); Lary May, *Screening Out the Past: The Birth of Mass Culture and the Motion Picture Industry* (New York: Oxford University Press, 1980), 98–100; Lewis Erenberg, *Steppin' Out: New York Nightlife and the Transformation of American Culture, 1890–1930* (Chicago: University of Chicago Press, 1981), 113–42; Lewis Erenberg, "Impresarios of Broadway Nightlife," in *Inventing Times Square: Commerce and Culture at the Crossroads of the World,* ed. William R. Taylor (New York: Russell Sage Foundation, 1991), 158–69; Kathy J. Ogren, *The Jazz Revolution: Twenties America and the Meaning of Jazz* (New York: Oxford University Press, 1989), 3–10, 57, 78; William R. Taylor, "Introduction," *Inventing Times Square,* xxv.

21. Warner Brothers, *Public Enemy,* 1931; Warner Brothers, *Special Agent,* 1935.

22. Universal, *Broadway,* 1929.

23. Warner Brothers, *Little Caesar,* 1930; Warner Brothers, *The Public Enemy,* 1931. See also Paramount, *Ladies Love Brutes,* 1930; Warner Brothers, *The Finger Points,* 1931; Warner Brothers, *Blondie Johnson,* 1933.

24. *Quick Millions* (Fox, 1931), quoted in Eugene Rosow, *Born to Lose: The Gangster Film in America* (New York: Oxford University Press, 1978), 30.

25. Coe, *The Other Half,* 300.

26. Walter Green, "Who's Who in Hooch," *Saturday Evening Post* 198 (12 June 1926): 23.

27. "'Bootleggers I Have Known'—By a Prohibition Officer," *Literary Digest* 73 (27 May 1922): 40, 42.

28. Will Irwin, "Gypped!" *Saturday Evening Post* 195 (15 July 1922): 23–24.

29. George P. Stone, "Chicago Seeks Help to Check Crime," *New York Times,* 7 March 1926.

30. Warner Brothers, *Doorway to Hell,* 1930.

31. Warner Brothers, *Little Caesar* 1930; Warner Brothers, *The Public Enemy,* 1931; United Artists, *Scarface,* 1932.

32. O. O. McIntyre, "Bad Man," 52.

33. Daniell, "Big Business of the Racketeers," 5. Lewis Erenberg observes that in the socially heterogeneous nightclubs of the 1920s "spending and

consumption seemed to expand the realm of the personal, promising to free people from authority, hierarchy, and the demands of social position" ("Impresarios of Broadway Nightlife," 167).

34. Reeve, *Golden Age of Crime*, 37.

35. William E. Weeks, *All in the Racket* (New York: Charles Boni, 1930), 23–24.

36. James C. Young, "Crime Gangs Organized as Big Business," *New York Times*, 4 April 1926.

37. Horowitz, *Morality of Spending*, 68–70, 110. Scholarship on the new consumerism has focused on its apparent blurring of class lines. Boorstin, *The Americans*, is the classic statement of the democratizing consequences of the new mass culture. Also see Stuart Ewen, *All Consuming Images: The Politics of Style in Contemporary Culture* (New York: Basic Books, 1988), 23; Gunther Barth, *City People: The Rise of Modern City Culture in Nineteenth-Century America* (New York: Oxford University Press, 1980), 110–47; May, *Screening Out the Past*, 147–66; Ronald Edsforth, *Class Conflict and Cultural Consensus: The Making of a Mass Consumer Society in Flint, Michigan* (New Brunswick, N.J.: Rutgers University Press, 1987), 88. Leach, *Land of Desire*, 117, suggests that businessmen, while increasingly monopolizing economic and political power, used the rhetoric of service "to give the impression . . . that consumption, not production, was the new domain of democracy." Recent studies emphasize the perseverance of distinctive class and ethnic spending patterns despite the development of a mass consumer economy. Lizabeth Cohen, *Making a New Deal: Industrial Workers in Chicago, 1919–1939* (Cambridge: Cambridge University Press, 1990), 99–158, persuasively argues that the flow of goods into workers' homes was less overwhelming than many historians assume and that many groups exploited consumer goods to preserve subcultures even as mass culture developed. Also see Frank Stricker, "Affluence for Whom?—Another Look at Prosperity and the Working Classes in the 1920s," *Labor History* 24 (Winter 1983): 5–33.

38. On the actual ethnic background of organized criminals in the period, see Humbert S. Nelli, *The Business of Crime: Italians and Syndicate Crime in the United States* (Chicago: University of Chicago Press, 1976); Mark H. Haller, "Urban Crime and Criminal Justice: The Chicago Case," *Journal of American History* 57 (1970): 619–35; Mark H. Haller, "Organized Crime in Urban Society: Chicago in the Twentieth Century," *Journal of Social History* 5 (1971–1972): 210–34; Jenna Weissman Joselit, *Our Gang: Jewish Crime and the New York Jewish Community, 1900–1940* (Bloomington: Indiana University Press, 1983); Dianne M. Pinderhughes, *Race and Ethnicity in Chicago Politics: A Reexamination of Pluralist Theory* (Chicago: University of Chicago Press, 1987), 141–80.

39. There were, of course, exceptions. See, for example, the openly xenophobic Warner Brothers, *Star Witness*, 1931; and Coe, *Other Half*, 194.

40. On the capacity of a single text to broadcast a multiplicity of widely divergent messages, see Melvin Patrick Ely, *The Adventures of Amos 'n'*

Andy: A Social History of an American Phenomenon (New York: The Free Press, 1991), 130–59.

41. Anonymous letter to Chicago Crime Commission, 10 April 1932, letter file, Chicago Crime Commission.

42. Conversely, members of ethnic minorities often took a very different lesson from the criminal exploits of members of their group. See Joselit, *Our Gang,* on the proud regard for gang leaders as exemplars of group initiative and ability.

43. Fred D. Pasley, *Muscling In* (New York: Ives Washburn, 1931), 136.

44. Jack Grey, "The New Underworld," *Outlook and Independent* 151 (20 March 1929): 476.

45. Young, "Crime Gangs Organized as Big Business."

46. "Home Life of the Gunman," cartoon reprinted in "The Flowery End of a Chicago Gangster," *Literary Digest* 83 (6 December 1924): 38.

47. United Artists, *Scarface,* 1932. Francois Truffaut contended Howard Hawks "deliberately directed Paul Muni to make him look like a monkey, his arms hanging loosely and slightly curved, his face caught in a perpetual grimace." Quoted in Pauline Kael, *5001 Nights at the Movies* (New York: Henry Holt, 1985), 514.

48. Warner Brothers, *Little Giant,* 1933. The same theme informed *Little Caesar*'s portrayal of its vain protagonist.

49. Daniell, "Big Business of the Racketeers," 5.

50. United Artists, *Scarface,* 1932.

51. The notion that refinement in consumption offered the solution to the problem of middle-class identity, especially common during and just after the First World War, is explored by Horowitz, *Morality of Spending,* 85, 101–2, 107, 118–20.

52. William McAdoo, "Causes and Mechanisms of Prevalent Crimes," *Scientific Monthly* 24 (May 1927): 415.

53. "Accounting for the 'Crime Wave,'" *Literary Digest* 70 (27 August 1921): 30. Horowitz, *Morality of Spending,* 124–26, argues persuasively that middle-class observers' postwar attacks on the supposed extravagance of workers reflected concerns about the blurring of class lines.

54. Mary Roberts Rinehart, "Can Women Stop Crime?" *Saturday Evening Post* 206 (18 November 1933): 101.

55. O. O. McIntyre, "Bad Man," Cosmopolitan (February 1931): 52.

56. Richard Washburn Child, "The Great American Scandal: Take This Case," *Saturday Evening Post* 198 (26 September 1925): 7.

57. Child, "Great American Scandal," 6–7, 182, 186.

58. On personality and the celebration of smooth conversation see Warren I. Susman, "'Personality' and the Making of Twentieth-Century Culture," chap. in *Culture as History: The Transformation of American Society in the Twentieth Century* (New York: Pantheon, 1984), 279.

59. F. Raymond Daniell, "The Big Business of the Racketeers," *New York Times Magazine,* 27 April 1930, 5.

60. Child, "Great American Scandal: Take This Case," 7.

61. Bruce Rae, "Will-O'-The-Wisps of the Underworld," *New York Times Magazine,* 18 August 1929, 7. Also see Grey, "The New Underworld," 446.

62. S. Tee Bee, "With the Gangsters," *Saturday Evening Post* 198 (26 June 1926): 100.

63. McIntyre, "Bad Man," 53.

64. Charles Francis Coe, "Pay-Off," *Saturday Evening Post* 204 (5 March 1932): 18–19, 105.

65. Susman, "'Personality' and the Making of Twentieth-Century Culture," 271–85. It was not only the criminal who acquired a charming personality. On the 1920s attribution of an engaging personality to Jesus see Susan Curtis, "The Son of Man and God the Father: The Social Gospel and Victorian Masculinity," in *Meanings for Manhood: Constructions of Masculinity in Victorian America,* ed. Mark C. Carnes and Clyde Griffen (Chicago: University of Chicago Press, 1990), 75–76.

66. Walter Davenport, "Whitey Was a Piker," *Collier's* 80 (28 May 1927): 16. See also George S. Dougherty, "The Criminal as a Human Being," *Saturday Evening Post* 196 (15 March 1924): 186.

67. Packard, *Big Shot,* 4.

68. Anon., *The Whole Truth About Racketeers* (New York: Macfadden, 1930), 4, 63.

69. Lloyd Lewis, "On the Chicago Front," *Outlook and Independent* 154 (19 February 1930): 290.

70. Grey, "New Underworld," 446.

71. Octavus Roy Cohen, "Pink Bait," *Collier's* 72 (7 July 1923): 5, 6, 30, 31.

72. Rae, "Will-O'-The-Wisps of the Underworld," 20. For other accounts of gigolo gangsters, see, for example, Grey, "New Underworld," 446, 476; Richard Washburn Child, "The Great American Scandal: The Criminal and the Citizen," *Saturday Evening Post* 198 (12 September 1925): 234; Warner Brothers, *Playing Around,* 1930.

73. Child, "Great American Scandal: The Criminal and the Citizen," 233.

74. "Accounting for the Crime Wave," 30.

75. Coe, "Pay-Off," 18.

76. Coe, *Other Half,* 104, 194.

77. Coe, *Other Half,* 206–09, 217.

78. Cohen, "Pink Bait," 30.

79. Horowitz, *Morality of Spending,* 73–79.

80. William G. Shepherd, "Damned Young," *Collier's* 77 (27 March 1926): 9.

81. Quoted in "The Rising Tide of Crime," *Literary Digest* 86 (15 August 1925): 5.

82. Richard Washburn Child, "The Great American Scandal: Youth and Felony," *Saturday Evening Post* 198 (29 August 1925): 18.

83. Child, "Great American Scandal: Youth and Felony," 133–34.

84. Evans Clark, "U.S. Indicted as the Most Lawless Country," *New York Times,* 2 November 1924.

85. See Erenberg, "Impresarios of Broadway Nightlife," 164–69, on the association of the nightclub, immorality, and criminality during the prohibition era.

86. "Our Bootleg Aristocracy," *Woman Citizen* 8 (19 April 1924): 18–19. Also see "The Bootlegger's Partner," *Woman Citizen* 8 (28 July 1923): 17; "The Bootlegger's Partner," *Woman Citizen* 8 (5 April 1924): 14.

87. "The Lindbergh Crime as a Challenge to America," *Literary Digest* 113 (28 May 1932): 6.

88. F. Scott Fitzgerald, *The Great Gatsby* (New York: Charles Scribner's, 1925), 2, 48, 100, 99, 65.

Chapter Four

1. Warner Brothers, *The Public Enemy* pressbook, 1931, Warner Brothers Pressbook Collection, State Historical Society of Wisconsin, Madison.

2. E. Anthony Rotundo, *American Manhood: Transformations in Masculinity from the Revolution to the Modern Era* (New York: Basic Books, 1993), 248–50.

3. Peter G. Filene, *Him/Her/Self: Sex Roles in Modern America,* 2nd. ed., (Baltimore: Johns Hopkins University Press, 1986), 69–93, 141; John Higham, "The Reorientation of American Culture in the 1890s," in *Writing American History: Essays on Modern Scholarship* (Bloomington: Indiana University Press, 1970), 73–102; Elaine Tyler May, *Great Expectations: Marriage and Divorce in Post-Victorian America* (Chicago: University of Chicago Press, 1980), 49–72.

4. Olivier Zunz, *Making America Corporate, 1870–1920* (Chicago: University of Chicago Press), 4, 8, emphasizes mid-level employees' enthusiastic participation in the creation of new corporate forms. Margaret Marsh, "Suburban Men and Masculine Domesticity, 1870–1915," in *Meanings for Manhood: Constructions of Masculinity in Victorian America,* ed. Mark C. Carnes and Clyde Griffen (Chicago: University of Chicago Press, 1990), 111–27, traces middle-class men's growing preference for companionate marriage and child rearing.

5. Rotundo, *American Manhood,* 232–35, 251–52, 265–70.

6. James C. Young, "Crime Gangs Organized as Big Business," *New York Times,* 4 April 1926.

7. Michael Fiaschetti, "The Apache's Moll," *Collier's* 75 (11 April 1925): 16.

8. Michael Fiaschetti, "The Man with the Hole in His Hand," *Collier's* 75 (14 February 1925): 17.

9. George S. Dougherty, "The Stick-Up and House Prowler," *Saturday Evening Post* 196 (7 June 1924): 66.

10. William G. Shepherd, "One Lie Beats Two Fists," *Collier's* 74 (29 November 1924): 14.

11. Carroll Smith-Rosenberg, "The Hysterical Woman: Sex Roles and Role Conflict in Nineteenth-Century America," *Disorderly Conduct: Visions of Gender in Victorian America* (New York: Oxford University Press, 1985), 197–216.

12. On the cultural associations of women and consumption, see Roland Marchand, *Advertising the American Dream: Making Way for Modernity, 1920–1940* (Berkeley: University of California Press, 1985), 66, 131, 162; William R. Leach, "Transformations in a Culture of Consumption: Women and Department Stores, 1890–1925," *Journal of American History* 71 (1984): 319–42; Susan Porter Benson, *Counter Cultures: Saleswomen, Managers, and Customers in American Department Stores, 1890–1940* (Urbana: University of Illinois Press, 1986), 76, 78–79; Nancy F. Cott, *The Grounding of Modern Feminism* (New Haven: Yale University Press, 1987), 172.

13. On turn of the century manifestations of "the fear of womanly men," see Rotundo, *American Manhood*, 265.

14. Charles Francis Coe, "Pay–Off," *Saturday Evening Post* 204 (27 February 1932): 84.

15. William G. Shepherd, "Meet the Colonel," *Collier's* 83 (2 March 1929): 8.

16. Walter Davenport, "Whitey Was a Piker," *Collier's* 79 (28 May 1927): 16.

17. W. R. Burnett, *Little Caesar* (New York: Signet, 1972 [1929]), 16–17; Warner Brothers, *Little Caesar,* 1930.

18. Young, "Crime Gangs Organized as Big Business."

19. Dashiell Hammett, *The Maltese Falcon* (New York: Vintage, 1984 [1930]), 234. Also see Donald Henderson Clarke, *Confidential* (Philadelphia: Triangle, 1944 [1936]), 218–19.

20. Rotundo, *American Manhood*, 273–79; Estelle B. Freedman, "Uncontrolled Desires: The Response to the Sexual Psychopath, 1920–1960," *Journal of American History* 74 (1987): 83–106. On the popular association of male homosexuality and effeminacy, see John D'Emilio, *Sexual Politics, Sexual Communities: The Making of a Homosexual Minority in the United States, 1940–1970* (Chicago: University of Chicago Press, 1983), 17.

21. O. O. McIntyre, "Bad Man," *Cosmopolitan* (February 1931): 52–53.

22. See Rotundo, *American Manhood*, 222–46 (Roosevelt quotation on p. 236). On the masculinizing of Jesus, also see Susan Curtis, "The Son of Man and God the Father: The Social Gospel and Victorian Masculinity," in Carnes and Griffen, *Meanings for Manhood*, 72–74.

23. Sinclair Lewis, *Babbitt* (New York: New American Library, 1980 [1922]), 29.

24. On the popularity of leisure activities that celebrated new notions of virile masculinity, see Higham, "The Reorientation of American Culture," 73–102; Filene, *Him/Her/Self*, 94–112; David I. Macleod, *Building Character in the American Boy: The Boy Scouts, YMCA, and Their Forerunners,*

1870–1920 (Madison: University of Wisconsin Press, 1983), 46–47; Rotundo, *American Manhood*, 227–29, 239–44.

25. See, for example, Jack Lait, *Put on the Spot* (New York: Grosset and Dunlap, 1930), 8.

26. Warner Brothers, *Doorway to Hell*, 1930. The inability of actor Lew Ayres, more often cast as a cherubic "juvenile lead," to play the part convincingly may explain the film's lack of commercial or critical success. See Carlos Clarens, *Crime Movies: From Griffith to the Godfather and Beyond* (New York: Norton, 1980), 54.

27. Warner Brothers, *Little Caesar*, 1930.

28. Lait, *Put on the Spot*, 176. Also see Rayner Seelig, "One Fine Day," *Liberty* 5 (15 February 1930): 22.

29. See, for example, F. Raymond Daniell, "The Big Business of the Racketeers," *New York Times Magazine*, 27 April 1930, 5.

30. First National, *Playing Around*, 1930. Also see Pathe, *The Racketeer*, 1929; United Artists, *New York Nights*, 1929.

31. Warner Brothers, *Little Caesar* pressbook, 1930, Warner Brothers Pressbook Collection, State Historical Society of Wisconsin, Madison.

32. Warner Brothers, *The Ruling Voice* pressbook, 1931, Warner Brothers Pressbook Collection, State Historical Society of Wisconsin, Madison.

33. Warner Brothers, *The Public Enemy* pressbook.

34. Cagney's tough-guy films of the early thirties, all from Warner Brothers, were *Sinners' Holiday*, 1930 (Cagney as a rumrunner and carnival hawker); *Doorway to Hell*, 1930 (as a gang lieutenant and leader); *The Public Enemy*, 1931 (as a gangster); *Smart Money*, 1931 (as a gambler); *Blonde Crazy*, 1931 (as a small-time swindler); *Taxi*, 1932 (as a leader of independent cabbies); *The Crowd Roars*, 1932 (as an automobile racer); *Winner Take All*, 1932 (as a boxer); *Hard to Handle*, 1933 (as a promoter); *Picture Snatcher*, 1933 (as an ex-con tabloid photographer); *The Mayor of Hell*, 1933 (as a gang leader and machine politician); *Lady Killer*, 1933 (as a movie usher, gang leader, and Hollywood star); *Jimmy the Gent*, 1934 (as a locator of heirs); *He Was Her Man*, 1934 (as a safecracker); *Here Comes the Navy*, 1934 (as an AWOL sailor); *The St. Louis Kid*, 1934 (as a trucker); *Devil Dogs of the Air*, 1935 (as a stunt pilot); *G-Men*, 1935 (as an FBI recruit). For brief discussions see Andrew Bergman, *James Cagney* (New York: Pyramid Publications, 1973).

35. See Robert Sklar, *City Boys: Cagney, Bogart, Garfield* (Princeton: Princeton University Press, 1992), 33; Clarens, *Crime Movies*, 65.

36. Warner Brothers, *Doorway to Hell*, 1930.

37. Warner Brothers, *Lady Killer*, 1933. A similar scene appeared in Warner Brothers, *Mayor of Hell*, 1933.

38. Warner Brothers, *Lady Killer*, 1933.

39. Warner Brothers, *Mayor of Hell*, 1933.

40. Warner Brothers, *The Public Enemy*, 1931.

41. Charles Francis Coe, "Pay-Off," *Saturday Evening Post* 204 (26 March 1932): 120.

42. Charles Francis Coe, *The Other Half* (New York: Cosmopolitan, 1930), 84–85.

43. See Cott, *Grounding of Modern Feminism*, on militant suffragism (26–28, 54–55, 59–60, 62), on the emergence of feminism (13–16, 36–40, 49–50), and on the movements for birth control (46–48), equal rights (120–29), and disarmament and world peace (243–60). Also see Rosalind Rosenberg, *Beyond Separate Spheres: Intellectual Roots of Modern Feminism* (New Haven: Yale University Press, 1982); David M. Kennedy, *Birth Control in America: The Career of Margaret Sanger* (New Haven: Yale University Press, 1970); and, on the struggle over equal rights, William H. Chafe, *The American Woman: Her Changing Social, Economic, and Political Roles, 1920–1970* (New York: Oxford University Press, 1972), 112–32.

44. See Cott, *Grounding of Modern Feminism*, 129–32, 148, 180–82, 217, 220, on women in white-collar work and the employment of married women. Also see Lois Scharf, *To Work and to Wed: Female Employment, Feminism, and the Great Depression* (Westport, Conn.: Greenwood Press, 1980), 5–16, on the changing jobs and demographics of employed women from the 1890s to the 1920s. Chafe, *American Woman*, 48–111, provides a useful overview.

45. Kenneth A. Yellis, "Prosperity's Child: Some Thoughts on the Flapper," *American Quarterly* 21 (1969), 44–64; Lois W. Banner, *American Beauty* (New York: Knopf, 1983), 279.

46. Mary P. Ryan, "The Projection of a New Womanhood: The Movie Moderns in the 1920s," in *Decades of Discontent: The Women's Movement, 1920–1940*, ed. Lois Scharf and Joan M. Jensen (Westport, Conn.: Greenwood Press, 1983), 116.

47. Paula S. Fass, *The Damned and the Beautiful: American Youth in the 1920's* (New York: Oxford University Press, 1977), 53–118, provides a useful overview. On the transition to an ethos of pleasure, see May, *Great Expectations*, 49–72; Ellen K. Rothman, *Hands and Hearts: A History of Courtship in America* (New York: Basic Books, 1984), 262–68; Lary May, *Screening Out the Past: The Birth of Mass Culture and the Motion Picture Industry* (New York: Oxford University Press, 1980), 200–236; and Lewis A. Erenberg, *Steppin' Out: New York Nightlife and the Transformation of American Culture, 1890–1930* (Chicago: University of Chicago Press, 1981), 155–58, 165–70. See Joanne Meyerowitz, *Women Adrift: Independent Wage Earners in Chicago, 1880–1930* (Chicago: University of Chicago Press, 1988), 117–39, for reactions to independent women. See Cott, *Grounding of Modern Feminism*, on companionate marriage (156–57), on divorce rates and their interpretation (147–48), and on the new woman's focus on self-development rather than familial duties (39).

48. John D'Emilio and Estelle B. Freedman, *Intimate Matters: A History of Sexuality in America* (New York: Harper and Row, 1988), 171–274, provides a good introduction. Also see Cott, *Grounding of Modern Feminism*,

42–45; Fass, *Damned and the Beautiful,* 260–90; John Modell, "Dating Becomes the Way of American Youth," in *Essays on the Family and Historical Change,* ed. Leslie Page Moch and Gary D. Stark (Arlington: University of Texas Press, 1983), 91–126; Bailey, *From Front Porch to Back Seat,* esp. 77–96.

49. See, in addition to the sources cited in the previous note, John C. Burnham, "The Progressive Era Revolution in American Attitudes toward Sex," *Journal of American History* 59 (1973): 885–908; James R. McGovern, "American Women's Pre–World War I Freedom in Manners and Morals," *Journal of American History* 55 (1968): 315–33; May, *Screening Out the Past,* 205–12; Erenberg, *Steppin' Out,* 134, 154–56; Ryan, "Movie Moderns in the 1920s," 115–19. See Kathy Peiss, *Cheap Amusements: Working Women and Leisure in Turn-of-the-Century New York* (Philadelphia: Temple University Press, 1986), 100–114, on sexually expressive working-class culture.

50. Coe, *Other Half,* 260.

51. Donald Henderson Clarke, *Louis Beretti* (New York: Vanguard, 1929), 13–14, 41.

52. Coe, *Other Half,* 1, 155.

53. Seelig, "One Fine Day," 24, 26.

54. United Artists, *Scarface,* 1932.

55. Warner Brothers, *20,000 Years in Sing Sing* pressbook, 1933, Warner Brothers Pressbook Collection, State Historical Society of Wisconsin, Madison.

56. Lawrence Saunders [pseud.], "The Payoff," *Liberty Magazine* 6 (1 February 1930): 50–54.

57. See, for example, review of *Skin Deep* in *Variety,* 2 October 1929, and review of *Born Reckless,* in *Variety,* 11 June 1930.

58. This generalization is based on a review of advertisements reproduced in the Warner Brothers Pressbooks Collection, State Historical Society of Wisconsin, Madison.

59. Warner Brothers, *Weary River,* 1929.

60. Warner Brothers, *The Public Enemy,* 1931.

61. Warner Brothers, *Lady Killer,* 1933.

62. Clarke, *Louis Beretti,* 8, 40, 55, 61.

63. Burnett, *Little Caesar,* 26.

64. See, for example, United Artists, *Alibi,* 1929; Warner Brothers, *Playing Around,* 1930; Pathe, *The Racketeer,* 1929; Fox, *Quick Millions,* 1931; Metro-Goldwyn-Mayer, *A Free Soul,* 1931; Metro-Goldwyn-Mayer, *Dance, Fools, Dance,* 1931; Warner Brothers, *Public Enemy's Wife,* 1936.

65. United Artists, *Scarface,* 1932. According to Eugene Rosow, *Born to Lose: The Gangster Film in America* (New York: Oxford University Press, 1978), 92, the gangster's irresistibility to women from respectable backgrounds also appeared in Famous Players, *The Exciters,* 1923; Metro-Goldwyn-Mayer, *While the City Sleeps,* 1928; Universal, *Come Across,* 1929; Paramount, *Ladies Love Brutes,* 1930.

66. Saunders, "Payoff," 50–54.

67. Jack Grey, "The New Underworld," *Outlook and Independent* 151 (20 March 1929): 446.

68. Bruce Rae, "Will-O'-The-Wisps of the Underworld," *New York Times Magazine,* 18 August 1929, 6–7.

69. Also see Fiaschetti, "Apache's Moll," 16–17, 40.

70. United Artists, *Scarface,* 1932.

71. R. L. Duffus "The Gunman Has an Intercity Murder Trade," *New York Times,* 8 July 1928.

72. Warner Brothers, *Playing Around,* 1930. Also see Arthur B. Reeve, *The Golden Age of Crime* (New York: Mohawk Press, 1931), 141.

73. Warner Brothers, *The Public Enemy,* 1931.

74. Warner Brothers. *Playing Around,* 1930. Also see United Artists, *Alibi,* 1929, for a similar treatment of the same themes.

75. Edward Doherty, "The Twilight of the Gangster," part 2, *Liberty* 8 (31 October 1931): 48.

76. Don Marquis, "As Crook Sees Crook," *Saturday Evening Post* 201 (27 October 1928): 121.

77. Fiaschetti, "Apache's Moll," 16–17.

78. *The Exciters* title card quoted in Rosow, *Born to Lose,* 92.

79. Warner Brothers, *The Public Enemy,* 1931.

80. Clarke, *Louis Beretti,* 61, 63.

81. Walter Noble Burns, *The One-Way Ride: The Red Trail of Chicago Gangland from Prohibition to Jake Lingle* (Garden City: Doubleday, Doran, 1931), 241.

82. Warner Brothers, *Big Shakedown* pressbook, 1934, Warner Brothers Pressbook Collection, State Historical Society of Wisconsin, Madison. For portrayals of the gangster's actual or threatened physical abuse of women, see, in addition to the films discussed below, Charles Francis Coe, "Vigilante," *Saturday Evening Post* 205 (11 March 1933): 20; Charles Francis Coe, "Percentage," *Saturday Evening Post* 206 (5 August 1933): 47; Doherty, "Twilight of the Gangster," part 2, 48; Frank L. Packard, *The Big Shot* (New York: P. F. Collier, 1929), 256, 258; Reeve, *Golden Age of Crime,* 141–45.

83. United Artists, *Alibi,* 1929. Also see Paramount, *Underworld,* 1927; Warner Brothers, *Those Who Dance,* 1930.

84. Warner Brothers, *Lady Killer,* 1933.

85. Metro-Goldwyn-Mayer, *A Free Soul,* 1931.

86. Reeve, *Golden Age of Crime,* 141.

87. Roy A. Giles, "Planning Big Crimes," *Scientific American* 126 (June 1922): 388.

88. Doherty, "Twilight of the Gangster," part 2, 48.

89. Marquis, "As Crook Sees Crook," 121.

90. Warner Brothers, *Playing Around,* 1930.

91. Clarke, *Louis Beretti,* 124.

92. Shepherd, "Meet the Colonel," 8; Davenport, "Whitey Was a Piker,"

16; McIntyre, "Bad Man," 52–53; Young, "Crime Gangs Organized as a Big Business."

93. Saunders, "Payoff," 50; Davenport, "Whitey Was a Piker," 17.

94. Burnett, *Little Caesar,* 80.

95. Warner Brothers, *Sweet Mama,* 1930.

96. Warner Brothers, *The Widow from Chicago,* 1930. Also see Warner Brothers, *Those Who Dance,* 1930; Columbia, *Murder on the Roof,* 1930; Paramount, *City Streets,* 1931.

97. Clarke, *Louis Beretti,* 6, 96–98. Also see Coe, *Other Half,* 54; Warner Brothers, *Petrified Forest,* 1936; Warner Brothers, *Public Enemy's Wife,* 1936.

98. Jack Lait, *Gangster Girl* (New York: Grosset and Dunlap, 1930), 1. Jack Lait and Lee Mortimer, *New York: Confidential!* (Chicago: Ziff-Davis, 1948), and *Chicago: Confidential!* (New York: Crown, 1950).

99. Lait, *Put on the Spot,* 6, 31.

100. Lait, *Gangster Girl,* 22.

101. Charles Francis Coe, "Repeal," *Saturday Evening Post* 206 (9 December 1933), 6, 7, 70. Accounts of the downfall of Big Jim Colosimo, Al Capone's reputed predecessor in Chicago, offered similar lessons about the enfeebling effects of romantic love. See Anon., *X Marks the Spot: Chicago Gang Wars in Pictures* (Chicago: Spot Publishing Co., 1930), 5; Richard T. Enright, *Al Capone on the Spot: Inside Story of the Master Criminal and His Bloody Career* (n. p.: Graphic Arts Corp. (Fawcett Publications), 1931), 37.

102. Lait, *Gangster Girl,* 173.

103. Warner Brothers, *The Public Enemy,* 1931.

104. Clarke, *Confidential,* 140.

105. Warner Brothers, *The Widow from Chicago* pressbook, 1930, Warner Brothers Pressbook Collection, State Historical Society of Wisconsin, Madison.

106. Charles Francis Coe, "Repeal," *Saturday Evening Post* 206 (16 December 1933): 20–21.

107. Warner Brothers, *The Public Enemy,* 1931; Warner Brothers, *Lady Killer,* 1933.

108. Saunders, "Payoff," 50–57.

109. See Cott, *Grounding of Modern Feminism,* on political attacks (61, 64, 246–51, 254–55, 258–61), on discrimination against career women (184–85, 191), and on the psychology-based backlash (153–55, 158–60). Also see Christina Simmons, "Modern Sexuality and the Myth of Victorian Repression," in *Passion and Power: Sexuality in History,* ed. Kathy Peiss and Christina Simmons (Philadelphia: Temple University Press, 1989), 164–67, 171; Carroll Smith-Rosenberg, "The New Woman as Androgyne: Social Disorder and Gender Crisis, 1870–1936," chap. in *Disorderly Conduct,* 257–62, 265–83; Rayna Rapp and Ellen Ross, "The Twenties' Backlash: Compulsory Heterosexuality, the Consumer Family, and the Waning of Feminism," in *Class, Race, and Sex: The Dynamics of Control,* ed. Amy Swerdlow and

Hanna Lessinger (Boston: G. K. Hall, 1983), 100–101. On hostility toward and discrimination against women workers, especially married and white-collar women workers, see Scharf, *To Work and to Wed,* 17–18, 43–44, 139–45; and Mary W. M. Hargreaves, "Darkness Before the Dawn: The Status of Working Women in the Depression Years," in *Clio Was a Woman: Studies in the History of American Women,* ed. Mabel E. Deutrich and Virginia C. Purdy (Washington: Howard University Press, 1980), 181. See J. Stanley Lemons, *The Woman Citizen: Social Feminism in the 1920s* (Urbana: University of Illinois Press, 1973), 209, on political attacks.

110. See, for example, Clarke, *Confidential,* 106–19; Warner Brothers, *Blondie Johnson,* 1933. See Simmons, "Modern Sexuality and the Myth of Victorian Repression," 157–77.

111. Warner Brothers, *Little Caesar,* 1930. In *The Public Enemy* the intense but apparently non-sexual connection of Matt and Tom results in Matt's death and thus the destruction of his idealized heterosexual relationship with Mamie.

112. United Artists, *Scarface,* 1932.

113. Saunders, "Payoff," 56–57.

114. Clarke, *Louis Beretti,* 142, 124, 123, 140, 156.

115. Clarke, *Louis Beretti,* 142. On the symbolic associations of women driving and female autonomy, see Virginia Scharff, *Taking the Wheel: Women and the Coming of the Motor Age* (New York: The Free Press, 1991), 24–25.

116. Warner Brothers, *Blondie Johnson* pressbook, 1933, Warner Brothers Pressbook Collection, State Historical Society of Wisconsin, Madison.

117. Warner Brothers, *Blondie Johnson,* 1933. Lait, *Gangster Girl,* 120–21, 174–77, implies a similar, though somewhat more ambiguous, domestication of its powerful heroine.

Chapter Five

1. Robert J. Casey, "Capone Goes to Trial on U. S. Charge," *Chicago Daily News,* 25 February 1931.

2. *Time* 15 (24 March 1930).

3. Edward Dean Sullivan, author of *Rattling the Cup on Chicago Crime* (New York: Vanguard, 1929), had a long newsroom career that included stints with the *Chicago Herald-Examiner* and the *New York Herald-Tribune.* Fred D. Pasley, author of *Al Capone: The Biography of a Self-Made Man* (New York: Ives, Washburn, 1930), was a reporter for the *Chicago Daily News.* Walter Noble Burns, author of *The One-Way Ride: The Red Trail of Chicago Gangland from Prohibition to Jake Lingle* (Garden City: Doubleday, 1931), had a long career as a newsman, most recently with the *Chicago Tribune.*

4. Carl S. Smith, "Fearsome Fiction and the Windy City; or, Chicago in the Dime Novel," *Chicago History* 7 (1978), 2–11, gives evidence of the city's unsavory image in one important type of nineteenth-century popular literature.

5. Henry Barrett Chamberlin, *'50-50' Fighting Chicago's Crime Trusts,* n. p., 1916, Chicago Historical Society, Chicago.

6. "Thefts and Gun Fights Mark Chicago's 'Wildest' Crime Orgy," *New York Times,* 25 November 1919.

7. R. L. Duffus, "Happy Hunting Ground for Racketeers," *New York Times Magazine,* 3 October 1930, 3. See "A Great Sunday Chronicle Scoop: Capone" (advertisement for a series in the *London Sunday Chronicle*), reprinted in *Chicago Daily Times,* 16 February 1931, located in Chicago Crime Commission clipping collection; "Edgar Wallace Puts Chicago 'On the Spot,'" *Literary Digest* 105 (21 June 1930), 19, on a British gangster play set in Chicago. Books by Edward Dean Sullivan and Fred D. Pasley discussed here appeared in British, French, German, and Spanish editions.

8. Janet A. Fairbank, "What's Wrong with Chicago?" *Woman Citizen* 12 (July 1927), 7.

9. On the symbolic importance of Chicago's railroads, stockyards, and skyscrapers see Carl S. Smith, *Chicago and the American Literary Imagination, 1880–1920* (Chicago: University of Chicago Press, 1984), 101–70.

10. Lee Alexander Stone, *Chicago: Greatest Advertised City in the World Not the Wickedest* (n.p., 1929), Chicago Historical Society, Chicago.

11. Smith, *Chicago and the American Literary Imagination,* 1–12. Ross Miller, *American Apocalypse: The Great Fire and the Myth of Chicago* (Chicago: University of Chicago Press, 1990), esp. 12–62, argues that Chicago's phenomenal growth, before and after the fire, led many Americans to see it as the archetypal modern city.

12. Sullivan, *Rattling the Cup,* xi.

13. Raymond Moley, "Behind the Menacing Racket," *New York Times Magazine,* 23 November 1930, 2.

14. Duffus, "Happy Hunting Ground for Racketeers," 3, 23.

15. Associated Press, "Chicago's Gang Wars Kill 125 in 9 Years," *New York Times,* 20 January 1929, 16.

16. Richard T. Enright, *Al Capone on the Spot: Inside Story of the Master Criminal and His Bloody Career* (n.p.: Graphic Arts [Fawcett Publications], 1931), 37; Anon., *Does Crime Pay? No! Life Story of Al Capone in Pictures* (Chicago: n.p., n.d. [1931]), 4. My discussion makes no attempt to evaluate the accuracy of these and other popular accounts.

17. Burns, *One-Way Ride,* 30–31.

18. Some accounts suggested that Torrio and Capone took an active role in their boss's demise. See *Scarface* (United Artists, 1932), the classic film written by Ben Hecht, directed by Howard Hawks, and produced by Howard Hughes.

19. Pasley, *Al Capone,* 9.

20. Sullivan, *Rattling the Cup,* 87.

21. Anon., *Does Crime Pay?,* 14.

22. Anon., *Does Crime Pay?,* 6.

23. Anon., *X Marks the Spot: Chicago Gang Wars in Pictures* (Chicago: Spot Publishing Co., 1930), 4.

24. Anon., *Does Crime Pay?*, 6.

25. Enright, *Al Capone on the Spot*, 37.

26. Pasley, *Al Capone*, 15.

27. Anon., *X Marks the Spot*, 4–5.

28. Anon., *Does Crime Pay?*, 6.

29. Enright, *Al Capone on the Spot*, 37. Also see Anon., *X Marks the Spot*, 4–5.

30. Anon., *Does Crime Pay?*, 7.

31. Sullivan, *Rattling the Cup*, 75.

32. See Anon., *Does Crime Pay?*, 8, on the putative inefficiencies of small gangs.

33. Pasley, *Al Capone*, 17, 15.

34. Burns, *One-Way Ride*, 21.

35. Sullivan, *Rattling the Cup*, 73.

36. Burns, *One-Way Ride*, 21, 112.

37. United Artists, *Scarface*, 1932.

38. Pasley, *Al Capone*, 5.

39. Burns, *One-Way Ride*, 22. Also see Pasley, *Al Capone*, 15; Sullivan, *Rattling the Cup*, 103.

40. Lewis W. Hunt, "The Rise of a Racketeer: A Portrait of Alphonse Capone," *Outlook and Independent* 156 (10 December 1930): 576.

41. Anon., *Life of Al Capone in Pictures! and Chicago's Gang Wars* (Chicago: Lake Michigan Publishing Corp., 1931), 6; Anon., *X Marks the Spot*, 19–20.

42. "Philadelphia Justice for Chicago's Al Capone," *Literary Digest* 101 (15 June 1929): 42. Also see Anon., *Does Crime Pay?*, 14; Enright, *Al Capone on the Spot*, 48.

43. Enright, *Al Capone on the Spot*, 18.

44. Burns, *One-Way Ride*, 28.

45. Pasley, *Al Capone*, 11.

46. Pasley, *Al Capone*, 11.

47. Enright, *Al Capone on the Spot*, 7. Also see Anon., *Life of Al Capone in Pictures*, 1–2.

48. Anon., *X Marks the Spot*, 3.

49. Anon., *Life of Al Capone in Pictures!*, 17.

50. Enright, *Al Capone on the Spot*, 14.

51. Anon., *Does Crime Pay?*, 5.

52. "Coming Out Party," *Time* 15 (24 March 1930): 15.

53. Pasley, *Al Capone*, 9, 11.

54. Burns, *One-Way Ride*, 33.

55. "Two Mighty Men—H. G. Wells and Al Capone," *Liberty* 8 (17 October 1931): 4.

56. Cornelius Vanderbilt, Jr., "How Al Capone Would Run This Country," *Liberty* 8 (17 October 1931): 18, 20–21. On the widespread appeal of Mussolini to conservative Americans see John P. Diggins, *Mussolini and*

Fascism: The View from America (Princeton: Princeton University Press, 1972), 26–31.

57. Pasley, *Al Capone*, 70.

58. Burns, *One-Way Ride*, 42.

59. Anon., *X Marks the Spot*, 3.

60. Sullivan, *Rattling the Cup*, 4, 10.

61. Burns, *One-Way Ride*, 84.

62. Burns, *One-Way Ride*, 87; Sullivan, *Rattling the Cup*, 8.

63. Anon., *Does Crime Pay?*, 13.

64. Anon., *X Marks the Spot*, 14.

65. Sullivan, *Rattling the Cup*, 12.

66. Pasley, *Al Capone*, 46.

67. Sullivan, *Rattling the Cup*, 102–3. The episode was memorably reenacted in Warner Brothers, *The Public Enemy*, 1931.

68. Anon., *Does Crime Pay?*, 13.

69. Sullivan, *Rattling the Cup*, 36.

70. Burns, *One-Way Ride*, 185.

71. Anon., *X Marks the Spot*, 19.

72. Anon., *The Morgue: The Gangster's Final Resting Place*, (n.p., 1933), no page numbers.

73. Anon., *Does Crime Pay?*, 13. On Weiss's temper, also see Enright, *Al Capone on the Spot*, 22.

74. Burns, *One-Way Ride*, 191. Also see Pasley, *Al Capone*, 126–27.

75. Anon., *Does Crime Pay?*, 13, 16.

76. Anon., *X Marks the Spot*, 3.

77. Enright, *Al Capone on the Spot*, 22.

78. Anon., *Does Crime Pay?*, 24.

79. Anon., *Life of Al Capone in Pictures!*, 38.

80. Pasley, *Al Capone*, 257.

81. Enright, *Al Capone on the Spot*, 29–30. Also see Boynton, *Gang Wars of Chicago*, 9.

82. See, for example, Burns, *One-Way Ride*, 83–84; Sullivan, *Rattling the Cup*, 11; Pasley, *Al Capone*, 47–48.

83. See, for example, Anon., *Does Crime Pay?*, 11; Enright, *Al Capone on the Spot*, 45.

84. John W. Ward, "The Meaning of Lindbergh's Flight," *American Quarterly* 10 (Spring 1958): 3–16.

85. Burns, *One-Way Ride*, 105.

86. See Robert Isham Randolph, "How to Wreck Capone's Gang," *Collier's* 87 (7 March 1931), p. 7; Anon., *Does Crime Pay?*, 50, 54; Anon., *Life of Al Capone in Pictures!*, 11, 17, 26, 36; Boynton, *Gang Wars of Chicago*, 18, 20, 22; Enright, *Al Capone on the Spot*, 51, 70, 90; Edgar Forest Wolfe, "The Real Truth About Al Capone," *Master Detective*, September 1930, 38.

87. Hunt, "Rise of a Racketeer," 574.

88. Burns, *One-Way Ride*, 28.

89. Pasley, *Al Capone*, 11. Also see Enright, *Al Capone on the Spot,* 37.

90. Enright, *Al Capone on the Spot,* 9 (also see page 31).

91. See Warren Susman, "'Personality' and the Making of Twentieth-Century Culture," chap. in *Culture as History: The Transformation of American Society in the Twentieth Century* (New York: Pantheon, 1984), 271–85.

92. Pasley, *Al Capone,* 11.

93. Pasley, *Al Capone,* 19.

94. Enright, *Al Capone on the Spot,* 14.

95. Anon., *Life of Al Capone in Pictures!,* inside front cover.

96. Anon., *Does Crime Pay?,* 50–51.

97. George F. Stone, "Chicago's Rum Runners Tell No Tales," *New York Times,* 9 May 1926.

98. Burns, *One-Way Ride,* 91–92. Also see Anon., *The Morgue,* no page numbers; Anon., *X Marks the Spot,* 14.

99. Pasley, *Al Capone,* 120, 334.

100. Burns, *One-Way Ride,* 32 (also see page 311); Pasley, *Al Capone,* 89; Anon., *Does Crime Pay?,* 108; Boynton, *Gang Wars of Chicago,* 22; Enright, *Al Capone on the Spot,* 73; "Coming Out Party," 15.

101. For Carnegie, Capone's insistence on his role as a public benefactor illustrated individuals' refusals to see themselves as blameworthy. Dutch Schultz, "Two Gun" Crowley, and John Dillinger offered similar insights. Dale Carnegie, *How to Win Friends and Influence People* (New York: Simon and Schuster, 1937), 30–31, 46.

102. Burns, *One-Way Ride,* 3–4.

103. Anon., *X Marks the Spot,* 5.

104. Burns, *One-Way Ride,* 5.

105. Sullivan, *Rattling the Cup,* 86.

106. Burns, *One-Way Ride,* 22; Sullivan, *Rattling the Cup,* 103.

107. Enright, *Al Capone on the Spot,* 47.

108. Anon., *Does Crime Pay?,* 12; Boynton, *Gang Wars of Chicago,* 2; Enright, *Al Capone on the Spot,* 47; Anon., *X Marks the Spot,* 15; Wolfe, "Real Truth About Al Capone," 41.

109. "The Flowery End of a Chicago Gangster," *Literary Digest* 83 (6 December 1924): 38, 40, 42. Also see Burns, *One-Way Ride,* 92–93; Anon., *X Marks the Spot,* 14–15.

110. Sullivan, *Rattling the Cup,* 15–16. Also see Anon., *Does Crime Pay?,* 12; Anon., *The Morgue,* no page numbers.

111. Enright, *Al Capone on the Spot,* 72.

112. Pasley, *Al Capone,* 89; Hunt, "Rise of a Racketeer," 595. Also see "Philadelphia Justice for Chicago's Al Capone," 39; Arthur B. Reeve, *The Golden Age of Crime* (New York: Mohawk Press, 1931), 65.

113. Burns, *One-Way Ride,* 311.

114. Enright, *Al Capone on the Spot,* 7.

115. "Coming Out Party," 15.

116. Hunt, "Rise of a Racketeer," 595. Also see "Philadelphia Justice for

Chicago's Al Capone," 39; Enright, *Al Capone on the Spot,* 12, 71; Anon., *Does Crime Pay?,* 36; Burns, *One-Way Ride,* 312.

117. Pasley, *Al Capone,* 84–85. Also see Sullivan, *Rattling the Cup,* 45–46.

118. Duffus, "Chicago in New War Against Gang Rule."

Epilogue

1. Richard Gid Powers, *G-Men: Hoover's FBI in American Popular Culture* (Carbondale: Southern Illinois University Press, 1983), 61, 113–38.

2. Warner Brothers, *Bullets or Ballots,* 1936. Also see Martin Mooney, *Crime, Incorporated* (New York: Whittlesey House, 1935).

3. Warner Brothers, *Angels with Dirty Faces,* 1938; United Artists, *Dead End,* 1937.

4. Warner Brothers, *Public Enemy's Wife,* 1936; Warner Brothers, *High Sierra,* 1941; Warner Brothers, *The Petrified Forest,* 1936; Warner Brothers, *Heat Lightning,* 1934.

5. See William Stott, *Documentary Expression and Thirties America* (New York: Oxford University Press, 1973), 52–53; and Richard H. Pells, *Radical Visions and American Dreams: Culture and Social Thought in the Depression Years* (New York: Harper Torchbooks, 1973), 199–200.

6. Warner Brothers, *The Petrified Forest,* 1936.

Index